with answers

English Vocabulary in Use

pre-intermediate and intermediate

Stuart Redman

CAMBRIDGE
UNIVERSITY PRESS

PUBLISHED BY THE PRESS SYNDICATE OF THE UNIVERSITY OF CAMBRIDGE
The Pitt Building, Triumpington Street, Cambridge CB2 1RP, United Kingdom

CAMBRIDGE UNIVERSITY PRESS
The Edinburgh Building, Cambridge CB2 2RU, UK
40 West 20th Street, New York, NY 10011–4211, USA
10 Stamford Road, Oakleigh, VIC 3166, Australia
Ruiz de Alarcón 13, 28014 Madrid, Spain
Dock House, The Waterfront, Cape Town 8001, South Africa

http://www.cambridge.org

First published 1997
Eight printing 2001

Printed in the United Kingdom by Redwood Books, Trowbridge, Wiltshire

A catalogue record for this book is available from the British Library

ISBN 0 521 55737 2

Contents

Connecting and linking

Topics

Introduction

Who is this book for?

English Vocabulary in Use (pre-intermediate and intermediate) has been written to help learners at this level to improve their English. It has been designed for students who are studying on their own, but it can also be used by a teacher in the classroom with groups of students.

How is the book organised?

The book has 100 two-page units. The left-hand page explains new words and expressions (most units contain approximately 25 new words or phrases), and the right-hand page gives you a chance to check your understanding through a series of exercises which practise the new vocabulary. In a very limited number of units e.g. Units 18 and 71, the right-hand page also includes a few new words and phrases which are not explained on the left-hand page.

There is an answer key at the back of the book. This not only gives *correct* answers to exercises with 'right' or 'wrong' solutions, but also *possible answers* and *sample answers* for exercises which do not have 'right' or 'wrong' solutions.

There is also an index at the back of the book. This lists all the new words and phrases introduced in the book and refers you to the unit or units where these words appear. The index also includes a phonemic transcription for many of the words, and on page 247 you are given special help with the pronunciation of approximately 200 words which present particular problems for many learners of English.

The left-hand page

This is the page that introduces the new vocabulary for each topic or area of language. First of all, the vocabulary is divided into a number of sections (A, B, C, etc.) with simple clear titles; and then within each section, new words are explained using a number of different techniques:

- A short definition. The definition follows directly after the word, or comes at the end of the phrase or sentence; it is in brackets and introduced by the symbol =.
  e.g. **unemployed** (= without a job); **feel like** (= want or desire *infml*)
  The abbreviations *fml* or *infml* tell you if a word is either 'formal' or 'informal'.

- A short explanation. This will be a complete sentence which often includes the new word, e.g. **effective**. (If something is **effective**, it works well and produces good results.)

- A synonym or opposite, e.g. **terrific** (= fantastic); **dirty** (≠ clean)

- In a situation. Some words are difficult to define and it is easier to see their meaning when they are put in context. The following is from a text about a motoring accident.
  e.g. 'The driver of the Mercedes was OK, but the other driver was **badly injured**, and both cars were **badly damaged**.'

- A picture or diagram. This seems the obvious way to explain a large number of concrete nouns and verbs.

e.g.

carrot   go along here and **turn left**.

For many of the new words there are also sentence examples which show the words in context in order to consolidate their meaning and illustrate any special syntactic features.

> My boyfriend gets very **jealous** when I talk to other boys.
> The plane **appeared** in the sky, then suddenly **disappeared** behind a cloud.
> He **admitted** stealing the woman's money. (admit + -ing)
> We were very busy but we **managed** to finish by 6 o'clock. (manage + inf.)

Finally, a big effort has been made to introduce new words alongside other words that often appear with them (this is called 'collocation').
e.g. miss the bus; a strong accent; the car broke down; it's vitally important; fasten your seat belt; go on holiday; give someone a hand; to a certain extent, a terrible pain, etc.

The right-hand page

This page contains the exercises to practise the new vocabulary presented on the left-hand page. In general the first exercise practises the form of some of the new words, and then there are further exercises which focus on the meaning. In most units there is at least one exercise which gives learners a chance to think about and practise new vocabulary in relation to their own lives, and/or a task which invites learners to do something with the vocabulary outside of the book (e.g. 11.4, 14.4, etc.). And in every unit, there is a range of exercise types to help maintain your interest.

Using the book

The first five units (or first six units if you go to an English class) teach you some important vocabulary, but they also help you with with useful ideas and techniques for vocabulary learning. Do these units first, and then work through the book studying the units which interest you.

Summary of abbreviations and symbols used in the book

n	noun
v	verb
adj	adjective
infml	informal word or expression
fml	formal word or expression
pl	word only used in the plural
(U)	uncountable word
(C)	countable word
≠	opposite
AmEng	American English word or expression
[NOT ~~I lost the bus~~]	indicates that a word or expression is wrong

---

Learning and revising with this book

Look at Exercise 1.1 on the next page before you read this page.

A Establish a routine

A **routine** means doing certain things regularly in the same way. And if you are using this book for **self-study** (= to study alone), it helps to have a routine. Decide how much time you can spend on the book each day or each week. If you are studying a unit for the first time, try to give yourself **at least** (= a minimum of) half an hour or forty-five minutes; if you are **revising** (= looking through a unit a second or third time), five or ten minutes each time is very useful. So, plan longer periods for new units, and shorter periods for **revision**.

B Working through the book

Do different things to **maintain your interest.**(= keep your interest high). For example:
- Don't work through the units **in sequence** (= in the order they appear in the book): look through the units and choose ones that interest you.
- When you do a unit, you can:
  read the whole of the left-hand page, then do the exercises.
  read part of the left-hand page, then do one or two exercises.
  try the exercises first, then use the left-hand page when you have a problem.
- Be <u>active</u> when you are learning. For example:
  While you are reading the left-hand page, use a **highlighter** pen to mark new or interesting vocabulary.
  Practise saying the words **silently** in your head (= without a noise), and also **out loud** (= making a noise, so it is possible for others to hear), to see if you can pronounce them.
  Put new words in your own notebook using some of the ideas from Unit 2 to do it **effectively**. (If something is **effective**, it works well and produces good results.)

C Revision

It is common to learn a word one day, then find you cannot remember it a day later. If you revise regularly (just for short periods), it helps you to remember words and make them part of your 'active' vocabulary. Here are some ideas for revising with this book.

- Do exercises in pencil. Check your answers when you have finished, then **rub them out** (= remove them using a rubber/eraser). Later, come back and do the exercises again, and just use the left-hand page if you cannot remember something.

- When you read a left-hand page for a second time, have a piece of card with you. When you reach a new word in **bold** which has a definition/explanation after it in **brackets** ( ), cover the definition quickly and try to say what it is. Then uncover it to see if you were right.

- Revise for short periods but do it often. Five minutes a day is probably better than half an hour a week; but half an hour a week is probably better than two hours a month.

- As with learning, be <u>active</u> when you revise. Look for different ways to revise: test yourself, create games for yourself; **set goals/targets** (= decide on things you want to be able to do by a particular time); decide when to work on something, e.g. meaning on Sunday, pronunciation on Monday, etc.

Exercises

1.1 **Think about these questions. On the opposite page you will find some answers. Do you agree with them?**

1 Is it better to plan regular self-study, or is it better just to study when you think you've got some free time?
2 Do you think you should work through the units in the same order as they appear in the book?
3 Do you think it's a good idea to write down new words in a notebook while you are studying a unit?
4 Is it necessary to revise vocabulary?
5 Is it better to revise vocabulary occasionally for long periods of time, or is it better to revise regularly for short periods of time?

1.2 **Finding your way round the book.**

Turn to the Topic units in the Contents on pages 1–3. Take a blank piece of paper and cover the right-hand side of the page giving the examples. Now read down the list of unit titles. For each one, try to write down your own examples – one or two for each unit. Are there any unit titles you don't understand? Are there any units where you can't think of examples? If so, turn to that unit and find out what it is about.

You could use similar titles in your own vocabulary notebook. (See Unit 2)

1.3 *True* or *False*? **If the sentence is** *false*, **rewrite it to make it** *true*. **Write your answers in pencil.**

1 In this book, new words are often shown in **bold** print.
2 Definitions/explanations of new words are often in **brackets** after the word.
3 A **routine** means doing certain things in a different way each time.
4 If you **maintain** something at a level, it means you keep it at the same level.
5 If something, e.g. a way of learning, is **effective,** it doesn't work very well.
6 **At least** 50 people means a maximum of 50 people.
7 If you write something then **rub it out**, you remove it from the page.
8 If you do something **silently,** you do it without making a noise.
9 **Revision** means studying something for the first time.
10 If you have a **goal** or **target,** you have something you want to be able to do or achieve by a particular point in the future.

Now check your answers on the opposite page and look at any wrong answers carefully. Then rub out your answers and come back to this exercise again tomorrow or within the next two or three days. Find out how much you can remember.

1.4 **Planning your self-study.**

Now start making your own plans to use this book. Decide how much time you can spend each week, plan some longer periods to study units for the first time, but also some shorter periods for revision. The first five units will teach you some important vocabulary; give you ideas on keeping a notebook; and give you help with pronunciation. After that, continue with the units that interest you most.
Good luck.

2 Keeping a vocabulary notebook

A Organising your notebook

Give each page or double page a title, e.g. sport, education, phrasal verbs, etc. Then, as you learn new words, record each one on a suitable page. You could also have a general index in the back of your book, with a space for each letter Then, as you learn new words, you enter them alphabetically with the title of the topic in brackets.

B What do I need to record?

These things are important but you won't need to record all of them for every word.

What?	How?	Example
Meaning	a translation	**lembrar** = to remember (Portuguese)
	b definition/explanation	A **pond** is an area of water smaller than a lake.
	c synonym or opposite	**awful** (= terrible); **ugly** (≠ beautiful)
	d picture	**saucepan**
	e example sentences	My hands were cold so I **put on** my **gloves.**
Pronunciation	phonetic symbols	**ache** /eɪk/
	or your own system	ache (like 'make')
Part of speech	(n), (v), (adj), etc.	gloves (n); remember (v); careful (adj), ache (n, v)
Grammar	make a note + example sentence	**enjoy** + -ing form; I enjoy going to parties. **weather** (U); We had lovely **weather** in Italy.
Common partners	phrase or sentence	**make a mistake; make a decision; make a mess**
Special style	make a note	purchase (*fml*); kids (*infml*)

Note: You won't learn everything about a word when you first record it, so always leave space in your notebook, then you can come back and add more information later.

C Organising words on the page

Certain words often appear together (common partners), so it is a good idea to record them together, and not just write lists of words on their own. You can do this in different ways:

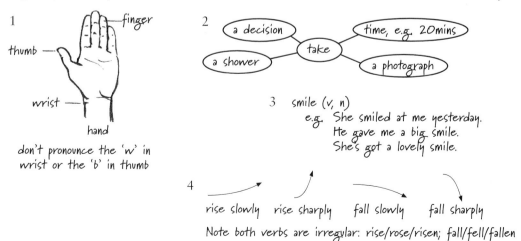

1
finger
thumb
wrist
hand
don't pronounce the 'w' in wrist or the 'b' in thumb

2
a decision — take — time, e.g. 20mins
a shower — take — a photograph

3 smile (v, n)
    e.g. She smiled at me yesterday.
          He gave me a big smile.
          She's got a lovely smile.

4
rise slowly   rise sharply   fall slowly   fall sharply
Note both verbs are irregular: rise/rose/risen; fall/fell/fallen

Exercises

2.1 Organise this list of words into three groups and give each one a title.

tie	put on	fare	blouse	homeless	train	get on
painful	scarf	jumper	jacket	journey	careful	station
helpful	jeans	platform	thoughtless	ticket	useless	

Find the units in this book which may include these words and add more examples.

2.2 Underline the correct answer or answers.

1 A pond is:
   a) bigger than a lake   b) smaller than a lake   c) the same size
2 I really enjoy:
   a) play tennis   b) to play tennis   c) playing tennis
3 When we were on holiday we had:
   a) lovely weathers   b) lovely weather   c) a lovely weather
4 The underlined letters in **a<u>ch</u>e** are pronounced the same as in:
   a) ma<u>ch</u>ine   b) cat<u>ch</u>   c) <u>ch</u>emist
5 She gave me a .... smile.
   a) strong   b) big   c) large
6 The past tense of **fall** is:
   a) fell   b) felt   c) falled
7 You can **put on**:
   a) gloves   b) a decision   c) shoes
8 **Rise sharply** means:

a)   b)   c)

2.3 Look again at the list a–e in B. Which would be the best way(s) to record the meaning of each word in the list below? What other information would be useful to record with this word (e.g. pronunciation, part of speech, grammar, common partners, etc.)? Use a dictionary to help you.

| dream | concentrate | beard | nearly |
| empty | forget | rescue | knife |

2.4 Fill the gaps with common partners for these verbs, then start a page in your own notebook for more examples. Turn to Unit 19 to help you.

take	a picture		make	a mistake
	....			....
	....			....
do	your homework		have	a rest
	....			....
	....			....

3 Using a dictionary

Using a dictionary

A   What dictionaries do I need?

If possible, you should buy two dictionaries: a good bilingual dictionary and a good English–English dictionary. The bilingual dictionary is quicker and easier for you to understand; the English–English dictionary may give you more information about a word or phrase, and it is also a good idea for you to work in English as much as possible. Here are some current recommended English–English dictionaries:

Large dictionaries
Cambridge International Dictionary of English
Longman Dictionary of Contemporary English
Collins COBUILD English Dictionary
Oxford Advanced Learner's Dictionary

Medium-sized dictionaries
Collins COBUILD Essential Dictionary
Oxford Wordpower Dictionary
Longman Active Study Dictionary

B   What information does a dictionary give me?

- the meaning, e.g. **homesick** = unhappy when you are away from home for a long time
- the pronunciation, e.g. **chaos** /keɪɒs/, **dreadful** /dredfʊl/, **island** /aɪlənd/
- the part of speech, e.g. **dirty** *adj* (= adjective), **lose** *v* (= verb), **law** *n* (= noun)
- any special grammatical features, e.g. **advice** (U) (= uncountable)
- common collocations (word partners), e.g. you **do homework** [NOT ~~you make homework~~]
- example phrases or sentences, e.g. It was such a big menu, I didn't know what to **choose**.
- opposites (where they exist), e.g. **polite** (≠ **impolite/rude**)

Note: In most English–English dictionaries for foreign learners, collocations are usually shown in **bold** or *italics*, or they are included in the examples given after the definition.

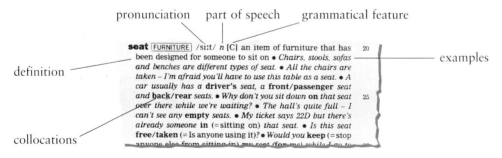

C   How should I use my dictionary?

Here are some ideas to help you.

- When you look up a word, put a ✓ next to it. Each time you return to a page with a ✓ look at it quickly to check that you remember the word.
- If you see an English word in a text, first try to guess the meaning, and carry on reading to see if your guess seems correct. Use your dictionary to check the meaning.
- If you look up a word in a bilingual dictionary and get several different words in your own language, look up the word in your monolingual dictionary. This should help you to decide which word in your own language is the nearest translation in this context.
- Remember that many words have more than one meaning, and the first meaning in the dictionary is not always the one you want. Read through the different meanings.

Exercises

If you find these exercises difficult, it may mean that you need to practise using a dictionary more often, or you need to buy yourself a better dictionary.

3.1 Use a dictionary to find/check the answers to these questions. (They are all based on words from the opposite page.)

1 What does **dreadful** mean?
2 How do you pronounce **lose**? (Is it the same as 'choose' or 'chose'?)
3 What part of speech is **choose**?
4 What part of speech is **homesick**?
5 **Homework** and **chaos** are both nouns, but what <u>type</u> of noun are they?
6 What adjectives are often used before **chaos**? (Give two.)
7 What two prepositions are often used after **choose**?
8 Write down a sentence example of **choose** used with a preposition.

3.2 When you look up a word, you can also use your dictionary to increase your vocabulary by learning related words and phrases. Find out if your dictionary helps you to answer these questions, also about words from the opposite page.

1 **Choose** is a verb, but what is the noun with the same meaning?
2 **Advice** is a noun, but what is the verb with the same meaning?
3 **Advice** is also uncountable, but you can make it countable using another word. Can you complete this sentence: 'He gave me a very useful .... of advice.'
4 What adjective is formed from **chaos**?
5 What is the opposite of **dirty**?
6 What is the difference between **homework** and **housework**?
7 What is the opposite of **lose a game**?
8 What is the opposite of **lose weight**?
9 **Law** often appears in the phrase **law and** .... What is the missing word?
10 If you want to sit at a table in a cafe and you see that one person is sitting there already, but another **seat** is empty, what can you say to the person sitting down?

3.3 In the word 'island' /aɪlənd/, the letter 's' is silent (= not pronounced). Use the pronunciation guide in your dictionary to find the silent letters in each of these words. (Do not include the letter 'e' at the end of a word.)

knife   bomb   psychology   receipt   castle   doubt   wrist   calm

Note: Students often ask if the letter 't' is pronounced in 'often'. Some people pronounce it, others don't. What does your dictionary say?

3.4 Look at the entry for *suit* on the right, then match the definitions with the sentences on the left.

1 I'm afraid black doesn't **suit** me – my hair is the wrong colour.
2 A: I'm not going, so don't ask me again.
    B: OK. **Suit** yourself.
3 If we have the meeting this afternoon, would 2.30 **suit** you?

> **suit²** *v* [T] **1** to be acceptable or CONVENIENT for a par- ☒
> ticular person or in a particular situation: *Finding a date* ☒
> *that suits us all is very difficult.* | *Buy a database program*
> *to suit your needs.* | **suit sb (fine)** *spoken* (=be completely
> acceptable) *"Eight o'clock?" "That suits me fine."* | **suit sb**
> **down to the ground** (=be exactly right for someone)
> *Yup, this little car suits me down to the ground.* **2** [not in
> passive] to make someone look attractive: *That coat re-*
> *ally suits Paul.* | *Red suits you.* —see FIT¹ (USAGE)
> **3 well/best/ideally suited** to have the right qualities to
> do something: *Dirk would be ideally suited to the job.*
> **4 suit yourself** *spoken* used to tell someone they can do
> whatever they want to, even though it annoys you: *"I*
> *don't really feel like going out after all." "Suit yourself."*
> **5 suit sb's book** *BrE informal* to fit well into someone's

4 English language words

A Parts of speech

nouns	e.g. chair, information, happiness
verbs	e.g. choose, tell, complain
adjectives	e.g. happy, tall, dangerous
adverbs	e.g. slowly, carefully, often
prepositions	e.g. in, at, on
pronouns	e.g. me, you, him, we, it, she
articles	e.g. definite article (the); indefinite article (a/an)

B Special terms

Uncountable noun: (U) a noun which has no plural form and cannot be used with the indefinite article, e.g. information. See Unit 27.

Plural noun: (*pl*) a noun which only has a plural form and cannot be used with the indefinite article, e.g. trousers. See Unit 27.

Infinitive: the base form of a verb, e.g. (to) work, (to) stop, (to) be.

Phrasal verb: a verb + adverb and/or preposition, e.g. turn on (verb + adverb), look after (verb + preposition), give up (verb + adverb), put up with (verb + adverb + preposition). See Units 16 and 17.

Idiom: a group of words with a meaning that is different from the individual words, e.g. never mind, hang on, a short cut, keep an eye on something.

Transitive verb: a verb which needs a **direct object**, e.g. Police caught the man ('the man' is the direct object of the verb 'caught'). See Unit 17.

Intransitive verb: a verb which does not need a direct object, e.g. The books arrived on time. (There is no direct object after arrive.) See Unit 17.

C Word building

In the word *uncomfortable, un-* is a **prefix**, *comfort* is a **root**, and *-able* is a **suffix**. Other common prefixes include: *re-, in-,* and *dis-*; common suffixes include: *-ity, -ment,* and *-ive*. Many words also have **synonyms**, which are words with the same meaning. For example, 'big' is a synonym of 'large'. The **opposite** is 'small'.

D Pronunciation

Dictionaries show the pronunciation of a word using **phonetic symbols**, e.g. book /bʊk/, before /bɪˈfɔː/, cinema /ˈsɪnəmə/, and so on.

Each word contains one or more **syllables**: 'book' has one syllable; 'before' has two syllables (be-fore); 'cinema' has three syllables (ci-ne-ma); 'education' has four syllables (e-du-ca-tion); and so on.

For pronunciation, it is important to know which syllable has the main **stress**. On 'before' it is the second syllable (be<u>fore</u>); on 'cinema' it is the first (<u>ci</u>nema); and on 'education' it is the third (edu<u>ca</u>tion).

Note: Dictionaries mark stress in different ways: in bold (re**turn**); or a ' before the main syllable (re'turn). Make sure you understand how your dictionary shows it.

E Punctuation

full stop   .   comma   ,   brackets   ( )   hyphen   -   question mark   ?

Exercises

4.1 There is one word missing in each line of this text. Where does the missing word go? What could it be? And what type of word is it (noun, verb, etc.)? Look at the example first.

Last year I went to/for my holiday. I spent the first
week Seville staying with a couple of friends, and
then I took a train to Barcelona where spent another
ten days. It is beautiful city and I had a marvellous
time. I stayed in a very hotel right in the centre, but
I didn't mind spending a lot money because it is a
wonderful and also very convenient. My brother was
the person who recommended it; he goes Spain a lot
and he stays anywhere else.

..Spain..(noun)..........
....
....
....
....
....
....
....
....

4.2 In the dialogue below, can you find at least one example of the following: an uncountable noun; a plural noun; a phrasal verb; an idiom?

A: What's the time?
B: 8 o'clock, so we'd better get a move on if we're going to meet your sister at the airport.
A: That's alright. Her flight doesn't arrive until 8.30.
B: Yeah, but it'll take us an hour to get there – you know what the traffic is like.
A: OK. I'll just go and get changed.
B: What's wrong with those shorts?
A: I don't like driving in shorts. I'm going to put some jeans on.

4.3 Look at the <u>underlined</u> verbs in these sentences. Which are transitive, which are intransitive?

1 She <u>broke</u> her leg.
2 I <u>got up</u> at seven thirty.
3 We <u>arrived</u> late.
4 <u>Take off</u> your jacket.
5 She doesn't <u>like</u> Chinese food.
6 He told me to <u>sit down</u>.

4.4 How many syllables are there in each of the words in the box?

English	noun	informal	education
understand	adjective	decide	pronunciation
before	opposite	preposition	comfortable

Now mark the main stress on each of the above words.

4.5 Look at these words, then answer the questions below.

happy   correct   lucky   sure   possible

1 What part of speech are these words?
2 Change each one into an adverb.
3 Can you write down a synonym for at least three of the words?
4 Which prefix do you need to form the opposite of each word? (three different ones)
5 Which word has the main stress on the second syllable?

5 Problems with pronunciation

A Phonetics

With many languages you can look at a word and know (more or less) how to pronounce it. With English this is not true: it is often very difficult to know the pronunciation from looking at a word. For example:

c<u>ough</u> (pronounced like 'off') en<u>ough</u> (like 'stuff') thr<u>ough</u> (like 'too') and d<u>ough</u> (like 'so')

The only way you can be sure about the pronunciation is to learn some phonetic symbols which tell you the pronunciation. Dictionaries use them, and there is a table of phonetic symbols, with examples, on page 246. Phonetic symbols are used next to many words in the index, and there is a special list of words on page 247, which cause pronunciation problems for speakers from different countries.

B Word stress

When a word has two or more syllables, one of them has the main stress. In these examples, the main stress follows the symbol ':

'accent   pre'fer   edu'cation   'necessary   Ja'pan   Japa'nese

If you put the stress on the wrong syllable, it may be difficult for listeners to understand what you are saying.

C /ə/

Probably the most important sound in English because it is often the pronunciation of the letters 'a', 'o' and 'e' if they are not part of a stressed syllable.

ma'chine /mə'ʃiːn/   'mother /'mʌðə/   po'tato /pə'teɪtəʊ/   'cinema /'sɪnəmə/

D Key letters and sounds

A common problem is that a single letter or combination of letters has more than one pronunciation, e.g. -ough in section A. Here are some more examples:

the letter 'o' is often /ɒ/, e.g. hot; or /ʌ/, e.g. some; or /əʊ/, e.g. no
the letter 'a' is often /æ/, e.g. hat; or /eɪ/, e.g. same; or /aː/, e.g. fast
the letter 'u' is often /ʌ/, e.g. run; or /ʊ/, e.g. put
the letter 'i' is often /ɪ/, e.g. sit; or /aɪ/, e.g. side

E Silent letters and short syllables

There are many words in English where a letter is not pronounced:

fas<u>t</u>en   plum<u>b</u>er   ca<u>l</u>m   <u>k</u>nee   <u>w</u>rong   com<u>b</u>

There are also many words where we almost 'eat' one of the syllables, and as a result a vowel sound almost disappears and a word, for example, with three written syllables may be two (or two and a half) in spoken English. For example:

interested /ɪntrəstɪd/   fattening /fætnɪŋ/   vegetable /vedʒtəbl/

Note: The exercises on the next page practise some words with difficult pronunciation.

Exercises

5.1 Try using some phonetic symbols. Using your dictionary or the index, fill in the pronunciation of these words (put the symbols between the / /). Then practise saying the words and make sure you can see and hear the difference in the pronunciation of the words in each pair.

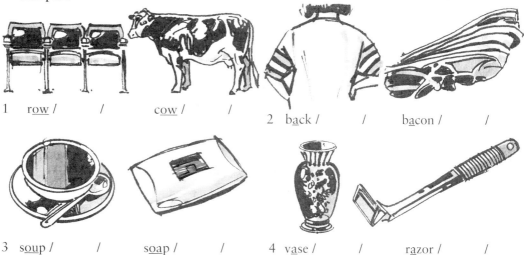

1 r<u>ow</u> / / c<u>ow</u> / / 2 b<u>a</u>ck / / b<u>a</u>con / /

3 s<u>ou</u>p / / s<u>oa</u>p / / 4 v<u>a</u>se / / r<u>a</u>zor / /

5.2 Look at the underlined letters in these words. Which one is the odd one out in each case?
1 br<u>ea</u>d   dr<u>ea</u>m   spr<u>ea</u>d   d<u>ea</u>d
2 sp<u>oo</u>n   r<u>oo</u>m   fl<u>oo</u>d   ch<u>oo</u>se
3 f<u>a</u>st   phr<u>a</u>se   bl<u>a</u>me   sunb<u>a</u>the
4 c<u>ou</u>sin   w<u>ou</u>nd (n)   r<u>ou</u>gh   tr<u>ou</u>ble
5 v<u>i</u>rus   p<u>i</u>lot   d<u>i</u>et   s<u>i</u>nce
6 h<u>y</u>phen   s<u>y</u>mptom   t<u>y</u>pe   ps<u>y</u>chology

5.3 Which syllable has the main stress in these words? Put them in the correct column.

cathedral   policy   palace
opposite   police   understand
advertisement   desert (n)
competition   organise
assistance   education

first	*second*	*third*

Now look at the words again. How many examples of the /ə/ sound can you find?

5.4 Look at the underlined letters in these pairs of words. Is the pronunciation the same or different?

<u>k</u>now / <u>k</u>nife   mu<u>sc</u>le / <u>sc</u>issors
i<u>s</u>land / I<u>s</u>lam   clim<u>b</u> / bom<u>b</u>
lis<u>t</u>en / wes<u>t</u>ern   <u>h</u>onest / <u>h</u>ope
ai<u>s</u>le / Chri<u>s</u>tmas   <u>wr</u>ong / <u>wr</u>ist
han<u>d</u> / han<u>d</u>some   cal<u>f</u> / ca<u>l</u>m

6 Classroom language

A Equipment

These are some of the things you may use in your classroom or school.

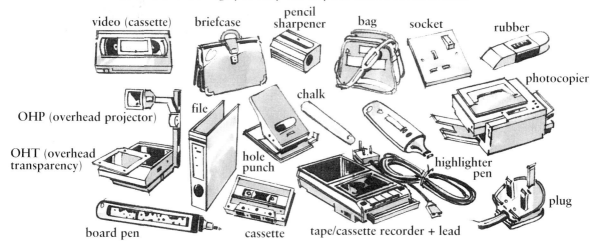

video (cassette) briefcase pencil sharpener bag socket rubber photocopier OHP (overhead projector) file chalk OHT (overhead transparency) hole punch highlighter pen plug board pen cassette tape/cassette recorder + lead

Note: We can use some of these nouns as verbs with little or no change: **to video** (= to record a programme on video), **to photocopy** (= to use the photocopier), **to highlight** and **to file** (= to put things in a file)

B Classroom activities

Here are some classroom activities. Look carefully at the verbs in bold.

Things you do in the classroom:

Look up a word if you don't understand it. (= find the meaning of a word in a dictionary)
Borrow someone's dictionary or rubber. (= use it and then return it)
Rub out mistakes in your notebook. (= erase mistakes / remove them using a rubber)

Things the teacher may do in the classroom:

Plug in the tape recorder. (= put the plug in the socket and turn on the electricity)
Turn up the tape recorder (= increase the volume) if the students can't hear it.
Rub things **off** the board. (= remove writing from the board)
Correct students' English. (= give the correct English if students make mistakes)

Things your teacher may ask you to do in the classroom:

Could you **clean** the board, Carlos? (= remove all the writing from the board)
Write these words **down**. (= write these words on a piece of paper / in a notebook)
Enrique, could you **swap** places (= exchange places) with Lorena?
Repeat this sentence (= say it again) after me.

C Questions about vocabulary

What does X mean? [NOT ~~what means X?~~]
How do you pronounce it?
How do you spell 'bicycle'?
How do you use 'anyway' in a sentence?
What's the difference between X and Y?

Exercises

6.1 Label these pictures then check your answers on the opposite page.

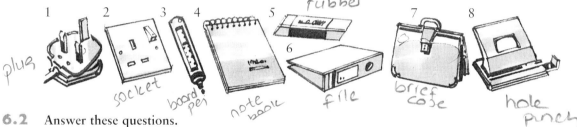

Handwritten labels: 1 plug 2 socket 3 board pen 4 note book 5 rubber 6 file 7 brief case 8 hole punch

6.2 Answer these questions.

1 What do you rub off the board?
2 What do you put in a tape recorder?
3 What do you put on an OHP?
4 What do you keep in a file?
5 What do you put in a briefcase?
6 What do you put in a socket?
7 What do you use a dictionary for?
8 What do you use a rubber for?
9 What do you use a photocopier for?
10 Why do you turn up a tape recorder?

6.3 Match the verbs on the left with the nouns on the right.

1 clean   places
2 turn up   a word
3 borrow   mistakes
4 swap   the board
5 video   a dictionary
6 do   the OHP
7 correct   the tape recorder
8 look up   a programme
9 plug in   an exercise

6.4 Think about your last lesson (in English or any other subject). Did you do any of these things?

clean the board   swap places with someone
use a rubber   look up a word
borrow something   make a mistake
watch a video   write something down in a notebook

6.5 Here are some answers. What are the possible questions?

A: ....?   B: It means to exchange places.
A: ....?   B: /swɒp/ Like 'cop' or 'stop'.
A: ....?   B: S-W-A-P.
A: ....?   B: I can't see the board from here. Will you swap places with me?

7 Prefixes

A With the meaning 'not'

Prefixes (**un-**, **in-**, **il-**, **ir-**, and **dis-**) are often used to give adjectives (and some verbs and nouns) a negative meaning. Here are common examples:

happy	**un**happy	like (v)	**dis**like (v)
possible	**im**possible	legal	**il**legal (= against the law)
correct	**in**correct	regular	**ir**regular, e.g. irregular verbs

un- is used with many different words, e.g. **unfriendly, unable, unemployed** (= without a job), **untidy** (= not in order; **in a mess**)

im- is used before some words beginning with **m** or **p**, e.g. **impolite** (= **rude**), **impatient** (somebody who is **impatient** wants things to happen now; they cannot wait for things)

il- is used before some words beginning with **l**, e.g. **illegible** (= cannot be read because the writing is very bad)

ir- is only used before some words beginning with **r**, e.g. **irresponsible**

dis- is used before some adjectives, e.g. **dishonest**, and a few verbs, e.g. **dislike, disagree**

in- is used before a limited number of words, e.g. **invisible** (= cannot be seen)

Note: A prefix does not normally change word stress, e.g. <u>hap</u>py/un<u>hap</u>py; <u>pos</u>sible/im<u>pos</u>sible. But the stress may change if you want to emphasise the negative or opposite:

A: Was he <u>hap</u>py about the change?
B: No, he was very <u>un</u>happy about it.

B Verb prefixes: un- and dis-

These prefixes have two meanings: they can have a negative meaning (as above), but they can also mean 'the opposite of an action' or 'to reverse an action'. This meaning is used with certain verbs.

I **locked** the door when I left, but I lost the key, so I couldn't **unlock** it when I got back.

I had to **pack** my suitcase (= put everything in it) very quickly, so when I **unpacked** (= took everything out) at the hotel, most of my clothes looked terrible.

The plane **appeared** in the sky, then suddenly **disappeared** behind a cloud.

In the morning you **get dressed** (= put on your clothes); when you go to bed you **get undressed** (= take off your clothes).

C Other verb prefixes with specific meanings

re- (= again)	My homework was terrible, so I had to **redo** it.
	The shop closed down but will **reopen** next month.
	I failed my exam but I can **retake** (or **redo/resit**) it next year.
over- (= too much)	I think my boss is **overdoing** it at the moment. (= working too hard; also **overwork**)
	I went to bed very late and I **overslept** (= slept too long) this morning.
	The shop assistant **overcharged** me. (= asked me for too much money)
mis- (= badly or incorrectly)	I'm afraid I **misunderstood** what he said.
	Two of the students **misread** the first question.

Exercises

7.1 Which prefix forms the opposite of these words? (The bottom line are all verbs, the rest are adjectives.)

.....happy   .....patient   .....polite   .....legal
.....correct   .....regular   .....visible   .....possible
.....legible   .....friendly   .....employed   .....honest
.....pack   .....lock   .....agree   .....like

7.2 Agree with these statements, using words from the left-hand page which have the same meaning as the underlined words.

Example: A: He <u>doesn't have a job</u>, does he?
         B: No, *he's unemployed.*

1 It's <u>against the law</u>, isn't it?
   Oh yes, *it's illegal*

2 His room is always <u>in a mess</u>, isn't it?
   Yes, *it's untidy*

3 He <u>took off his clothes</u>!
   Yes, *he gets undressed*

4 This handwriting is <u>impossible to read</u>.
   Yes I know, ...

5 She <u>can never wait for five minutes, can she?</u>
   No, ...

6 I thought it was <u>rude</u>, didn't you?
   Yes, it was very ....

7.3 Complete the verbs in these sentences.

1 I'm sorry, I mis..................... her message completely.
2 We un..................... as soon as we got to the hotel, then went out for a walk.
3 She was here a minute ago, but then she dis...................... I'm afraid I don't know where she is now.
4 We normally have similar opinions but I dis..................... with him totally on the subject of drugs.
5 My homework was so bad that I'll have to re..................... it.
6 Apparently her alarm clock didn't ring and she over......................
7 She finally managed to un..................... the door and we were able to go inside.
8 I dis..................... the film, but the others enjoyed it.
9 I don't think I'll pass the exam, but I can always re..................... it in September.
10 The post office shuts for lunch but it should re..................... at 2.00 p.m.
11 She's over..................... at the moment. She really needs a holiday and a complete break from her job.
12 My sister wrapped up my present so well that it took me about five minutes to un..................... it.

7.4 Keep several pages in your notebook for verbs or adjectives which combine with these prefixes. Each time you add a new word, read through your list of words with that prefix, then close your book and see how many you can remember.

8 Noun suffixes

A Verb + suffix

Many nouns are formed in this way.

Verb	Suffix	Noun
improve (= get better)	-ment	improvement
manage (e.g. a shop or business)	-ment	management
elect (= choose somebody by voting)	-ion	election
discuss (= talk about something seriously)	-ion	discussion
inform (= tell someone something)	-ation	information
organise	-ation	organisation
jog (= running to keep fit or for pleasure)	-ing	jogging
spell (e.g. S-P-E-L-L)	-ing	spelling

Note: Sometimes there is a spelling change. The most common is the omission of the final 'e' before the suffix **-ion** or **-ation**: translate/translation; organise/organisation

B Adjective + suffix

Nouns are also formed by adding a suffix to an adjective. Two suffixes often added to adjectives to form nouns are **-ness** and **-ity**.

Adjective	Suffix	Noun
weak (≠ strong)	-ness	weakness
happy	-ness	happiness
dark (e.g. at night, when you can't see)	-ness	darkness
stupid (≠ intelligent, clever)	-ity	stupidity
punctual (= always arrives at the right time)	-ity	punctuality
similar (= almost the same; ≠ different)	-ity	similarity

C Pronunciation

The addition of these suffixes may change the pronunciation.

Nouns ending **-ion** or **-ity** have the main stress on the syllable before, so the pronunciation may be different from the verb or adjective:

Verb	Noun	Adjective	Noun
educate	education	similar	similarity
translate	translation	stupid	stupidity
discuss	discussion	punctual	punctuality

D -er/-or and -ist

These are common noun suffixes added to existing nouns or verbs, and they describe people and their jobs.

-er	-er	-or	-ist
dancer	driver	actor	artist
singer	manager	director	economist
murderer	footballer	translator	psychologist
farmer	employer	operator	journalist

Note: Notice the common spelling changes:
translate/translator, operate/operator, economy/economist, psychology/psychologist.

Exercises

8.1 Complete the tables and mark the stress on each word. The last two in each column are not on the opposite page, but do you know or can you guess the noun formed from them?

Verb	Noun
educate	
improve	
jog	
spell	
hesitate	
arrange	

Adjective	Noun
stupid	
dark	
weak	
similar	
punctual	
sad	
popular	

8.2 Combine the suffixes on the right with the verbs or adjectives on the left, and then complete the text below. (Remember you may need to make a small spelling change.)

| improve¹ televise elect |
| educate² weak manage |
| govern³ stupid |

| -ment | -ity | -ion | -ation | -ness |

In his first broadcast on (1) _____ since he won the (2) _____ last month, the Prime Minister promised to make health and (3) _____ two of his top priorities. And in a strong attack on the previous (4) _____, he said that the present (5) _____ of the British economy was caused entirely by their (6) _____ and bad (7) _____. He said he would act immediately and he hoped the British people would be able to see clear signs of an (8) _____ in the economy by the end of the year.

8.3 Write down the name of the person who does these things.

Example: farm ...*farmer*.........

1 act .... 4 sing .... 7 economics ....
2 employ .... 5 murder .... 8 translate ....
3 football .... 6 psychology .... 9 manage ....

8.4 Look at the two examples and then complete the rest of the definitions.

Example: An actor is a person who ...*acts in films, plays and on TV*.....
A murderer is a person who ...*murders someone*....

1 A journalist is a person who ....
2 A ballet dancer is a person who ....
3 A film director is a person who ....
4 A bank manager is a person who ....
5 An employer is a person who ....
6 A pop singer is a person who ....
7 A translator is a person who ....
8 A lorry driver is a person who ....
9 A photographer is a person who ....
10 An artist is a person who ....

9 Adjective suffixes

Suffixes change word class, e.g. from verb to noun or noun to adjective, but they can also change meaning (see sections B and C below).

A Noun or verb + suffix

Noun or *Verb*	*Suffix*	*Adjectives*
danger, fame	-ous	dangerous, famous (= well-known)
music, politics	-al	musical, political, industrial,
industry, economics		economical (= saves you money)
cloud, fog, sun, dirt	-y	cloudy, foggy, sunny, dirty (≠ clean)
attract, create	-ive	attractive (= pretty, nice to look at); creative (= able to produce new ideas; with imagination)

Note: Sometimes there is a spelling change. Here are common examples:
double the consonant, e.g. sun/sunny, fog/foggy
leave out the final 'e', e.g. create/creative, fame/famous
leave out the final 's' before 'al', e.g. politics/political; economics/economical
change 'y' to 'i' before 'al', e.g. industry/industrial

B -able /əbl/

This suffix (also -ible in some words) is used to form many adjectives from nouns or verbs: **enjoyable, comfortable, knowledgeable** (= knows a lot), **suitable** (= right/correct for a particular situation).

Quite often, -able (and -ible) has the meaning 'can be done'. For example, something that is **washable** 'can be washed'. Other examples include:

drinkable, comprehensible (= can be comprehended or understood), **reliable** (= can be relied on or trusted, e.g. a car or other machine that never goes wrong or breaks down).

Words ending -**able** quite often express the opposite meaning by adding the prefix **un-**:

undrinkable, unreliable, unbreakable (= cannot be broken), **unsuitable, uncomfortable**

Words ending -**ible** add the prefix **in-**:

incomprehensible, inflexible (somebody who is **inflexible** has a fixed idea about something and cannot change quickly or easily; an **inflexible** timetable cannot be changed easily); **inedible** (= cannot be eaten).

C -ful and -less

The suffix -**ful** often means 'full of' + the meaning of the adjective: **careful**, you are full of care; if you are **helpful** you are full of help. Other examples are: **painful** (= hurts a lot), **useful**, and **thoughtful** (= someone who is **thoughtful** is kind and always thinks about others; a **thoughtful** action shows care for others)

The suffix -**less** means 'without' + the meaning of the adjective: if you are **careless**, you do something 'without care'. Other examples are: **painless, useless** (= has no use or function) **thoughtless, jobless** and **homeless** (= with nowhere to live)

Note: You can see that -**ful** and -**less** are often used with the same words to form opposites. This is not always true: a person with a home is NOT ~~homeful~~.

Exercises

9.1 Write down an adjective (or adjectives) formed from these nouns or verbs. Cover the opposite page first.

thought	dirt	pain	comfort
attract	care	knowledge	fame
create	danger	suit	rely
fog	politics	sun	wash
home	enjoy	music	break
use			

9.2 Fill the gaps with suitable adjectives from the opposite page.

1 You must be very .... when you drive in wet weather.
2 It was so .... this morning that I couldn't see more than twenty metres in front of me.
3 Everyone in my country has heard of her; she's very ....
4 The people in the tourist information office were very .... and answered all our questions without any problems.
5 This is a very .... road; there were at least three serious accidents on it last year.
6 It was very .... when I hit my leg against the corner of the table.
7 This bag is very .... because I can use it for work or when I go on holiday.
8 We've never had any problems with our TV in ten years; it's been very ....
9 The factory is in the middle of the .... part of the city, surrounded by other factories.
10 I made some coffee but it was horrible. In fact, my sister said it was ....
11 I'm afraid my working hours are very ....; I have to start at exactly the same time every day and finish at the same time every day.
12 It seems terrible to me that there are so many .... people living in a city with thousands of empty houses.

9.3 How many of these words can form opposites with the suffix -less?

painful   wonderful   useful   careful
beautiful   tactful   awful   thoughtful

Can you think of words which mean the opposite of the other words (the ones without -less)?

9.4 From the adjectives on this page and the opposite page, choose three which could describe each of these people or things. (You can use the same adjective more than once.)

1 the weather ....
2 someone who is a very bad driver ....
3 Wolfgang Amadeus Mozart ....
4 a large city ....
5 Albert Einstein ....
6 a new car ....
7 a speech ....
8 yourself ....

10 Zero affixation

son ek / onek (handwritten)

A What is zero affixation?

Many words in English can function as a noun and verb, or noun and adjective, or verb and adjective, with no change in form. The meaning is not always the same, but this unit looks at examples where the words do have the same meaning.

What's the **answer**? (noun)   I must **clean** my room. (verb)
Answer the question. (verb)   It's a **clean** room. (adjective)

I don't like the **cold**. (noun)   I didn't **reply** to the letter. (verb)
I don't like **cold** weather. (adjective)   I wrote a **reply** to the letter. (noun)

Note: Other examples in the book are marked like this: ache (n, v), damage (n, v), dry (v, adj). Keep a record of them in your notebook.

B Noun and verb

You may know these words in one form but not the other. (The definitions are for the verb.)

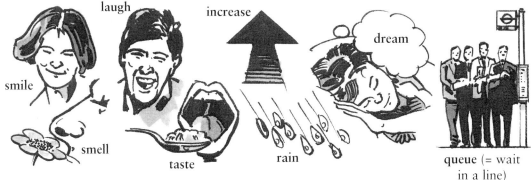

brake (= stop a car using the **brake** on the floor)   **ring** (= phone)
diet (= eat less and lose weight)   **push** (≠ **pull**)
guess (= give an answer without knowing the facts)   **murder** (= kill someone)

Note: Other words in this group include: **stay, drink, rest, look, cost,** and **wait.** Use a dictionary if you need to check the meaning. Here are a few examples:

We **queued** for half an hour.   We waited in **a queue** for half an hour.
This orange **smells/tastes** strange.   This orange has got a strange **smell/taste**.
I didn't know the answer, so I **guessed**.   I didn't know the answer, so I **had a guess**.

C Which verb?

When you use these words as nouns, you need to choose the correct verb to use with it.

Verb   *Noun*
We stayed in Paris for a short time.   We **had** a short stay in Paris.
We rested for a while.   We **had** a short rest.
She braked quickly.   She **put on** the brakes quickly.
He needs to diet.   He needs to **go on** a diet.
I'm going to ring him.   I'm going to **give** him a ring.
I looked in the paper.   I **had** a look in the paper.
He pushed me.   He **gave** me a push.
I dreamt about you last night.   I **had** a dream about you last night.

Exercises

10.1 Rewrite these sentences using the underlined nouns as verbs. The meaning must stay the same. Look at the example first.

Example: There was a lot of <u>rain</u> yesterday.
.............It rained a lot yesterday..............

1 We had a long <u>wait</u>.
....

2 I had a <u>dream</u> about you last night.
....

3 We waited in the <u>queue</u> for half an hour.
....

4 The <u>cost</u> of the holiday was about £500.
....

5 I wrote a <u>reply</u> to his letter yesterday.
....

10.2 Now rewrite these sentences using the underlined verbs as nouns. The meaning must stay the same.

1 I'll <u>ring</u> him this evening.
....

2 I <u>diet</u> if I put on weight.
....

3 It was very hot, so we <u>rested</u> for a while after lunch.
....

4 I <u>braked</u> but I still couldn't stop in time.
....

5 He <u>pushed</u> me.
....

6 Did you <u>look</u> in the paper?
....

10.3 Sometimes the same word form can be a verb and noun but with a very different meaning. Read these pairs of sentences. Does the verb have the same meaning as the noun, a similar meaning, or a completely different meaning?

1 We had a long <u>wait</u> for the bus.
  If we <u>wait</u> any longer, we may miss the train.
2 Could we have another bottle of <u>water</u>, please?
  I asked her to <u>water</u> the garden.
3 I gave him the <u>book</u>.
  Did you <u>book</u> the table in the restaurant?
4 They always take a <u>break</u> after an hour's work.
  Did he <u>break</u> his arm skiing?
5 I go for a <u>run</u> most mornings.
  I was late so I had to <u>run</u> to get to school on time.

11 Compound nouns

A Formation

A compound noun is formed from two nouns, or an adjective and a noun. Here are some common examples.

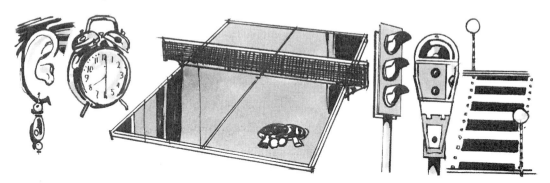

alarm clock	dining room (= the room where you eat meals)
credit card	film star (e.g. Tom Cruise, Jodie Foster)
table tennis	brother-in-law (= your sister's husband, your husband's brother)
T-shirt	income tax (= the tax you pay on your salary)
earring	writing paper (= paper for writing letters)
sunglasses	washing machine (= the machine for washing clothes)
traffic lights	cheque book (= a book which has cheques)
tin opener	baby-sitter (= he/she looks after children when parents are out)
parking meter	*mother tongue (= your first language)
*first aid	*science fiction (= stories about the future)
*pedestrian crossing	*box office (= where you buy tickets in cinemas and theatres)

B One word or two?

Compound nouns are usually written as two words (e.g. credit card), but sometimes they are joined by a hyphen (e.g. baby-sitter), or written as one word (e.g. sunglasses). Unfortunately there is no rule for this, so you may need to check in a dictionary.

C Pronunciation

The main stress is usually on the first part (e.g. parking meter) but sometimes it is on both parts (e.g. mother tongue). In A, the compounds marked *all have the stress on both parts. Some dictionaries show the stress on compounds.

D Forming new compounds

Quite often, one part of a compound forms the basis for a number of compound nouns.

post/ticket/box office   traffic lights/warden/jam   film/pop/rock star

brother/sister/father/mother -in-law   dining/sitting/waiting room

Note: A **traffic jam** is a long line of cars which are moving slowly because the road is busy; and **traffic wardens** patrol the streets to make sure you are not parked in the wrong place illegally. You buy theatre tickets at the **box office** and train tickets at the **ticket office**.

Exercises

11.1 Find compound nouns on the opposite page connected with each of these topics.

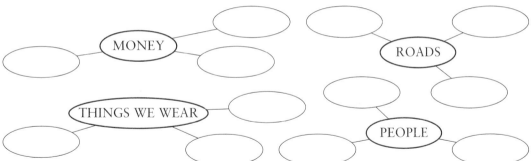

11.2 Complete these sentences with suitable compound nouns, then see if you can find them on the opposite page.

1 I'm late because there was a terrible .... in the centre of town.
2 Humphrey Bogart was a famous .... in the forties and fifties.
3 My .... didn't ring this morning and I didn't wake up until 9.30.
4 When I got to the surgery, I had to sit in the .... for forty minutes before I could see the dentist.
5 Mary really wanted to see the film but she couldn't find a .... for the children, so she had to stay at home.
6 When I'm driving I always wear .... if it's very bright and sunny.
7 You have to pay .... on your salary in Britain; the amount depends on how much you earn.
8 I often have the same problem: I park the car next to a ...., and then I discover that I don't have the right money.
9 In some countries you have to have a .... box in your car for minor injuries and illnesses.
10 My brother loves ...., but I prefer true stories about the present or the past.

11.3 Take one word (the first part or the second part) from each compound and create a new compound. Use a dictionary to help you if necessary.

Examples: brother-in-law   ...*mother-in-law*......
              table tennis   ...*table leg*.............

dining room   ....   traffic lights   ....
film star   ....   sunglasses   ....
credit card   ....   post office   ....
toothpaste   ....   hairdryer   ....

Now mark the main stress on each of the compound nouns you have created.

11.4 Try creating your own compound nouns. Choose two or three common words and then try to form compound nouns from them. When you have two or three possibilities, check in a dictionary to see if your words exist. Start with these.

.... book   *or*   book ....
.... card

12 Compound adjectives

A **Formation and pronunciation**

A compound adjective is formed from two different words, and occasionally three. They are usually written with a hyphen (e.g. good-looking, well-known), and the stress is usually the same on both parts of the compound.

B **Describing people**

Many compound adjectives describe a person's appearance, character, and situation.

This is William. He isn't **well-known** (= famous), he isn't **well-off** (= rich), and I've never heard anyone say he was **good-looking** (= handsome/attractive). But he's a very nice man – kind, friendly and very **easy-going** (= relaxed). In this picture he's wearing a **short-sleeved** shirt and a **brand-new** (= completely new) hat.

C **'Well' and 'badly'**

These adverbs combine with many past participles to form compound adjectives. You can use 'well' or 'badly' in front of the adjective (except **well-known**, which has no opposite).

a well-directed film	a badly-paid job (= a low salary)
a well-made pair of shoes	a badly-behaved child (= acting in a bad way)
a well-written story	a badly-dressed young man (= wearing horrible clothes)

D **A 'five-minute' walk**

It is common to combine a number and a singular noun to form a compound adjective.

It's a **fifteen-minute drive** to the centre. (= a drive of fifteen minutes)
He works in a **four-star** hotel. (= a hotel with a rating of four stars)
I gave her a **five-pound** note. (= a note with a value of five pounds)
The winner was a **ten-year-old** girl. (= a girl who is ten years old)
There was a **two-hour** delay on our flight. (= the plane was two hours late)

E **Common compounds**

She had a **full-time** job in a bank, but after the baby was born she changed to a **part-time** job and just worked in the mornings.
The hotel is **north-west** of here, about ten miles away. (also **north-east**, **south-east**, and **south-west**)
Most of the population are **right-handed**, but about 10% are **left-handed**.
On trains and planes you can buy a **first-class** ticket if you are happy to pay a lot more.
Mary bought a **second-hand** BMW. (= the car was not **brand-new**, but was a new car for her)

Note: As with compound nouns, you can often combine different words with one part and form many different compound adjectives.

Exercises

12.1 Match words from the box on the left with words from the box on the right to form 12 compound adjectives.

good	well
easy	north
ten	short
brand	badly
part	left
first	second

new	known
written	class
looking	sleeved
hand	handed
going	east
time	pound

12.2 For each word below, find two words which will combine with it to form different compound adjectives. Cover the left-hand page first.

....
well   badly   handed
....

....
          time   east
....

12.3 Complete the compound adjectives in these sentences.
1 They were both wearing short-.............. shirts.
2 We stayed in a five-.............. hotel.
3 There is a shop in London which sells things for left-.............. people.
4 He's just bought a brand-.............. car.
5 The airport is about ten miles south-.............. of the city centre.
6 One little girl was very badly-..............; she kept shouting during lunch and then threw food all over the floor.
7 She's just got a ....-time job; she works three hours a day on Mondays, Wednesdays and Fridays.
8 It was a very badly-.............. article: I noticed several punctuation mistakes and lots of spelling mistakes.
9 They're very well-.............., so they can afford to go to expensive restaurants.
10 It's a twenty-.............. walk to the house, but it takes much less than that in the car.
11 She's got a little stall in the market where she sells second-.............. things.
12 When I saw her last night, she was dancing with a very good-.............. young man in a white suit.
13 I was astonished when the man at the next table gave the waiter a ten-.............. note as a tip.
14 Have you ever met a well-.............. actor or politician?
15 I had a nice time with my cousin – he's good company and very easy-...............

12.4 Write ten sentences about yourself and use a different compound adjective from the opposite page in each one. You can describe yourself, your personality, your family, your clothes, the place where you live, the journeys you make, etc. Try to do this exercise with a friend and see who can finish first.

13 Collocation (word partners)

A What is collocation?

If you want to use a word naturally, you need to learn the other words that often go with it (word partners). These can be very different from language to language. For example, in English we say:

I **missed the bus** (= I didn't **catch the bus**) [NOT ~~I lost the bus~~]
She **made a mistake** [NOT ~~she did a mistake~~]
A **heavy smoker** (= someone who smokes a lot) [NOT ~~a strong smoker~~ *or* ~~a big smoker~~]
It was a **serious illness** [NOT ~~a big illness~~ *or* ~~a strong illness~~]

B Verb + noun

The meaning of many of these examples may be clear, but did you know these verbs and nouns go together? Is it the same or different in your language?

start the car (= turn on the engine)   start a family (= think about having your first child)
tell a story   tell the truth (≠ tell a lie)
tell a joke   run a shop/company (= manage/control it)
get on a bus (≠ get off)   get in(to) a car (≠ get out (of) a car)
miss a person (= be unhappy because that person is not there)
miss a lesson (= when you don't come to a lesson)

C Adjective + noun

Common adjectives often combine with a wide range of nouns.

a soft drink (= non-alcoholic drink)   a soft voice (≠ a loud voice)
dry wine (≠ sweet wine)   dry weather (≠ wet weather)
strong coffee (≠ weak coffee)   a strong accent (≠ a slight accent)
hard work (= hard physically or mentally) a great success (= very successful)
heavy traffic (= a lot of cars)   heavy rain (= raining a lot)

Look at some of these phrases in example sentences.

I can't understand his English because he has such a **strong accent**.
It was **hard work** organising the conference, but I think it was a **great success**.
You always get **heavy traffic** during the rush hour.

D Adverb + adjective

In these examples, all the adverbs mean **very,** but we choose to use them with certain adjectives. (You could still use **very** in all of these examples if you wish.)

I was **terribly sorry** to hear about your accident.
He's **highly unlikely** to come now. (= I'm almost sure he will not come)
She is **fully aware** of the problem. (= she knows all about the problem)
It is **vitally important** that you make a note of common collocations in your notebook.

E Collocation in dictionaries

All good dictionaries now include examples of common collocations but they do it in different ways: sometimes they are in **bold print** after the definition; sometimes in *italics* after the definition; and sometimes in the definition and examples. (See Unit 3, Section B.)

Exercises

13.1 You can keep a record of common collocations by using 'spidergrams'. These are very clear on the page and you can add to them. Complete these.

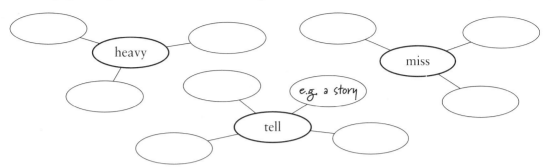

13.2 Write the opposite of these phrases and expressions.
1 sweet wine
2 a strong accent
3 strong coffee
4 a soft voice
5 get on the bus
6 tell the truth
7 catch the bus
8 get in the car

13.3 Find a suitable adjective, verb or adverb from the opposite page to complete these sentences.
1 I'm .... sorry I'm late, but I .... the bus and had to wait ages for another one.
2 He .... everyone the same joke, and nobody laughed.
3 We had lots of snow in the night and I had a problem .... the car this morning.
4 Michael is the owner, but his brother John .... the company, and he has about 50 employees working for him.
5 I think they want to get married and .... a family.
6 That's the third mistake she's .... today.
7 It's .... important that we finish this work by the end of the week.
8 If this .... rain continues, I think he's .... unlikely to come.
9 I don't drink .... coffee at night because it keeps me awake.
10 I really .... my family when I stayed in Australia on my own last year.

13.4 The adjectives on the left can all mean 'very big', but we often use them specifically with the nouns on the right. Use a good dictionary to find the correct collocations, and then complete the sentences below.

| wide | large | | shoulders | range |
| broad | vast | | majority | size |

1 I used to be medium but I need a .... now because I've put on weight.
2 Fortunately the shop I go to has a .... of shirts and jumpers to choose from.
3 I've also got very ...., but my waist is quite small.
4 A few men can't find clothes to fit them, but the .... are small, medium or large.

14 Verb or adjective + preposition

A Verb (+ preposition)

Here are some common examples of verbs which are usually followed by a particular preposition. You will probably know most of these verbs, but do you always get the preposition right? Pay special attention to any that are different in your language.

I often **listen to** the radio.
My brother never **agrees with** me. (= he never has the same views/opinion as me)
I may go to the match; it really **depends on** the weather. (= the weather will decide for me)
He **suffers from** (= has the unpleasant/bad experience of) a type of diabetes.
He **got married to** a girl he met in France.
I'm going to **apologise** (= say sorry) **for** the mistakes we made.
She has **applied** (= made a written request) **for** a new job.
They were **waiting for** me when I arrived.
Don't **worry** (= be nervous) **about** your exam; it'll be OK.
She **complained** (= said she was not satisfied) **to** the waiter **about** the food. (You complain
    to someone **about** something.)
He s**pends** a lot of money **on** clothes and discos.
That dictionary **belongs to** Rolf. (= it is Rolf's dictionary)

B Changes of meaning

Sometimes a verb may be followed by different prepositions, and the meaning changes.

He **threw** the ball **to** me.
(= for me to catch it)

He **threw** the ball **at** me.
(= in order to hit me;
perhaps he was angry)

He **shouted to** me. (= in order to communicate with me)
He **shouted at** me. (= he was angry with me)

C Adjective (+ preposition)

I was never very **good at** mathematics.
She is **afraid of** (= frightened of) flying.
I'm very **keen on** Italian food. (= I like Italian food very much)
She is **similar to** (= almost the same as) her older sister, but very **different from** her brother.
He's very **interested in** antique furniture.
I was **surprised at** (or **by**) the weather; it rained nearly every day.
I think she is **aware of** (= knows about) the problems in her class.
I'm **tired of** studying foreign languages. (= I've had enough and I want to stop)
The streets are **full of** rubbish. (= there is rubbish everywhere in the streets)
There is something **wrong with** this TV. (= the TV is not working/functioning correctly)

Exercises

14.1 Finish these questions with the correct preposition, then write a short answer for each one.

1 A: What exactly is she worried ....? B: ....
2 A: What subjects is she good ....? B: ....
3 A: Who is she waiting ....? B: ....
4 A: What job is she applying ....? B: ....
5 A: What programme is she listening ....? B: ....
6 A: What did she complain ....? B: ....
7 A: What did she apologise ....? B: ....
8 A: Who does this car belong ....? B: ....
9 A: I know she was angry but who was she shouting ....? B: ....
10 A: What kind of films is she interested ....? B: ....
11 A: What will the decision depend ....? B: ....
12 A: What is she afraid ....? B: ....

14.2 Match the sentence beginnings on the left with the endings on the right.

1 He suffers ⊂
2 She wasn't aware e
3 He threw the book
4 She complained
5 She said it was similar
6 She applied
7 She shouted
8 He said it depends
9 The suitcase was full
10 She's tired
11 She apologised
12 I was very surprised

a at me, but it missed.
b for a job in Australia.
c from a rare illness.
d to the man across the lake.
e for the mistake.
f at his choice.
g of clothes.
h to the one she has.
i of working at weekends.
j of her mistakes.
k on me.
l about the bad service.

14.3 Complete these sentences in a way that is logical and grammatically correct. If possible, compare your answers with someone who has also done this exercise.

1 My steak was overcooked, so I complained ....
2 When I was a child I sometimes wore clothes that belonged ....
3 I want to help poor people, so I have decided to apply ....
4 I work quite hard but I'm not very good ....
5 In the summer a lot of people suffer ....
6 I've always been interested ....
7 I'm very keen ....
8 A lot of people are afraid ....
9 People in my country are very different ....
10 When I went to ...., I was very surprised ....

14.4 A good dictionary will tell you if a verb or adjective is usually followed by a special preposition. Sometimes the preposition is shown after the verb or adjective; sometimes it is illustrated in the example sentences. Use a dictionary to find the preposition that often follows these words.

fond (adj)   concentrate (v)   responsible (adj)   rely (v)

15 Preposition + noun

A Common patterns

There are many expressions formed by a preposition + noun, and sometimes a preposition is used with a particular meaning in a number of expressions, so they are very common.

A book **by** Stephen King, a film **by** Steven Spielberg, a song **by** Elton John.
You can go **for** a walk, **for** a drive, **for** a run, **for** a swim.
You can go **in** the morning, **in** the afternoon, **in** the evening (but **at night**).
You can travel **by** car, **by** plane, **by** bus, **by** coach, **by** train, **by** taxi (but **on foot**).
I heard it **on** the radio; I saw it **on TV**; I spoke to her **on the phone** (but I read it **in the newspaper, in a magazine**).
The man **in** the dark suit (= wearing the dark suit); the woman **in** the red dress.

B Fixed expressions

Sometimes it is difficult to know why a particular preposition is used, and you must learn these as fixed expressions.

I took his pen **by mistake**. (= I thought it was my pen)
I did all the work **by myself**. (= **on my own**; without help from others)
The shoes are made **by hand**. (= not by machine)
The workers are **on strike**. (= they refuse to work because of a problem over pay, hours, etc.)
I met them **by chance**. (= it wasn't planned – it was luck)
The children are **on holiday**. (= they are having a holiday)

He broke the plate **by accident**.
    (= he did not want to do it – it was an error/mistake)

She could not talk to me for long because she was **in a hurry**.
    (= she had to go quickly – she didn't have much time)

He broke the plate **on purpose**. Αναειρεγειιλιηει
    (= he wanted to do it and intended to do it)
        /ηιγετ

There are two million **out of work**. (= without a job)
There were **at least** fifty people at the party. (= a minimum of 50)

C In time or on time?

Sometimes two prepositions can be used with the same noun, but the meaning is different.

Lessons begin at 8.30 and I always arrive **on time**. (= at 8.30)
Lessons begin at 8.30 and I always get there **in time**. (= before 8.30; I'm not late)

In the end we went home. (= finally, after a long period)
At the end of the book they get married.

The two men are **in business**. (= they are businessmen)
The two men are in Germany **on business**. (= they are there for work and not for a holiday)

I'll see you **in a moment**. (= very soon)
I can't speak to you **at the moment**. (= right now)

Exercises

15.1 Complete these sentences with the correct preposition. Cover the opposite page first.

1 I saw it .... TV.
2 They came .... car.
3 They are all .... strike.
4 He is here .... business.
5 I did it .... my own.
6 It was written .... Goethe.
7 We went .... a walk.
8 I read it .... a magazine.
9 He's .... holiday this week.
10 She took it .... mistake.
11 I went .... the afternoon.
12 He came .... foot.
13 The clothes are made .... hand.
14 She broke it .... accident.
15 He did it .... purpose.
16 I'll see you .... a moment.
17 I'm very busy .... the moment.
18 It's very quiet .... night.
19 We met .... chance.
20 She's .... least 25 years old.

15.2 Replace the underlined words with a suitable prepositional phrase. Look at the example first.

Example: The meeting was planned for 11 a.m. and we got here <u>at 11 a.m.</u> *on time*

1 I wrote the reports <u>without any help from anyone else</u>.
2 Did you get to the cinema <u>before the film started</u>?
3 Thousands of people are <u>without jobs</u> in my town.
4 She's <u>making a phone call</u>.
5 I saw the advertisement <u>when I was watching TV</u> last night.
6 He opened her letter <u>because he thought it was addressed to him</u>.
7 It was a very long journey but <u>finally</u> we got there.
8 He gets killed <u>in the last scene</u> of the film.
9 I'm afraid I'm very busy <u>right now</u>.
10 I saw her yesterday <u>but I didn't plan to see her</u>.

15.3 Respond to these questions with a negative answer and a suitable prepositional phrase. Look at the example first.

Example: Was it the man wearing the blue shirt?
        No, the man in the white shirt.

1 Did she hit him on purpose?
   ....

2 Did they go by car?
   ....

3 Are they here on holiday?
   ....

4 Did you read about the accident in the newspaper?
   ....

5 Did the others help him?
   ....

6 Do you want to sit down and have a rest?
   ....

15.4 Look at the prepositional phrases on the opposite page again, and make a list of the ones which are not exact translations from your own language. Put the list in your pocket and carry it around with you. Test yourself as often as possible by thinking of a translation and/or explanation and/or example sentence for each one.

16 Phrasal verbs: form and meaning

A Formation

A phrasal verb is a verb combined with an adverb or preposition, and occasionally with an adverb and preposition.

The price of petrol may **go up** (= increase) again next week.
He **fell over** (= fell to the ground) when he was running for the bus.
She's promised to **find out** (= learn/discover) the name of that new hotel.
Who is going to **look after** (= take care of) the children when she goes into hospital?
If you don't understand the meaning, you can **look** it **up** (= find the meaning in a book – in this case a dictionary).
He doesn't **get on with** (= have a good relationship with) his parents. (verb + adv + prep)

B Meaning

Sometimes the meaning of a phrasal verb is very similar to the base verb, and the adverb just <u>emphasises</u> the meaning of the base verb, e.g. **stand up, wake up, save up, hurry up, sit down, lie down** and **send off** (e.g. a letter). On other occasions, the adverb adds the idea of completing the action of the verb, e.g. **drink up** (= finish your drink), **eat up** (= finish eating), **finish off**.

But more often, the meaning of a phrasal verb is very different from the base verb, e.g. **go up** doesn't mean the same as **go**; **look after** is different from **look**; and **look after** is also quite different from **look up**. An adverb or preposition can therefore change the meaning of a verb a great deal.

Here are some more examples of this type of phrasal verb.

It took her a long time to **get over** (= get better / recover from) her illness.
He told me to **carry on** (= continue) as far as the traffic lights.
I persuaded my wife to **give up** (= stop) smoking.
I can't make any sandwiches because we've **run out of** bread. (= the bread is finished / all used, so we have no bread)
In the end my next-door neighbour had to come and **put out** (= extinguish/stop) the fire.

C Multiple meaning

Many phrasal verbs have more than one meaning, so you must be careful when you see a phrasal verb you think you know, or look up the meaning in a dictionary. In the examples marked *, the phrasal verb is much more natural than the explanation in brackets.

It was hot so I decided to *****take off** (= remove) my jacket.
I am always nervous when the plane *****takes off** (= leaves the ground).

I don't think I'll **get through** (= finish) this report before five o'clock.
I think she'll **get through** (= pass) the exam.

I *****picked up** the rubbish (= took it from the ground or a low place) and put it in the bin.
I had to go to the shop to **pick up** (= collect) my photos.

My alarm clock didn't **go off** (= ring) this morning.
The bomb could **go off** (= explode) at any minute.
The fish will *****go off** (= go bad) if you don't put it in the fridge.

Exercises

16.1 Fill the gaps to complete the phrasal verb in each sentence.

1 We went round the school and .... **up** all the rubbish.
2 I don't think they ever .... **out** how the man escaped.
3 This milk smells horrible; I think it has .... **off**.
4 Do you think they'll .... **through** the exam next week?
5 They had a bad relationship at first, but she .... **on** very well **with** him now.
6 The price has .... **up** three times this year.
7 I agreed to .... **after** my sister's cat when she goes to France.
8 We can .... **on** until the teacher tells us to stop.
9 Why didn't your alarm clock .... **off** this morning?
10 I'm afraid this photocopier has .... **out of** paper, but you can use the other one in my office.

16.2 Complete these sentences in a logical way.

1 It will take her a long time to get over ....
2 I'm afraid we've run out of ....
3 He had to look it up ....
4 I don't really get on with ....
5 She came in and took off ....
6 I had to put out ....
7 Who is going to look after ....
8 I went to the garage to pick up ....
9 The plane took off ....
10 My rent is going up ....

16.3 Look at the dictionary entry for *pick up*, and match the meanings with the sentences below.

> **pick up** *v adv* **1** [T] (**pick** sbdy./sthg.↔ **up**) to take hold of and lift up: *Pick up the box by the handles.* —see picture on page 669 **2** [T] (**pick** sthg.↔ **up**) to gather together; collect: *Please pick up all your toys when you've finished playing.* **3** [I] to improve: *Trade is picking up again.* **4** [T] (**pick** sthg.↔ **up**) to gain; get: *Where did you pick up that book/your excellent English?* **5** [I;T (**pick** sthg.↔ **up**)] to (cause to) start again: *to pick up (the conversation) where we left off* **6** [T] (**pick** sbdy./sthg.↔ **up**) to collect; arrange to go and get: *Pick me up at the hotel.|I'm going to pick up my coat from the cleaner's.* **7** [T] (**pick** sbdy./sthg.↔ **up**) to collect in a vehicle **8** [T] (**pick** sbdy.↔ **up**)

1 I said I would pick her up at the airport.
2 I picked up most of the rubbish that was on the floor.
3 Where did he pick up that strange accent?
4 Business was bad at the beginning of the year but it's picking up now.
5 I hurt my back when I tried to pick up that chair.

16.4 Write two sentences for each of these phrasal verbs to show their different meanings.

pick up   take off   go off   get through

17 Phrasal verbs: grammar and style

Look at Unit 16 on the form and meaning of phrasal verbs before you do this unit.

A Grammar: intransitive verbs

Some phrasal verbs are intransitive and do not need a direct object.

The children are **growing up**. (= getting older and more mature)
The doctor told me to **lie down** on the bed.
Don't wait out there. Please **come in**. (= enter)
I'm going to **stay in** (= stay at home) this evening.

With these verbs, you cannot put another word between the verb and adverb.

B Grammar: transitive verbs

But many phrasal verbs are transitive and do need a direct object. With some of these, you can put the object between the verb and adverb:

Put on your shoes ✓   **Turn on** the TV ✓
Put your shoes **on** ✓   **Turn** the TV **on** ✓

If the object is a pronoun, it must go between verb and adverb.

Put them **on** ✓ [NOT ~~Put on them~~]   **Turn** it **on** ✓ [NOT ~~Turn on it~~]

Note: A dictionary will show you if you can put a word between the verb and adverb:

> **turn** *(obj)* [SWITCH] /£tɜːn, $tɜːrn/ *v* [always + adv/prep] to
> use a control to switch (a piece of equipment) on or off or to   70
> increase or reduce what it is producing • *Turn* **off/out** *the*
> *light.* [M] • *Who turned the telly* **on***?*[M] • *I asked him to turn*
> **down** *the heating.* [M] • *Turn the sound* **up** *– I can't hear*
> *what they're saying.* [M] • *This programme's boring – shall I*
> *turn* **over** (=change the station) *to BBC?* [I] • *This sort of*   75
> *heater turns* **off** (=can be switched off) *at the mains.* [I] •

C Style: formal or informal

Some phrasal verbs can be used equally in written or spoken English. Sometimes this is because there is no other easy way to express the meaning of the phrasal verb.

I always **wake up** early, even at weekends.
The car **broke down** (= went wrong; stopped working) on the motorway.
The plane couldn't **take off** because of bad weather.
Thieves **broke into** (= entered by force and illegally) the house and took money, credit cards and all my jewellery.

D Informal phrasal verbs

But most phrasal verbs are informal and are more common in spoken English. In written English there is often a more formal word with the same meaning.

We had to **make up** a story. (= invent/create from our imagination)
I can usually **get by** on about £200 a week. (= manage)
You can **leave out** question 7. (= omit, i.e. you don't need to do question 7)
They've got a problem and they asked me to **sort it out**. (= resolve (it) / find a solution / do something about it)

Exercises

These exercises also practise and test some of the phrasal verbs from Unit 16.

17.1 Complete these sentences in a logical way.

1 I'm not very good at making up ....
2 Could you lie down .... ?
3 She asked me to turn on ....
4 Two men tried to break into ....
5 We have asked an engineer to come and sort out ....
6 Are you going to stay in .... ?
7 Why did you leave out .... ?
8 I'm afraid we broke down ....
9 Can you get by .... ?
10 I grew up ....

17.2 Is it possible to separate the two parts of the phrasal verb in the sentences below? Look at the examples first, and use a dictionary to check your answers. (You can also check your answers in the answer key.)

Examples: I forgot to **get off** the bus. NO (get the bus off ✗)
             Why did he **take off** his trousers? YES (take his trousers off ✓)

1 She decided to **carry on** working.
2 He had to **put out** the fire.
3 Could you **turn on** the radio?
4 I had to **lie down** for a few minutes.
5 Could you go to the shop for me? We've just **run out of** coffee.
6 I think she **made up** that story.
7 I can't **get by** on the money my parents give me.
8 Children **grow up** very quickly these days.
9 I **turned off** the light when I went to bed.
10 Can we **leave out** this question?

17.3 Make these texts more informal by changing some of the verbs to phrasal verbs with the same meaning. (There are three in each text.)

1 The cost of living is increasing all the time and I find it quite difficult to manage on my salary. But I think I can probably continue for a few months.
2 She told us to enter, but then we had to remove our shoes and I had to extinguish my cigarette.
3 The teacher told the class to invent a story to go with the picture in their books, and then continue with exercise 4. She said they could all omit exercise 5.

17.4 There are many phrasal verbs in other units. Can you find:

1 three phrasal verbs in Unit 21 on page 46?
2 three phrasal verbs in Unit 47 on page 98?
3 three phrasal verbs in Unit 48 on page 100?
4 three phrasal verbs in Unit 56 on page 116?
5 three phrasal verbs in Unit 62 on page 128?
6 three phrasal verbs in Unit 75 on page 154?

18 Idioms and fixed expressions

A What is an idiom?

An idiom is a group of words with a meaning that is different from the individual words, and often difficult to understand from the individual words. Many of the phrasal verbs in Units 16 and 17 were idiomatic. Here are some more common idioms.

The teacher told us to **get a move on**. (= hurry; be quick)
My wife and I **take it in turns** to cook. (= I cook one day, she cooks the next, etc.)
I don't know the answer **off-hand**. (= without looking it up or asking someone)
It's not far. We can take **a short cut** (= a quick way) through the park.
I'm not very good at **small talk**. (= social talk; not about serious things)
I'm sorry I can't **make it** (= come) on Friday.
I asked her to **keep an eye on** (= watch / look after) my suitcase while I went to the toilet.

B Fixed expressions

There are also expressions in English where the meaning is easy to understand, but the same idea in your language may need a completely different expression. In other words, if you just translate from your language, you may say something in English which is completely wrong. For this reason, you need to learn some expressions as idioms. For example:

A: What was wrong with the hotel?
B: Well, **for a start** it was next to a motorway and very noisy. And **to make matters worse**, there were factories on the other side of the road, which stayed open 24 hours a day.

It's not a problem **in the short term** (= at the moment) but **in the long term** (= for the longer future) we will need to think about it and probably spend some money on it.

C Using idioms

Idioms are important but they can be difficult to use correctly.

- With many idioms, if you make just a small mistake, it can sound strange, funny, or badly wrong. For example: get a move; a small talk; put an eye on, off-hands, etc.
- Idioms often have special features: they may be informal or funny or ironic; they may only be used by certain people (e.g. young children, or teenagers, or elderly people); they may only appear in limited contexts; they may have special grammar. For these reasons, you can often 'learn' the meaning of an idiom but then use it incorrectly. For example: After her husband died she was **down in the dumps**. (This idiom means 'sad and depressed' but is completely wrong here: the situation is too serious and the idiom is too informal.)

D Easy idioms to use

Some idiomatic expressions are used on their own, or with just one or two other words. These are often the easiest to use.

A: Are you coming?
B: Yes, **hang on**. (= wait)

A: **What's up?** (= what's the matter?)
B: Nothing.

A: Can I borrow your dictionary?
B: Sure, **go ahead**. (= help yourself; take it; do it)

A: I don't know which one to choose.
B: Well, **make up your mind**. (= make a decision)

A: I'm really sorry but I've forgotten to bring the book you lent me.
B: That's OK. **Never mind**. (= it's OK, don't worry; it's not important)

Exercises

18.1 It can be difficult to guess the meaning of an idiom, especially if you do not have the full context. Look at these examples (they are not presented on the opposite page).

1 I **feel like** a drink.
2 They've gone **for good**.
3 I'm **tied-up** all afternoon.
4 She was **pulling my leg** when she said that.
5 I can probably **make do** with a smaller flat.

Here is a fuller context for each of the above idioms. Can you guess the meaning now?

1 A: Are you hungry?
  B: No, but I feel like a drink.
2 A: Do you think they'll ever come back to England?
  B: No, they've gone for good.
3 A: Do you have a lot of clients to see?
  B: Yes, I'm tied-up all afternoon.
4 A: Did she tell you there were no bathrooms in the hotel?
  B: Yes. I think she was pulling my leg when she said that.
5 A: Do you really need a large flat?
  B: Well, it's nice to have a big place, but I can probably make do with a smaller flat.

18.2 Replace the underlined words in each dialogue with a suitable idiomatic expression from the opposite page. (But try to answer the questions before looking at the opposite page.) Can you think of similar expressions in your own language?

1 A: Is Rebecca here?
  B: Yes, <u>wait a minute</u>. I'll get her.
2 A: Does it take long to get there?
  B: No, I know a <u>quick way</u>.
3 A: Could I borrow this for a minute?
  B: Yes, <u>take it</u>.
4 A: Sorry I can't <u>come</u> on Thursday.
  B: That's OK. <u>Don't worry</u>.

5 A: What's <u>the matter</u>?
  B: Nothing. Why?
6 A: <u>Look after</u> my things for a minute?
  B: Yeah, sure.
7 A: Do we have to go now?
  B: Yes, <u>hurry up</u>, otherwise we'll be late.
8 A: You'll have to <u>decide</u> soon.
  B: Yes I know, but it's very difficult.

18.3 Complete the expressions in these sentences.

1 It wasn't a very successful holiday. **For a** .... the beach was a long way from our hotel; then **to make** .... **worse,** the car broke down on the third day and we had to walk to the beach the rest of the time.
2 We **take it in** .... to look after the dog.
3 She asked me about the times of the trains but I couldn't tell her **off-**...............
4 I don't enjoy parties where you just stand around and make .... **talk** with lots of people you don't know.
5 We can probably **make** .... with a three-roomed flat for the moment, but **in the long** .... we will have to think about moving into a bigger place.

18.4 Can you find at least three idiomatic expressions in this text? What do they mean?

> I went to stay with my cousin last week. We are the same age but have very little in common: he loves sport and I hate it; I'm mad about music and he's not interested in it. As you can imagine, we didn't have a very good time together, and by about Thursday we were really getting on each other's nerves, so I decided to come home.

19 Make, do, have, take

There are many common expressions with these verbs, and often they are different in other languages, so you need to learn them.

A Things we make

a mistake (= an error)	He **made** a few **mistakes** in the exam.
a meal (= prepare and cook something to eat)	I had to **make** my own **dinner** last night.
money (= become rich)	He **made** a lot of **money** when he worked in America.
friends	It's not always easy to **make friends** in a foreign country.
a decision	We can have the red ones or the green ones, but we must **make a decision** (choose the red or green) before 6 p.m.
a noise	I can't work when the children **make** a lot of **noise**.
progress (U) (= improvement)	Her English is good now; she has **made** a lot of **progress**.

B Things we do

homework (U)	I forgot to **do** my English **homework** last night.
the housework (U) (= cleaning)	My mother **does** all **the housework** in our house.
subjects (= study subjects)	Did you **do English** at school?
a course	I **did** a one-week **course** in word processing.
the shopping (= buy food)	I always **do the shopping** at the weekend.
research (U) (= detailed study in one subject)	He's **doing research** in physics at Rome University.
(someone) a favour (= do something to help someone)	I don't have any coffee. Could you **do me a favour** and lend me some?
something/anything/nothing	I didn't **do anything** last night. That boy has **done nothing** all day

C Things we have

a rest (= relax / do nothing)	They **had a** long **rest** after the game.
food (= eat food) and drink	I **had steak** but Paul just **had a cup of tea**.
a drink (= drink something)	Let's **have a drink** before dinner.
a bath/shower	I always **have a bath** when I get up.
a party	I'm **having a party** for my birthday.
a baby (= be pregnant or give birth)	Mary is **having a baby** next month.
a (nice/great/terrible) time	We **had a very nice time** in Switzerland last year.

D Things we take

an exam (also 'do an exam')	I'm going to **take** four **exams** next month.
a photo	She **took lots of photos** on holiday.
a decision (also 'make')	I'm not very good at **taking decisions**.
a shower (also 'have')	I'm just going to **take a shower** before lunch.
a bus/train/plane/taxi	We were late, so we **took a taxi** to the airport.

Note: Notice the use of **be + adjective** [NOT ~~have + noun~~] in these expressions:

She **was lucky**   I'm **hungry** (= I want to eat)   I'm **thirsty** (= I want a drink)

Exercises

19.1 Cross out the incorrect verbs in these sentences. Both verbs may be correct.

1 I couldn't do/make the homework last night.
2 She's going to make/have a party for her birthday.
3 Did he do/make many mistakes?
4 I often make/do the housework.
5 Did you make/take many photos?
6 When do you take/do your next exam?
7 I want to do/make a course in English.
8 We must take/make a decision soon.
9 He is doing/making research in chemistry.
10 They did/made a lot of noise during the party.

19.2 Replace the underlined word(s) with a suitable word or expression from the opposite page.

Example: I want to eat something.   I'm hungry

1 Let's drink something.
2 I'm going to prepare lunch tomorrow.
3 I'll clean the house at the weekend.
4 I ate a pizza in the restaurant.
5 I want a drink.

6 I usually buy my food on Saturday morning.
7 They both want to become rich.
8 When are they going to decide?
9 I think she enjoyed herself last night.
10 She is definitely improving. How many driving lessons has she had now?

19.3 Look at the four split pictures. Describe what happened using at least two expressions from the opposite page in each one. Look at the example first.

Last Friday evening I had a party but the next-door neighbour complained and said we were making too much noise.

1

2

3

19.4 Test yourself. Without looking at the opposite page, write down six things you can:

Examples:
make .a mistake.   do .the housework.   have .a rest.

20 Give, keep, break, catch, see

These common verbs have many different meanings (some of them in other parts of this book). This unit looks at some important meanings of these verbs, and in some cases they combine with specific nouns, e.g. give someone a ring, break the law, etc. You can learn these as expressions.

A Give

I'll **give** you **a ring** this evening. (= phone you this evening)
Could you **give** me **a hand**? (= help me)
Please **give my regards to** Paul. (= please say 'hello' to him from me) *or*
    If you see Paul, please **give him my regards**.

B Keep

The coat will **keep** you **dry**; the gloves will **keep** your hands **warm**. (= the coat/gloves will help you to stay dry/warm) [keep + noun/pronoun + adjective]
I **keep** losing my glasses; I **keep** getting backache. (= I lose my glasses / get backache again and again) [keep + -ing]
Please **keep in touch**. (= don't forget to stay in contact, e.g. phone or write to me sometimes)
The school **keeps a record** (= clear written information) of the number of times that students are absent.

C Break

He **broke the** world **record** again. (= created a new record, e.g. He ran the 100 metres in 9.85 seconds, which is 0.1 seconds faster than anyone else.)
Most people **break the law** at some point in their life. (= do something wrong / against the law)
In my first lesson with a new class, I usually do something to **break the ice**. (= to make people feel more relaxed when they first meet strangers)

D Catch

We can **catch a bus** down the road. (= take a bus/travel by bus)
How did you **catch that cold**? (= get that cold/virus)
Catch the ball and throw it to James.

E See

A: This part of the picture doesn't look right compared with the other part.
B: Yes, **I see what you mean**. (= I understand what you are saying)

A: Do you think we need to hire a car?
B: I don't know. **I'll see** (= I'll ask and find out) what the others say.

I **don't/can't see the point of** practising six hours a day. (= I don't understand the reason for practising six hours a day; I think it's crazy)

Exercises

20.1 Match the nouns on the right with the verbs on the left to form common word partnerships. (There is one noun you need to use twice.)

break (2)	keep (2)
catch (3)	give (2)

the ball	the law	a cold
me a hand	a bus	in touch
a record	my regards to ...	

20.2 Fill the gaps with the correct verb in these sentences.

1 I don't .... the point of spending a lot of money on tickets when we can watch the concert on television.
2 These boots should .... your feet warm and dry.
3 Please .... my regards to your mother when you go back home.
4 Before we make a decision, let's .... what Patricia says.
5 If it's too far to walk, we can .... a bus.
6 I don't know what the problem is, but I .... getting headaches.
7 When I meet people on holiday I always promise to .... in touch, but I never do.
8 I didn't really enjoy the holiday because I .... a cold on the second day and spent most of the week sneezing and blowing my nose.
9 When you organise a conference or a course, I think you need something to .... the ice, otherwise people are a bit nervous of each other.
10 I don't .... the point of spending a lot of money on children's clothes because they only last for a few months and then they're too small.

20.3 What expressions are represented by these pictures? Can you complete the sentences below? Look at the example first.

Example: I'll *give you a ring*

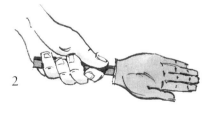

1

2

3

4

1 How did you ....?   3 I decided to ....
2 He agreed to ....   4 He finally ....

20.4 Look through the key expressions in bold on the opposite page again. Can you translate these expressions into your own language? If so, do you use the same verb in your own language? Concentrate on the ones that are different.

21 Get: uses and expressions

A Meanings

Get is an informal word, so it is more common in spoken English than written English. It has many meanings. Here are some of the basic ones.

receive	I got a letter this morning.
	You get a certificate at the end of the course.
obtain	She's trying to get a new job.
(sometimes = buy)	Where did you get those shoes?
become	It gets dark very early at this time of year.
(= a change in state)	My hands are getting cold.
arrive	When did you get here?
	I'll phone when I get home.
fetch	Could you get the books from the cupboard?
	She went to get the children from school.

B 'Get' + past participle

We sometimes use the more informal '**get**' + **past participle**:

get married (= marry)	She got married in France.
get divorced (= divorce)	They got divorced last year. (= the marriage has ended officially)
get dressed (= dress)	I got dressed quickly and went out.
get undressed (= undress)	He got undressed and got into bed.
get changed (= change clothes)	When I got home I went to my room and got changed.
get lost (= lose one's way)	I got lost on my way to the station.

C Common collocations

Get is so common with certain words (often describing a change of state) that it is a good idea to learn them as expressions.

It's getting	hot/cold	I'm getting	hot/cold
	dark/light		tired
	late		better/worse
	better/worse		hungry
	busy		ready (= preparing)

Note: The expression **getting better at** something can describe an improvement in your ability to do something, e.g. I'm getting better at English/swimming; it also describes an improvement in your health, e.g. She was very ill but she's **getting better** now. (≠ **getting worse**)

D Phrasal verbs and special expressions with 'get'

I **get on** very well **with** my sister. (= I have a very good relationship with my sister)
How are you **getting on**?   (a) (= a general question: how is life?)
                              (b) (= what progress are you making, e.g. with your English?)
It's difficult to **get to know** people in a foreign country. (= meet people and make friends)
I want to **get rid of** all my old records. (= sell them or throw them away or give them away)
My alarm wakes me up at 7 a.m., but I don't usually **get up** (= get out of bed) until 7.15.

Exercises

21.1 Write a synonym for *get* in each of these sentences.

1 Where can I get something to eat round here?
2 I'm just going to get some paper from the office. I'll be back in a minute.
3 What time did they get here last night?
4 He got very angry when I told him what you did with his CDs.
5 I couldn't get a room; all the hotels were full.
6 We normally get five weeks' holiday.
7 This book is getting quite interesting.
8 I must get some stamps before I go home.
9 He sent the letter last week but I didn't get it until yesterday.
10 Do they often get here early?

21.2 Write appropriate sentences using *I'm getting + adjective* or *it's getting + adjective*.

1 A: ....
   B: Yes it is. I'll turn on the heating.
2 A: ....
   B: OK, let's have something to eat, then.
3 A: ....
   B: Yes me too. I'll open the window.
4 A: ....
   B: Yes it is. I think I'll go to bed.
5 A: ....
   B: Yes. I'll put the lights on.
6 A: ....
   B: No you're not. You're getting much better. You understand a lot now.

21.3 Rewrite each of these sentences using an expression with *get*. The meaning must stay the same.

1 They're preparing to go out.
   They're ....
2 I had to put on my clothes very quickly.
   I had to ....
3 How do you meet people and make friends in this country?
   How do you ....?
4 I have a good relationship with my boss.
   I ....
5 We're going to throw away most of these chairs.
   We're going to ....
6 Someone told me you're doing a new course. How's it going?
   Someone told me you're doing a new course. ....?

21.4 Write down examples of 'get' that you see or hear, then try to group your sentences according to the different meanings. This will help you to get (= obtain) an idea of the ways in which this important word is used in English.

22 Go: uses and expressions

A Come vs. go

Go usually expresses a movement away from the position the speaker is in now; **come** expresses a movement towards the speaker.

Imagine you are at school. The time is 9.30 a.m.

I had to **go** to Jimmy's to pick up some books; then I **went** to the post office before I **came** to school.

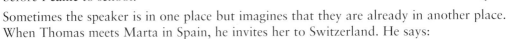

Sometimes the speaker is in one place but imagines that they are already in another place. When Thomas meets Marta in Spain, he invites her to Switzerland. He says:

'Would you like to **come** and visit me in Bern?' (He imagines he is there and so her movement is towards him.)

We can also imagine that the listener is in a different place. Talking to Marta, Thomas says:

'I'll **come** to your flat at 7.30 p.m.' (She will be at home, so his movement is towards her.)

Note: It is a similar difference between **bring** and **take**:
I think I'll **take** my bike to the match and Peter can **bring** it back here tomorrow.

B Different meanings of 'go'

- When you leave a place <u>in order to do an activity</u>, you often express it either with **go + -ing noun** or **go (out) + for a + noun**. Here are some common examples:

  We could go shopping.
  They went   riding (on horses).
               sightseeing.
               swimming (also 'for a swim').

  She wants to go (out) for a walk.
                  (out) for a drink.
  Let's go   (out) for a drive.
                  (out) for a meal.

- **Go** is followed by certain adjectives to describe a change in state (usually to a worse state) with the meaning 'become' (**get** is also used with some adjectives).

  My brother's hair is **going grey**, and my father is **going bald**. (= losing all his hair)
  The company **went bankrupt** last year. (= lost all its money and had to stop operating)
  My grandmother is **going deaf**. (deaf = cannot hear)
  He'll **go mad** (= get very angry *infml*) if you wear his jacket.

- It is often used to describe the speed something is travelling (also **do**):

  We were **going** about 80 kph when the accident happened.

- When you want to say/ask if a road or form of transport takes you somewhere:

  Does this bus **go** to (= take me to) the National Gallery?
  I don't think this road **goes** to (= leads to) the station.

C Expressions

I've never tried bungee jumping but I'd love to **have a go**. (= try it)

How's it going? (= How are you? *infml*) And you can use the same question if you want to know if something is easy, difficult, enjoyable, etc. For example, if you are doing an exercise in class, your teacher may ask: **How's it going?** (also **How are you getting on?**)

It's my **go** (also it's my **turn**). This expression is used in games such as chess or monopoly where you move from one player to another, then back.

Exercises

22.1 Complete the dialogue with suitable forms of these verbs: *come, go, bring, take.* (There are two verbs that can be used in one of the answers.)

A: What time are you (1)................. to Jim's party this evening?

B: I'm not sure because Christopher is (2)................. here first, and then we'll (3).................
together.

A: Right. Do you know what's happening about the music?

B: Yeah. I'm going to (4)................. some CDs, and Sue is (5)................. her guitar. I'll
probably leave quite early though, so do you think you could (6)................. my CDs back
here tomorrow?

A: Yeah sure. What time.

B: Well, I want to (7)............. to the shops in the morning. Could you (8)............... before ten?

A: No problem.

22.2 Replace the underlined words and expressions. The meaning must stay the same.

1 It's hard to say exactly but I think the lorry was <u>going</u> about 60 kph.
2 Some people aren't interested in scuba diving but I've always wanted to <u>have a go</u>.
3 Come on John, it's your <u>go</u>.
4 Hi Sue. How<u>'s it going</u>?
5 Excuse me. Does this road <u>go</u> to the bus station?
6 A: How<u>'s it going</u>?
   B: Not bad. We've nearly finished the first exercise.

22.3 Complete these sentences with an *-ing noun* (e.g. riding), or *for a + noun* (e.g. for a walk).

1 I went .... this morning and bought some books and clothes.
2 We didn't have much food in the house so we decided to go out ....
3 Why don't we go .... in that nice new bar near the square?
4 I wanted to go .... because I had never been to Venice before, but the
others wanted to hire a car and go .... in the countryside.
5 The pool was at the end of the road , so we decided to go ....
6 There are some stables near where we live with about a dozen horses, and we go
.... most weekends.

22.4 Complete these sentences with a suitable word. Use a dictionary to help you.

1 You can wear a hearing aid if you go ....
2 If business doesn't improve they could go ....
3 You can dye (= change the colour of) your hair if you start going ....
4 And you can wear a wig if you go ....
5 If she sees the dog destroying her flowers, she'll go ....

22.5 Look back at the different meanings of *go* (as verb and noun) on the opposite page. Translate these meanings into your own language. How many meanings use the word for *go* in your language? How many are expressed with a different word or in a different way? Compare with someone who speaks the same language if possible.

22.6 Now look up *go* in a good English dictionary. You will find many meanings (including phrasal verbs and idioms), but just concentrate on two or three that you think may be useful to you. Try to learn them. Write down the meanings with example sentences in your notebook. Write a translation as well if you want.

23 Apologies, excuses, and thanks

A Apologies (= saying sorry)

We can **apologise** (= say sorry) in different ways in different situations:

	Situation
(I'm) sorry. I beg your pardon (*fml*).	A general apology, e.g. you close the door in someone's face, interrupt someone, etc.
I'm very/terribly/so/awfully sorry.	A stronger apology, e.g. you step on someone's foot or take their coat by mistake.
I'm very/really sorry I'm late.	When you are late for an appointment.
Sorry to keep you waiting. I won't be long. (= I will talk to you soon)	Someone is waiting to see you and you are busy, e.g. with someone else.

Note: In formal situations (especially in writing), we often use **apologise** and **apology**:
I must **apologise for** (being late). I would like to **apologise for** (the delay. Unfortunately, ...)
Please accept our apologies for the mistakes in your order. We tried to ...

B Excuses and promises

If the situation is quite important we usually add an explanation or **excuse** after the apology. An **excuse** is the <u>reason</u> for the apology, which may or may not be true. (If it is not true, it should still be a reason that people will believe.) Here are some common excuses:

I'm sorry I'm late but **I was delayed/held up** at the airport.
I'm sorry I'm late, but my train was **cancelled**. (= the train was timetabled but did not run)

Note: **To be/get delayed** or **be/get held up** (*infml*) both mean to be late because of a problem that is out of your control.

If you are responsible for a problem, you can offer or promise to do something about it.

I'm sorry about the mess in here. **I'll clear it up.** (= I'll tidy it up)
I'm sorry about the confusion, but **I'll sort it out.** (= I will solve the problems)

C Reassuring people

When people apologise to us, it is very common to say something to **reassure** them (= tell them that 'everything is OK'), and that we are not angry. These are all common expressions. Note that we often use two of them to emphasise the fact that 'it's OK'.

A: I'm sorry I'm late.   B: **That's OK. Don't worry.** *or* **Never mind. It doesn't matter.** *or* **That's OK. No problem.**

D Thanks

These are the most common ways of thanking people in everyday situations:

A: Here's your pen.   B: Oh, **thank you / thanks (very much)**.
A: I'll answer that.   B: Oh, **thanks a lot** (*infml*).
A: I'll post those letters for you.   B: Oh, thank you. **That's very kind of you.**

If you go to someone's house for dinner, or stay with people in an English-speaking country, you will need to thank them for their **hospitality** (= when people are kind and friendly towards their guests). You could say something like this:

Thank you very much for inviting me. It's been a lovely evening.
Thank you very much for everything. You've been very kind.

Exercises

23.1 The opposite page includes a number of expressions, or groups of words that often appear together. How many can you remember? Complete these dialogues in a suitable way.

1 A: I'm .... sorry.
   B: That's OK.
2 A: I'm sorry .... late. I'm afraid I got .... up.
   B: That's OK. No ....
3 A: Sorry to .... you waiting.
   B: That's OK. Never ....
4 A: I'll carry your bags for you.
   B: Oh, thank you. That's very .... of you.
5 A: I must .... for missing the meeting.
   B: That's OK. It doesn't ....
6 A: I'm busy right now but I won't be ....
   B: .... mind. I'll come back later.
7 A: I .... your pardon.
   B: It's OK. Don't ....
8 A: I think the boss has got a real problem.
   B: Yes, but don't worry, he'll .... it out.

23.2 What could you say in these situations? (If it is an apology, give an explanation/excuse if you think it is necessary.)

1 You get on a bus at the same time as another person and he/she almost falls over.

2 You arrange to meet some friends in the centre of town but you are twenty minutes late.

3 You are pushing your car into a side road and a stranger offers to help you.

4 A friend borrows a pen from you and then loses it. When they apologise, you want to reassure them.

5 Some English friends invite you to dinner. How could you thank them as you leave their house at the end of the evening?

6 A colleague at work tells you that a number of files are in a mess: papers are all in the wrong order and he doesn't know what to do. When he apologises to you for this mess, how can you reassure him, and what offer can you make?

7 You are unable to go to a meeting you arranged with a client at their office, and now you must write to them to explain.

8 Your company promised to send some information about new products to a customer last week. You still haven't sent the information and must now write to explain.

23.3 Do you apologise, reassure, explain and thank people in similar ways in your own language? Read the left-hand page again and think about any differences between English and your language.

24 Requests, invitations and suggestions

A Requests and replies

We use different expressions to introduce a request – it depends who we are talking to, and the 'size' of the request ('big' or 'small'). These are some of the most common (the 'small' requests first), with suitable positive and negative replies.

A: **Could you** pass me the salt?
B: Yes, **sure**.

A: **Could I (possibly)** borrow your dictionary?
B: Yes, **of course.** *or* Yes, **help yourself** (= yes, take it) *or* **Go ahead.**

A: Do you think you could possibly lend me two or three pounds?
B: Yes sure *or* I'm afraid I can't.
          I'm afraid not.
          I wish I could but, / I'm sorry but, | I haven't any money on me at all.

A: **I was wondering if I could (possibly)** leave work half an hour early today. *or* **Would you mind if I left** work …
B: Yeah, **no problem.** *or* Well **I'd rather you didn't (actually)**, because …

B Invitations and replies

A: **Would you like to** go out this evening?
B: Yeah **great / lovely / I'd love to** *or* **I'm sorry I can't.**

A: We're going to a restaurant and **we were wondering if you'd like to** come with us?
B: **I'd love to, but I'm afraid I** can't.
Oh, **I'm afraid I** have to look after my younger sister.

C Suggestions and replies

Here are some common ways of asking for and making **suggestions** (= ideas for things to do/say/make, etc.) and suitable replies.

Asking for suggestions
What shall we do tonight?   **Where shall we go** this evening?

Making suggestions
How about (or **what about**) going to the cinema? (*Note:* How/What about + -ing)
We could go to the leisure centre and watch the basketball.
Why don't we try that new club in the main square?

Responding
Yeah, **great / fine / OK / that's a good idea.**
Yeah, **if you like.** (= if you want to go, then I am happy to go)
Yes, **I don't mind.** (= I have no preference)
I think **I'd rather** (= I **would prefer to**) go out for a meal.

Note: In this situation, learners often say 'it's the same for me'. We don't use this expression in English; we say **I don't mind.**

Exercises

24.1 Correct the mistakes in this dialogue.

A: Do you like to go out this evening?
B: I'm afraid but I haven't got any money.
A: That's OK, I'll pay. How about go to see a film?
B: No, actually I think I'd rather to stay at home and do my homework.
A: Why you don't do your homework this afternoon?
B: I'm busy this afternoon.
A: OK. How about tomorrow evening, then?
B: Yeah good.
A: Great. What film shall we go to?
B: For me it's the same.

24.2 Complete these dialogues with a suitable word or phrase.

1 A: Could you .... open that window? It's very hot in here.
  B: Yeah, ...
2 A: Clive and Sally are here at the moment and we were .... if you'd like to come over and join us for a meal this evening?
  B: Yes, I'd ....
3 A: What .... we do this evening?
  B: I don't know really. Any ideas?
  A: Why .... go to the cinema? We haven't been for ages.
  B: Yeah, that's a ....
4 A: OK. Where .... we go on Saturday?
  B: .... going to the beach if the weather is good?
  A: Yeah. Or we .... try that new sports centre just outside town.
  B: Mmm. I think I'd .... go to the beach.
  A: Yeah OK, if you ....
5 A: What .... you like to do this weekend?
  B: I don't .... You decide.

24.3 Here are eight requests, invitations or suggestions. Respond to each one as fast as you can with a suitable reply. If possible, do this activity with someone else: one of you asks the questions, the other answers.

1 Could I borrow a pen for a minute?
2 Do you think you could post a letter for me?
3 I was wondering if you've got a suitcase you could lend me?
4 Would you like to go out this evening?
5 I've got some tickets for a concert of classical music and I was wondering if you'd like to go with me?
6 How about going to a football match at the weekend?
7 Why don't we meet this afternoon and practise our English for an hour?
8 We could invite some other people from our English class to meet us as well.

24.4 There will be many situations when you make requests, invitations and suggestions in your own language, and respond to the requests, invitations and suggestions of others. Try using English expressions in place of your first language. If your friends don't understand, you can teach them a bit of English.

25 Opinions, agreeing and disagreeing

A Asking someone for their opinion

What do you **think of** his new book?
How do you **feel about** working with the others?
What are your **feelings** (*pl*) **about** the change in the timetable?
What's your **honest opinion of** that painting?

B Giving your opinion

I think Charles had the best idea.
I don't think he knew very much about the subject.
Personally, I think his first book is terrible.
In my opinion we should sell the old car and buy a new one.
As far as I'm concerned the whole evening was a waste of time.

Note:
- If you want to say something isn't a good idea you make 'think' negative:
  I don't think it's a good idea. [NOT ~~I think it's not a good idea.~~]
- **Personally** and **As far as I'm concerned** are more common in spoken English.
- **As far as I'm concerned** can mean, 'this is my opinion and I don't care what others think'.

C Giving the opinion of others

According to one of the journalists on television (= in the opinion of this journalist), the Prime Minister knew nothing about it.
The newspaper **says** that the Prime Minister knew weeks ago. (*Note:* we still use the verb **say** when referring to a written opinion)

D Agreeing with someone

We often agree by continuing with the same opinion or adding to it.

A: I think we should concentrate on this one project.
B: Yes, it's better to do one thing well than two things badly.

But if we want to make it clear we agree, we can use these expressions:

Yes, I **agree** (**with you**). (*Note:* **agree** is a verb in English. [NOT ~~I am agree~~])
Yes, I **think you're right**.

E Disagreeing with someone

It is very common in English to begin with a short expression of agreement, and then give a different opinion. Here are some expressions used to introduce the disagreement:

	perhaps/maybe/possibly,	but don't you think …
Yes,	that's true,	but I'm not sure that …
	you could be right,	but don't forget …

If you **disagree strongly** with someone you can say: I'm afraid **I totally disagree** (with you).

Note: When we want to disagree but not completely, we can use these phrases:

Yes, I **partly** agree (with you), but …
I agree **to some extent / a certain extent**, but …

Exercises

25.1 Complete these sentences in at least three different ways to ask people their opinion.

1 .... the proposed changes?
2 .... the new building?
3 .... the transport system?
4 .... the new divorce law?
5 .... the government's decision to make parents responsible?

25.2 Fill the gaps with the correct word. (One word only.)

1 A: What did you think .... it?
   B: Well, ... I didn't like it.
2 .... to the radio, we won't know the result until tomorrow morning.
3 I agreed with him to a certain ....
4 As far as I'm ...., we need to buy a new photocopier immediately.
5 I'm afraid I .... disagree with you.

25.3 Rewrite these sentences without using the underlined words and phrases. The meaning must stay the same.

1 <u>In my opinion</u> you can't learn a language in three months.

   ....

2 <u>I think</u> the club needs to buy new players.

   ....

3 Yes, I <u>think you're right</u>.

   ....

4 <u>According to</u> the newspaper, terrorists started the fire.

   ....

5 I agree with her <u>to some extent</u>.

   ....

25.4 Continue these short conversations. You can either agree with the point of view and add to the argument; or introduce a different point of view. If you introduce a different point of view, remember to start with a short expression of agreement first.

1 A: A lot of women are quite happy to stay at home and be housewives.
   B: ....
2 A: The state shouldn't give money to people who don't want to work.
   B: ....
3 A: People from developing countries need all the help we can give them.
   B: ....
4 A: We should think about legalising cannabis.
   B: ....
5 A: It can be very dangerous if people become too nationalistic.
   B: ....

26 Specific situations and special occasions

You will know many of these expressions but may not be sure exactly how they are used.

A Greetings: 'hello'

Hi/Hello. How are you?	This is the normal greeting when you meet someone you know. (also: **How's it going?** *infml*) The usual reply is: **Fine thanks. And you?** Or possibly, **Not bad. How about you?**
Good morning, good afternoon, good evening	These expressions are used at different times of the day (most people say **Good morning** until lunchtime). British people do not usually say **Good day**, but Australians do.
How do you do?	For formal situations when you meet someone for the first time. The reply can be the same (How do you do?) or **Pleased/nice to meet you.**

B Farewells: 'goodbye'

Nice to meet you. (Nice to have met you.)	For formal situations, when you say goodbye to someone you have just met for the first time.
Bye. See you later.	If you plan to see someone you know later the same day.
Bye. See you soon.	When you know you will see them again, but have no specific plans to meet them.
Goodnight	When you say goodbye to someone late at night, or if you (or they) are going to bed.
A: **Have a nice weekend.** B: **Yes. Same to you.**	The statement and reply when you say goodbye to a colleague/friend at work, school or college on Friday afternoon.

C Happy occasions and celebrations

Happy Birthday	To someone on his/her birthday. You can also say **Many Happy Returns,** and write either expression in a birthday card.
Happy/Merry Christmas	To someone just before or on Christmas Day. You also write this in a card.
Happy New Year	To someone at the beginning of the year.
Congratulations	To someone who has just done something, e.g. passed an exam or got a job. In many situations we can also say **Well done.**

D Special conventions

Excuse me	(a) To get someone's attention (b) When you want to get past, e.g. in a crowded place (c) To tell others you are going to leave the room.
Sorry	(a) To say **sorry**, e.g. you stand on someone's foot. You could also say **I beg your pardon** in this situation. And (b) When you want someone to repeat what they said.
Cheers	To express good wishes when you have a drink with other people. Informally it can also mean 'goodbye' (also **cheerio**) and 'thank you'.
Good luck	To wish someone well before a difficult situation, e.g. a job interview, an exam, a driving test, etc.
Bless you	To someone when they sneeze. They can reply by saying **Thank you.**

Note: In English there is no special expression when people start eating. If you want to say something, you can use the French expression **Bon appetit**, but it is not common.

Exercises

26.1 **What message could you say on the phone or write in a card to these people?**

1 A friend. Next week is 25 December.
2 A friend who is 21 tomorrow.
3 A friend on January 1st or soon after.
4 A very good friend who has just passed some important exams.
5 A friend who is going to take his driving test in three days' time.
6 A friend you know you are going to meet in the next few days/weeks.

26.2 **Complete the conversations in a suitable way.**

26.3 **What could you say in these situations?**

1 You are in a meeting. Someone enters the room and says you have an important telephone call. What do you say as you leave?
2 Someone says something to you but you didn't hear all of it. What do you say?
3 You met a new business client for the first time fifteen minutes ago, and now you are leaving. What do you say?
4 You are in a crowded bus. It is your stop and you want to get off. What do you say to other passengers as you move past them?
5 You are staying with some English friends. What do you say to them when you leave the room in the evening to go to bed?
6 You are in the street. A woman walks past you and at the same time something falls out of her bag. She has her back to you. What do you say?
7 A friend tells you they have just won a competition.
8 Another friend is going for a job interview this afternoon.

26.4 **Here are some more special expressions. When do we use them and do you have equivalent expressions in your own language?**

hard luck   say 'cheese'   watch out   I've no idea

27 Uncountable nouns and plural nouns

A Uncountable nouns

Uncountable nouns (e.g. information):

- don't have a plural form (informations);
- are used with a singular verb (the information are); _is_
- cannot be used with the indefinite article 'a/an'. (I want an information) _some_

These uncountable nouns are often countable in other languages. Look at them carefully.

He refused to give me more **information** about the hotel.
She gave me lots of **advice** about the best dictionary to buy.
We are going to sell all the **furniture**. (= tables, chairs, armchairs, desks, etc.)
My **knowledge** of German is very limited.
You need a lot of **equipment** for camping (e.g. tent, sleeping bag, things for cooking, etc.)
She is making good **progress** in her English. (= her English is improving / getting better)
We had fabulous **weather** in Italy.
The teacher gave us a lot of **homework** last night.
I never take much **luggage** (= bags and suitcases) when I go on holiday.

B In dictionaries

Countable nouns are usually shown with a (C) after them; uncountable nouns have (U) after them; and some nouns can be countable with one meaning and uncountable in another.

book (C)   The books are on the table.
housework (U)   I did a lot of housework this morning.
hair (U)   My hair is getting very long and untidy. I need to get it cut.
hair (C)   There is a hair on my dinner plate.

C Plural nouns

Plural nouns (e.g. trousers):

- only have a plural form and cannot be used with 'a/an' (a trouser) _trousers_
- usually have a plural verb (the trousers is ...) _are_
- some plural nouns can be made singular using **a pair of**, e.g. a pair of trousers/sunglasses

Other words which are usually plural include:

I bought a pair of **jeans** yesterday.
These **shorts** are too long.
I bought a new pair of **pyjamas** when I went into hospital.
The **scissors** are on the table.
When it's sunny I wear **sunglasses** for driving.
These **stairs** are dangerous.
You can weigh yourself on those **scales** over there.
The **headphones** on my new walkman are great.

Exercises

27.1 Correct the mistakes in these sentences.

1 I need some informations.
2 We had a lovely weather.
3 The furnitures are very old.
4 I'm looking for a new jeans.
5 Your hairs are getting very long.
6 Do you have a scissors?
7 We had a lot of homeworks yesterday.
8 Do you think she's making a progress with her English?
9 These trousers is too small.
10 She gave me some good advices.

27.2 Are these nouns countable, uncountable, or countable with one meaning and uncountable with another? Use a dictionary to help you. If they can be countable and uncountable, write sentence examples to show the difference.

butter	cup	housework	insurance
spaghetti	coffee	grape	money
television	coin	work	travel

27.3 Complete these dialogues using a suitable plural noun or uncountable noun from the opposite page. Make sure the form of each word is correct. Look at the example first.

Example: A: It's too hot for jeans.
          B: You need ..*a pair of shorts.*....

1 A: I have to cut this paper into three pieces.
   B: You need ....
2 A: I can't see because the sun is in my eyes.
   B: You need ....
3 A: I don't know what to do when I leave school.
   B: You need ....
4 A: My room looks so empty.
   B: You need ....
5 A: I want to find out how much I weigh.
   B: You need ....
6 A: I can't play my music loud because my mother always complains.
   B: You need ....
7 A: I'm starting to feel cold in bed.
   B: You need ....
8 A: My teacher said my English wasn't getting any better.
   B: You need ....

27.4 Read this text from a radio broadcast. Can you find two more uncountable nouns and two more plural nouns? (These words are not included on the opposite page.)

```
Traffic has been bad throughout the day because of roadworks on the
A40 at Uxbridge which are causing long delays for motorists heading
into London. The authorities are advising drivers to avoid the area
if at all possible, and we will, of course, keep you informed of the
situation with the latest news every half hour, so don't go away.
```

28 Verbs + -ing form or infinitive

A Verb + -ing form

Some verbs are followed by an **-ing** form if the next word is a verb:

enjoy   finish   imagine
(don't) **mind**   **can't stand** (= hate)   **feel like** (= want/desire *infml*)
give up (= stop doing something for the last time)
avoid (If you **avoid** something, you keep away from it; if you **avoid** someone, you stay away
     from them. You do these things by intention.)
admit (If you **admit** something, you agree it is true, and usually it is something bad.)
deny (= the opposite of admit; in other words, you say something isn't true)

Look at these sentences to help you with the meaning of the more difficult verbs.

I stayed in last night but I **feel like** going out this evening.
At the police station, he **admitted** stealing the woman's money but **denied** hitting her.
Cigarettes are very expensive, so he's decided to **give up** smoking.
I've lived in New Zealand all my life; I can't **imagine** living anywhere else.
Some people **can't stand** working at the weekend but I **don't mind**. (= it's not a problem)
I always try to **avoid** driving through the city centre during the rush hour.

B Verb + infinitive

Some verbs are followed by an infinitive if the next word is a verb:

offer   want   seem   decide   hope   forget
mean (= intend, plan)   **expect** (= think or believe something will happen)
manage (= be able to do something, even when it is difficult)
refuse (= say 'no' when someone asks you for something)
promise (= say you will definitely do something, or that something will definitely happen)

Look at these sentences to help you with the meaning of some of the verbs.

We were very busy but we **managed** to finish before 6 p.m.
It was getting late and there were no buses so I **offered** to take them home in my car.
He hit one of the boys but he didn't **mean** to do it; I **meant** to go but I forgot.
I asked her to carry the suitcases but she **refused** to help.
I don't **expect** to see them before next week.
They **promised** to phone as soon as they arrive.

C Verb + infinitive without 'to'

There are two common verbs followed by an object + infinitive without 'to'. They are:
make someone do something, and **let** someone do something.

My parents **make** me do my homework every night. (= they **force** me **to do** my homework)
My parents **let** me go out after I've done my homework. (= they **allow**/permit me **to go** out)

D Verb + -ing form or infinitive

Some verbs can be followed by an -ing form or infinitive, but the meaning is very similar,
e.g. **love**, **like**, **hate**, and **prefer**. But with some verbs there is a difference in meaning:

I **remembered** to buy a present for my brother. (= I <u>didn't forget</u> to buy a present)
I **remember** buying her a present. (= it's in my memory; it happened and I remember)

Exercises

28.1 Cross out the incorrect answers.

1 We decided <u>to work / working</u> during our holiday.
2 She promised <u>to help / helping</u> us.
3 I don't feel like <u>to go / going</u> for a walk at the moment.
4 He forgot <u>to take / taking</u> the cake out of the oven.
5 Do you really hate <u>to drive / driving</u> when it's wet?
6 I can't imagine <u>to eat / eating</u> pasta every day of the week.
7 Most of the time she prefers <u>to work / working</u> on her own.
8 I don't remember <u>to go / going</u> to the zoo when we stayed in Madrid.
9 He hopes <u>to finish / finishing</u> his thesis by the end of the month.
10 I don't mind <u>to help / helping</u> you if I'm not busy.

28.2 Complete part c) of each number in a suitable way.

1 Most people want:
   a) to be rich   b) to get married   c) ....
2 A lot of people can't stand:
   a) getting wet   b) getting up early   c) ....
3 Most people enjoy:
   a) going to parties   b) lying on a beach   c) ....
4 On hot days most people don't feel like:
   a) working   b) eating big meals   c) ....
5 Most people expect
   a) to be happy   b) to find a job they will like   c) ....
6 A lot of people don't mind:
   a) washing-up   b) ironing   c) ....
7 Some parents make their teenage children:
   a) wear certain clothes   b) do housework   c) ....
8 Other parents let their teenage children:
   a) wear what they like   b) stay out all night   c) ....

Now think about each of the above statements. Are they true, and are they (or were they) true of you? If possible, compare and discuss your answers with someone else.

28.3 Read the story and answer the questions below.

> When Julie was 17, her father said she could go on holiday with two school friends. He also said that he would lend her the money for a hotel, but she must pay for the air fare and her entertainment. Julie was delighted and said she would bring him back a wonderful present and pay him back in six months. But first they had to decide where to go. They looked at lots of brochures and finally agreed on a two-week holiday in the south of France. They had a great time, but unfortunately Julie spent all her money and forgot to buy a present for her father.

1 What did Julie's father let her do when she was 17?   He let ....
2 And what did he offer to do?   He offered ....
3 But what did he refuse to do?   He refused ....
4 In return what did Julie promise?   She promised ....
5 What did the three girls decide?   They decided ....

29 Verb patterns

A Verb + object

subject	verb	object	
She	proposed (= suggested *fml*)	the plan	at the meeting.
The travel agent	confirmed (= said it was sure)	my reservation.	
They	discussed (= talked about)	the film	for hours.

B Verb + object + question word

subject	verb	object	question word	
I	told	them	where	to find it.
She	asked	us	why	we wanted it.
He	showed	everyone	what	to do.

Note: A common mistake is: 'He explained <u>me</u> what to do.' After explain + question word, there is no direct object. We say: 'He explained what to do / what I had to do.'

C Verb + object + infinitive

subject	verb	object	infinitive	
She	asked	everyone	to leave.	
They	told	us	to wait	outside.
The doctor	advised	him	to stay	in bed.
I	wanted	the others	to help	us.
He	persuaded	me	to go	to the party.
She	warned	them	to be	careful.

persuade = make somebody change their mind.
John wanted to get an IBM but I **persuaded** him to buy an Apple Macintosh.
warn = tell someone of a possible danger, and often tell them what they should(n't) do.
She **warned** the children not to swim near the rocks.

D Verb + (object) + (that) clause

subject	verb	object	(that) clause
He	said	–	(that) it was good.
She	suggested	–	(that) we go together.
He	insisted	–	(that) we work until 5 p.m.
They	told	him	(that) it was expensive.
She	warned	me	(that) it was dangerous.

insist = demand something strongly and not accept refusal.
She **insisted** that I stay with them (= she did not want me to stay in another place).

We can also use **-ing** after **suggest**, e.g. She suggested going there together.

E Verb + (object) + preposition

He **insisted on** paying for the hotel. (*Note:* use the -ing form of the verb after a preposition)
They **blamed** the driver **for** the accident. (= they said he was responsible / it was his **fault**)
He **complained** (to the manager) **about** the bad service. (= he said he was not satisified)
The manager **apologised** (to the customer) **for** the bad service. (= the manager said sorry)

Exercises

29.1 Correct the mistakes in these sentences. (Most are the result of translating from the first language.)

1 She said me the film was terrible.
2 He told it's not possible.
3 Can you explain me what to do?
4 She suggested us to go to an Italian restaurant.
5 Can we discuss about my report?
6 I want that he leaves.
7 I need to confirm me the booking.
8 I apologised my mistake.
9 She advised me buy a dictionary.
10 She insisted to pay.

29.2 What is the missing verb in each of these sentences? (There may be more than one answer.)

1 I didn't understand how the photocopier worked but she kindly .... me.
2 She wasn't satisfied with her course, so she went to see the Principal to
   ....
3 It was a terrible thing to say to him, but she refused to ....
4 He knew it was dangerous but he didn't .... me.
5 I didn't want to go at first but she .... me.
6 She advised them to stay here but they .... on going.
7 I booked the room by phone but they asked me to .... it in writing.
8 I don't think it was my fault but they still .... me.
9 She didn't know the way but I .... how to get there.
10 They watched the film together and then they .... it in small groups.

29.3 Complete these sentences in a logical way.

1 Some of us were getting hungry so I suggested ....
2 They were making a lot of noise next door and I told ....
3 She went to that new Italian restaurant and said ....
4 We read the book for homework and discussed ....
5 The streets are quite dangerous at night so I insisted ....
6 It was only a few minutes to the beach, but I still couldn't persuade ....
7 She wasn't feeling very well and the teacher advised ....
8 The whole team played badly but most of the newspapers have blamed ....
   ....
9 The water there can make you ill and I warned ....
10 If you don't understand the instructions, someone will explain ....

29.4 When you learn new verbs, you may need to know the constructions that are used with them. So, look at the grammar information about a word in a good dictionary, and always look carefully at the example sentences, then write one or two of your own. Do it for these three examples. What patterns from the opposite page are used after these verbs?

order   recommend   prevent

30 Adjectives

A 'Scale' and 'limit' adjectives

← ————————————————————————————————————— →

(absolutely) terrible	(very) bad	OK	(very) good	(absolutely) marvellous
awful				wonderful
dreadful				great
				terrific

We can use **very** before 'scale' adjectives e.g. very good, very bad; we can use **absolutely** before 'limit' adjectives e.g. absolutely awful, absolutely great. (You cannot say 'very wonderful'; you cannot say 'absolutely good'.) Here are some more examples.

Scale	Limit	Scale	Limit
big	huge/enormous	hot	boiling
small	tiny	cold	freezing
tired	exhausted	crowded (= full of people)	packed
interesting	fascinating	frightened (= afraid of sth.)	terrified
surprised	astonished	hungry	starving (*infml*)

B Adjectives ending -ing and -ed

There is a large group of adjectives which can have an -**ing** or -**ed** ending. The -**ing** ending is used on adjectives which describe a person or thing or situation; the -**ed** ending is on adjectives which describe the effect this person, thing or situation has on us.

It was such a **boring** party; I was **bored**, and so was everyone else.
I didn't think the film was very **frightening**, but my younger brother was **frightened** by it.
I think the students are **depressed** largely because the weather is so **depressing**.

Other examples of common adjectives ending -**ing** and -**ed** include:

surprising/surprised	exciting/excited
exhausting/exhausted	terrifying/terrified
confusing/confused	tiring/tired
frightening/frightened	fascinating/fascinated
astonishing/astonished	embarrassing/embarrassed
interesting/interested	disappointing/disappointed

Look at these examples to help you with the meaning of some of these words.

John wasn't very good at maths, so I was very **surprised** when he passed the exam. And I
    was **astonished** when I discovered that he'd got 98%.

In London there are lots of streets with the same name and it's very **confusing** if you are a
    tourist. Another problem is that it's a huge place. We walked everywhere on our last trip
    and we were **exhausted** at the end of each day. But it's an **exciting** city, with so much to
    do.

It's been a terrible week for Greg. He was very **disappointed** last Saturday because he played
    badly in an important match. Then on Monday, his girlfriend left him for someone else,
    so he's very **depressed** at the moment.

One of our teachers can never remember our names. It seemed funny at first, but now it's
    getting a bit **embarrassing**.

Exercises

30.1 Write at least one limit adjective for these scale adjectives. Cover the opposite page before you begin.

big	....	hot	....
small	....	cold	....
tired	....	bad	....
surprised	....	hungry	....
interesting	....	frightened	....

30.2 Rewrite this postcard using limit adjectives where possible to give a more positive and/or more extreme effect.

Arrived on Sunday. The hotel is good — we've got a big room and the food is nice. It's been hot every day so far, so we've spent most of the time on the beach, along with everyone else — it's very crowded. But the sea is actually cold — that's because it's the Atlantic coast, I suppose.
Tomorrow we're going to walk to a small seaside village about ten kilometres from here — I imagine I'll be really tired by the time we get back, but it does sound an interesting place and I'm looking forward to it.
I'll write again in a couple of days and tell you about it. Until then, love, Benita

30.3 Complete these dialogues using the correct limit adjective in the correct form (*-ing* or *-ed*).

1 A: Was it very tiring?
   B: Yes we were absolutely ....
2 A: I was very interested in her talk.
   B: Yes it was absolutely ....
3 A: Maria said it was a frightening film.
   B: Yes it was absolutely ....
4 A: It was a surprising decision, wasn't it?
   B: Yes I was absolutely ....
5 A: Was it very cold?
   B: Oh yes, it was ....

30.4 Can you think of an adjective from the opposite page to describe how the people felt in each of these situations?

1 They walked about ten miles in the morning, then spent the afternoon helping some friends to cut down some trees.
2 From the description in the travel brochure, they expected a beautiful big villa by the sea. In actual fact it was quite small, not very nice, and miles from the beach.
3 They decided to wear jeans to the party but when they arrived everyone else was wearing formal evening dress.
4 One person told them the street was on the left, another told them to turn right, and a third person said they had to go back to the station.
5 When they got home there was a new car outside their house. They went inside and there was a new sofa in the lounge and a new dining table in the dining room.

3 1 Prepositions: place

A At, On, In

Learn these rules.

at a point/place	**x**	e.g. I met her at the bus stop. She lives at 43 Duke Road. He's at work (i.e. not at home). They're at a party tonight.
on a surface	**x**	e.g. The book is on the desk. We sat on the floor.
in an area or space	**x**	e.g. Malawi is a country in Africa. She lives in Milan. He's in the kitchen. The key's in my pocket. Put it in the box.

B Opposites

Some prepositions form pairs of opposites.

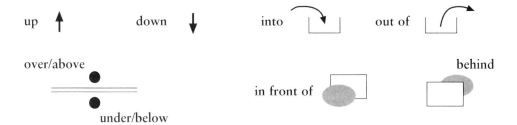

up   down   into   out of

over/above   behind

in front of

under/below

Note: **Over/above** are often synonymous, so are **under/below**, but **over** and **under** sometimes suggest movement.

When we flew **over** Paris we couldn't see much because we were **above** the clouds. **Below** us was the river which ran **under** the bridge.

C Here are some more common prepositions of place

We drove **along** the river, **round** the lake, **past** the old castle, and **through** the village.

We came **over** the bridge, and parked **next to** the house, which was **opposite** the hotel.

Our house is **between** two shops and it is **near** a bus stop; you just go **across** the road and walk **along** the other side **towards** the church.

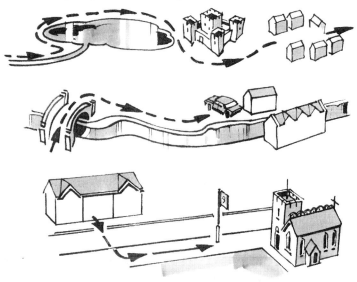

Exercises

31.1 Fill the gaps with *at*, *on* or *in*.

1 I put the books .... the table.
2 The butter is .... the fridge.
3 We saw them .... the bus stop.
4 I met her .... a party.
5 She works .... Barcelona.
6 The dictionary is .... my desk.
7 I sat .... the bed and wrote the letter.
8 I left my books .... school.
9 There was still a lot of snow .... the ground when I arrived.
10 He lives .... a very nice area.

31.2 Answer the questions using the opposite preposition.

1 Was he standing in front of the picture?
No, ...
2 Is it up the hill to his house?
No, ...
3 Did you climb over the fence?
No, ...
4 Did you see her get into the car?
No, ...
5 Did you fly below the clouds?
No, ...
6 Does she live in the flat above you?
No, ...

31.3 Look at the map and complete the description of the route you took on the first day.

We took the boat (1).......... the channel, then we drove (2).......... France and (3)..........
Switzerland, where we spent the first night (4).......... a small town quite (5).......... Lucerne.

Now look at the diagram and complete the description of the second day.

The next morning we walked (6).......... a river which ran (7).......... two mountains. We had
lunch (8).......... a small restaurant and then walked (9).......... the lake and (10).......... the small
town of Stans, before going back.

32 Adverbs: frequency and degree

A Frequency (= how often)

←———→

| always | frequently | regularly
quite often | sometimes | occasionally | seldom (*fml.*)
hardly ever
rarely | never |

Note:

- Adverbs of frequency go before the <u>main</u> verb with the exception of the verb 'to be':

  I **occasionally** see them.   They **hardly ever** go to the cinema now.
  She is **often** late these days.   I've **never** tried Korean food.

- **Sometimes, occasionally** and **often** can go at the beginning or end of the sentence:

  They go to the zoo **quite often**.   I play tennis **occasionally**.
  Sometimes my parents give me money.   **Occasionally** I work at the weekend.

B Degree (= how much)

| | *positive* | *OK* | *negative* |

←———→

| extremely | very | rather | fairly | | slightly | fairly | rather | very | extremely |
| incredibly | | pretty | quite | | a bit | | quite | pretty | | incredibly |

Note:

- **Rather** is more *formal* than the other words and <u>often</u> describes a negative situation:

  We had **rather** bad weather.   The food was **rather** expensive.

- For a positive situation, **rather** often indicates that something is better than we expected:

  Her cooking is **rather** good actually. (I didn't expect that, so it was a <u>very</u> nice surprise.)

- **Incredibly, pretty** and **a bit** are *informal* and mostly used in spoken English; **a bit** is mostly used before negative adjectives (not positive ones) or adjectives with a negative prefix.

  The food was **pretty** good. (= nearly 'very' good)   That Ferrari is **incredibly** expensive.
  The hotel was **a bit** disappointing, actually.   I thought she looked **a bit** unhappy.

C Almost/nearly

It's **almost/nearly** five o'clock. (= it is probably about 4.57)
I **almost/nearly** lost the match. (= I won but only just; only by a small amount)

Note: <u>almost</u> the same NOT ~~quite the same~~

D Hardly

Hardly + a positive often has the same meaning as **almost** + a negative:

I **hardly** had **anything** to eat for lunch. (= I had almost nothing)
She could **hardly** walk after her operation. (= she almost couldn't walk)

Note: In the above sentences you can also use **barely** with the same meaning.

Exercises

32.1 Organise these mixed up words into correct sentences.

1 brother often us Sunday visits on my
2 me ever phones she hardly
3 have leg my broken never I
4 visit saw I hardly his him during
5 get occasionally I early up
6 always she Monday on early is work for a

32.2 Replace the underlined adverb with a different adverb that has the same meaning.

1 She <u>seldom</u> goes to conferences now.
2 I can <u>barely</u> remember the first house we lived in.
3 There were <u>almost</u> fifty people there, you know.
4 I thought it was <u>a bit</u> disappointing, didn't you?
5 I'm afraid I'm <u>extremely</u> busy next week.

32.3 Respond to these sentences using 'rather' to show surprise. (You can also add 'actually' at the end of the sentence.)

1 A: Was it a boring evening?
   B: No, it ....
2 A: Were the children very noisy?
   B: No, they ....
3 A: I've heard it's a very dirty town. Is that true?
   B: No, it ....
4 A: Was the weather awful?
   B: No, it ....

32.4 Change the underlined adverbs to make the first two sentences slightly more positive, and the last three sentences slightly less negative.

1 I thought they were <u>very</u> good.
2 He's been getting <u>quite</u> good marks in his exams.
3 John said the flat was <u>very</u> small.
4 They said it was <u>fairly</u> boring.
5 The clothes were <u>very</u> expensive.

32.5 Put a frequency adverb into each of these sentences to make a true sentence about yourself. Make sure you put the adverb in the correct place. Compare your answers with someone else if possible.

1 I buy clothes I don't like.
2 I clean my shoes.
3 I remember my dreams.
4 I give money to people in the street if they ask me for money.
5 I speak to strangers on buses and trains.
6 I'm rude to people who are rude to me.

Now think about each of your answers to the above sentences. Do you think they are:

a) very typical?   b) fairly typical?   c) slightly unusual?   d) extremely unusual?

If you compared your answers with someone else, how would you describe their answers?

33 Time and sequence

A When and as soon as

I'll phone my uncle **when** I get home. / **As soon as** I get home I'll phone my uncle.
When you've finished you can go home. / You can go home **as soon as** you've finished.

Note: The meaning is the same, but **as soon as** suggests it is more *immediate*. Note also that both items can be followed by the present tense or the present perfect (but not *will*).

B Two things happening at the same time

Pat wrote some letters **while** I cooked the dinner. (two actions in the same period of time)
The accident happened **while** I was on my way to work. (Here there is a longer action 'on my way to work' and a shorter action 'the accident'. We can also use **when** or **as** here.)
I saw him (**just**) **as** I came out of the office. (For two very short actions we use **as** (not **while**), and we often use **just as** to emphasise that these two short actions happened at exactly the same moment: He opened the door **just as** I touched the handle.)

C One thing after another

We met the others in the cafe, and **then** we went to the match.
I finished my homework, **after that** I played a couple of computer games.
After my visit to New York, I decided to have a rest.
We had something to eat **before** we went out.

Note: We can also follow before and after with an **-ing** form:

After visiting New York, I ...   We had something to eat **before** going out.

D A sequence of actions

We had a great holiday. **First of all** we spent a few days in St. Moritz. **Then** / **After that** we drove down to the Italian Riviera and stayed in Portofino for a week. **Finally,** we went back to Switzerland and visited some old friends in Lucerne.

Note:
- If one action happens soon after the other, we often use **afterwards** in place of **after** (**that**): First of all we met the others for a meal, and **afterwards** we went to the disco.
- If you want to say that something happened after a lot of time and/or a lot of problems, you can use **eventually** or **in the end**.

  We took several wrong turnings and the traffic was awful, but **eventually** we got there.

E A sequence of reasons

There are different combinations of words and phrases we can use here:

SON: Why can't we go away this weekend?
DAD: **First(ly)** because I'm busy this weekend. **Second(ly)** you've got a lot of school work to do. And **third(ly)** we're planning to go away <u>next</u> weekend.

Note:
- We can also start with the phrases **to begin with** / **to start with**.
- In spoken English we can start with **for one thing**, followed by **and for another** (**thing**).
- For the second or final reason, we sometimes use (**and**) **besides** or **anyway** (*infml*):

  We can't go to that club because it's too far. And **besides,** I'm not a member.

Exercises

33.1 Cross out the incorrect answers. Sometimes both answers are correct.

1 I'll give them your message as soon as I <u>get / will get</u> there.
2 Maria cleaned the kitchen <u>as/while</u> I did the bathroom.
3 We must go to that gallery before <u>leave/leaving</u>.
4 I had a lot of problems at the shop but <u>eventually/finally</u> they agreed to give me a refund.
5 The phone rang <u>while / just as</u> I was leaving the house.
6 The letter arrived <u>while/as</u> we were getting ready.

33.2 Complete these sentences in a suitable way.

1 We had a game of squash and afterwards ....
2 I'll meet you as soon as ....
3 I must remember to lock the back door before ....
4 I think I dropped the letter as ....
5 I looked up half of the words in my dictionary while ....
6 We had to wait for hours but eventually ....
7 My car is too big for you to drive. And besides, ...
8 I saw him break the window just as ....

33.3 Add a final sentence (starting with a suitable link word or phrase) to each of these texts.

1 A: Why do you want to stay in this evening when we could go to Karl's party?
  B: Well, for one thing because my ex-boyfriend will be there and I really don't want to see him. ....

2 A: What did you do?
  B: First of all we spent a few days in Paris. After that we took the train down to Marseilles and stayed with friends. ....

3 A: Why can't we send one of our staff to the conference?
  B: Well, to start with, I don't think that the company should send anyone to the conference. And ....

33.4 You spent a week at a hotel and had these problems:

– There was very little variety in the food.
– The service was very slow.
– When you mentioned this to the staff, they were very rude.

The manager was on holiday during your stay, so you have decided to send a letter of complaint. Write the next part of this letter and then look at the model answer for the whole letter in the answer key.

```
Dear Sir/Madam

I have just returned from a week's break at The
Royal Malvern Hotel, and I am writing to express my
dissatisfaction with the food and service provided
in your restaurant.
```

34 Addition and contrast

A In addition, etc. (X and Y)

When you add a second piece of information in a sentence to support the first piece of information, you often use **and**, e.g. The food is excellent **and** very good value. When you put this information in two sentences, these link words and phrases are common:

The food is usually very good. **Furthermore**, it is one of the cheapest restaurants in town.
The set menu is £10, which is excellent value. **In addition**, you get a free glass of wine.
The restaurant has a reputation for excellent food. It's **also** very good value.
The food is excellent in that restaurant. It's very good value **as well** (or **too**).
You get very good food in that place. **What's more**, it's excellent value.

Note: The first two examples are more formal and more common in written English. The last two examples are more common in spoken English.

B Although, in spite of, etc. (X but Y)

When you want to contrast two pieces of information in <u>a single sentence</u> and say that the second fact is surprising after the first, you can use these link words:

She still won the game **although / though / even though** she had a bad knee.
They still went for a walk **in spite of the fact that** it was pouring with rain.
The service is worse **despite the fact that** they have more staff.

Note:
In these examples you can also begin the sentence with the link word:

Although she had a bad knee, she still won the game.

It is very common to use **still** in these sentences to emphasise the surprise (as in examples).

In the last two example sentences you can use a noun or -ing form:

They went for a walk **in spite of** the rain. The service is worse **despite** hav**ing** more staff.

After **although**, you can only have a noun/pronoun + verb (i.e. although she had a bad knee / her knee was bad).

C Whereas

This word is used to connect a fact or opinion about a person, place or thing, with something different about another person, place or thing (you can also use **whilst**). In other words, the second fact is a contrast with the first, but not always a surprise (as in B above).

John is very careful **whereas** Christopher makes lots of mistakes.
The south is hot and dry **whereas** the north gets quite a lot of rain.

D However

You can use **however** to contrast two ideas in <u>two sentences</u>, and say that the second sentence is surprising after the first (as in B); and you can use **however** or **on the other hand** to make a contrast between different people/places or things (as in C above):

I don't agree with a lot of his methods. **However**, he is a good teacher.
We didn't like the hotel at all. **However**, we still enjoyed ourselves.
Marcel thought it was a great film. Joe, **however / on the other hand**, thought it was stupid.
Most big cats, such as tigers and leopards, are very solitary creatures. Lions, **however / on the other hand**, spend much of their time in groups.

Exercises

34.1 **Cross out the incorrect answers. Both answers may be correct.**

1 <u>Although / in spite of</u> we left late, we still got there in time.
2 It was a fantastic evening <u>although / in spite of</u> the terrible food.
3 We have decided to go <u>in spite of / despite</u> the cost of the tickets.
4 They enjoyed the course <u>even though / whereas</u> it was very difficult.
5 I love the sea <u>furthermore/whereas</u> most of my friends prefer the mountains.
6 We found a lovely villa near the lake that we can rent. <u>In addition / Furthermore</u> it has its own swimming pool, and we have free use of a car provided by the owners.
7 We both told John the car was too expensive. <u>However / On the other hand</u>, he still decided to buy it.
8 Most people we met tried to help us. They were very friendly <u>too / as well</u>.
9 During the week the town centre is very busy. At the weekend <u>on the other hand / whereas</u>, it is very quiet and almost empty.
10 My uncle is the owner of the factory opposite. He <u>also/however</u> runs the restaurant next door and the car hire company down the road.

34.2 **Combine parts from each column to form five short texts.**

A	B	C
He went to school today	even though	the pay isn't very good.
He always did his best at school	in spite of	he's the most experienced.
He's got the right qualifications.	However	the help I gave him.
He didn't pass the exam	whereas	he didn't feel very well.
He decided to take the job.	What's more	most of his schoolfriends were very lazy.

34.3 **Fill the gaps with a suitable link word or phrase.**

1 .... taking a map, they still got lost.
2 It took me two hours to do it .... the others finished in less than an hour.
3 The hotel has a very good reputation. ...., it is one of the cheapest in the area.
4 She managed to get there .... she had a broken ankle.
5 It's not the best dictionary you can buy; ...., it's better than nothing.
6 She's younger than the others in the group, and she's better than most of them ....

34.4 **Complete these sentences in a logical way.**

1 I was able to follow what she was saying even though ....
2 I was able to follow what she was saying whereas ....
3 We enjoyed the holiday in spite of ....
4 If you buy a season ticket, you can go as often as you like. Furthermore, ...
   ....
5 The exam was very difficult. However, ...
6 Although it was a very long film, ...

34.5 **Answer the questions and test yourself on these different link words and phrases.**

1 Write down all the link words and phrases from the opposite page that you can remember.
2 Organise them into groups according to their meaning.
3 Write your own examples for each one and keep them on one page in your notebook. In future, you can add more examples as you meet them.

35 Similarities, differences and conditions

A Similarities

These are ways of saying that two or more things are similar, or have something the same.

Peter is **similar to** (= **like**) his brother in many ways. Peter and his brother are very **similar**.
Peter and his brother are quite **alike**.
Maria and Rebecca **both** passed their exams. (= Maria passed and Rebecca passed)
But **neither** wants to go to university. (= Maria doesn't want to go and Rebecca doesn't want to go either)
The two boys **have a lot in common**. (= they have many things e.g. hobbies, interests, beliefs, that are the same or very similar) See also section B.

B Differences

These are ways of saying that two or more things are different.

His early films are **different from** his later ones.
Paula is **quite unlike** (= very different from) her sister.
They **have nothing in common**. (= they have no interests or beliefs that are the same)

C Using 'compare'

We want to **compare** the prices of all the televisions before we decide which one to buy.
They made a **comparison of** average salaries in different parts of the country.
Our new flat is very big **compared with/to** our old one. (= if you compare it with the other)
If you **compare** this one **with** the others, I'm sure you'll see a difference.

D Exceptions

When we make a general statement about things or people and then say that <u>one</u> thing or person is not included or is different from the others, we use these words and phrases:

It snowed everywhere **except** on the west coast.
The two girls are very similar **except** that Louise has slightly longer hair.
The museum is open every day **except** (**for**) / **apart from** Sunday(s).
Everyone heard the fire alarm **except** (**for**) / **apart from** the two boys in room 7.

Note: **Except** can be followed by different words (nouns, prepositions, etc.), but **except for** and **apart from** are followed by nouns or noun phrases.

E Conditions

Here are some words/phrases which introduce or connect conditions. Like 'if', they are used with certain tenses, and the rules are quite difficult. For the moment, notice the tenses underlined in the examples, and use them in this way until you meet other examples.

We <u>will be</u> late **unless** we <u>hurry</u>. (= we'll be late if we don't hurry)
Unless the weather <u>improves</u> (= if the weather doesn't improve), we <u>won't be able</u> to go.
I must go now **otherwise** (= because if I don't) <u>I'll</u> miss the last bus.
You can borrow it **as long as** (= **on condition that**) you <u>bring</u> it back by Thursday.

Note: The meaning is very similar to **if** here, but the use of **as long as** shows that the condition is very important to the speaker.

Take your umbrella with you **in case** it <u>rains</u>. (= because of the possibility it may rain later)
I brought food **in case** we <u>get</u> hungry. (= because of the possibility we may be hungry later)

Exercises

35.1 Read the information, then complete the sentences using the words/phrases from A and B.

MICHEL ...
is 21 and lives with his parents. He has worked in a shop. He is shy, hard-working and very good at sport. He would like to become the manager of a sports shop.

PHILIPPE ...
is 22 and lives alone. He is at university. He is clever but lazy, and spends most of his time at parties. He has no plans for the future.

PAUL ...
is 18 and lives with his parents. He is a trainee in a bank, but one day would like to be the manager. He is a very good footballer.

1 Michel and Paul are very ....
2 Philippe is quite .... the other two.
3 Paul and Michel have ....
4 Paul and Philippe have almost nothing ....
5 Paul and Michel both ....
6 Neither of them ....

35.2 Rewrite these sentences. You must start with the words you are given and use the words in brackets. The meaning must stay the same. Look at the example first.

Example: He's like the others.
He's ..*very similar to the others*.... (similar)

1 Martin is quite unlike his brother.
  Martin is very .... (different)
2 When you see the houses, you realise that the flats are very good value.
  The flats are very good value .... (compare)
3 In her class, Carla was the only one who didn't pass the exam.
  Everyone .... (except)
4 The two boys have completely different interests.
  The two boys have .... (common)
5 You don't have to wear a tie except for Saturday(s).
  You don't have to wear a tie .... (apart)

35.3 Fill the gaps with the correct link word or phrase from E opposite.

1 You must write these words down .... you may forget them.
2 I've made extra food for the party .... more people come than we expect.
3 I can meet you for dinner on Friday evening .... I have to work late at the office.
4 We agreed to buy my daughter a dog .... she takes it for a walk every day.

35.4 Complete these sentences in a suitable way.

1 I want to finish this report today otherwise I'll ....
2 You can't get in that disco unless you ....
3 You can borrow the money as long as you ....
4 I've cleaned the spare room and made the bed in case ....
5 I'm not going to work on Saturday unless ....
6 I'm going to take my cheque book with me in case ....

35.5 How many different sentences can you write beginning with these words?

Compared with Britain, my country ....

36 Reason, purpose and result

A Reason

I went home early **because/as/since** I was feeling a bit tired.

Note: With **as** or **since**, the reason (in this example 'feeling tired') is often known to the listener or reader, so it is less important. It is also common to put **as/since** at the beginning of the sentence: 'As/since I was feeling tired, I went home early'. In spoken English, many native speakers would use **so** after the reason: I was feeling a bit tired, **so** I went home early.

We can also use **because of**, but with a different construction. Compare:

We always go there **because** the weather is absolutely wonderful. (because + noun + <u>verb</u>)
We always go there **because of** the wonderful weather. (because of + (adjective) + noun)

Due to and **owing to** have the same meaning as **because of**, but they are more formal, and are often used in sentences which explain the reason for a problem:

The plane was late **due to** bad weather. (**due to** is often used after the verb 'to be')
Due to / Owing to the power cut last night, I missed the late film on TV.

B 'Cause' and 'result' verbs

There are some verbs which we can use in similar ways to the words above:

Police think the bus **caused** the accident. (= **was responsible for** the accident)
The extra investment should **lead to** more jobs. (= **result in** more jobs)

'Cause' and 'result' verbs sometimes appear together in this way:

Police think that a cigarette **caused** the fire which **resulted in** the destruction of the building.

C Purpose

A 'purpose' is an intention, an aim or a reason for doing something:

The purpose of buying this book **was** to improve my English.

But we often introduce a purpose using **so** (**that**):

I bought this book **so** (**that**) I can improve my English.
They went home early **so** (**that**) they could watch the match on television.
We moved house **so** (**that**) we could send our children to this school.

Note: In spoken English, people often just say **so** (without **that**). It is also very common (as in the examples) to use a modal verb, e.g. can or could, after **so that**.

D Result

These words introduce a result:

I left the ticket at home, **so** I'm afraid I had to buy another one.
I forgot to send the letters. **Consequently**, some people didn't know about the meeting.
She was extremely hard-working and **therefore** deserved the promotion.
Both the manager and his assistant were ill. **As a result**, there was no-one to take decisions.

Note: So is the most common, and usually links ideas in a single sentence. **As a result** and **consequently** are more formal, and usually connect ideas in two separate sentences (as in the examples). **Therefore** (also more formal), can be used in a single sentence (as in the example), but may also connect two sentences.

Exercises

36.1 Combine the two sentences into one sentence using *so*, *so that*, *because*, *as*, or *since*. More than one answer is possible in some sentences.

1 I didn't phone you. It was very late.
2 I turned up the radio in the lounge. I could hear it in the kitchen.
3 The restaurant was full. We went to the bar next door.
4 I stayed at home. I was expecting a phone call.
5 It's a very large city. You have to use public transport a lot.
6 I learned to drive. My mother didn't have to take me to the riding school every week.

36.2 Transform these sentences using *because of*. Make any changes that are necessary.

Example: He couldn't play because he had an injured shoulder.
          He couldn't play because of his injured shoulder.

1 She got the job because her qualifications are excellent.
2 The weather was terrible, so we couldn't eat outside.
3 She had to stay at home because she has a broken ankle.
4 The light was very bad, so the referee had to stop the game.
5 The flowers died because it was so dry.
6 The traffic was very heavy. I was half an hour late.

36.3 Read this memo from a manager to the staff. Fill the gaps with suitable words or phrases.

> To: All staff
> From: The Manager
> Date: 9.8.96
> Subject: Temporary roadworks
>
> From next Monday (and continuing throughout the week), there will be
> roadworks on all major approach roads to the factory. (1)_____ this will (2)_____
> considerable delays, could I please ask staff to leave home a few minutes early in
> the morning (3)_____ everyone arrives on time.
> I have been told that these roadworks could also (4)_____ severe traffic
> congestion. (5)_____ it may be advisable to leave your cars at home and use
> public transport instead.
> Thank you for your cooperation in this matter.
> DP

36.4 These sentences are all about learning English. Complete them in a logical way.

1 I want to improve my English because ....
2 I bought myself a walkman so that I ....
3 I study English at the weekend as ....
4 I always write words down in my notebook so that ....
5 I don't get many opportunities to practise my English. Consequently, ...
   ....
6 My brother has got a number of American friends. As a result, ...
   ....
7 If he could speak almost perfect English, it could lead to ....
8 Some people find English difficult because of ....

37 The physical world

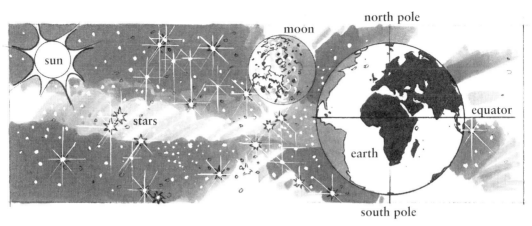

A Physical features

continents	e.g. Asia, Europe
countries	e.g. China, Brazil
islands	e.g. Sicily, Corsica, Hong Kong
group of islands	e.g. The Bahamas, The Balearics
oceans	e.g. The Atlantic Ocean, The Pacific Ocean
seas	e.g. The Red Sea, The Dead Sea
lakes	e.g. Lake Tanganyika, Lake Titikaka
rivers	e.g. The Nile, The Mississippi
falls	e.g. Niagara Falls, The Iguacu Falls
mountains	e.g. Mount Everest, Mount Fuji
mountain ranges	e.g. The Andes, The Alps
jungles	e.g. The Amazon (also called The Amazon rainforest)
forests	e.g. The Black Forest
deserts	e.g. The Sahara, The Gobi

Note: Sometimes you need the definite article 'the', e.g. The Atlantic Ocean, The Alps; sometimes no article is used, e.g. Mount Everest and Lake Titikaka. Compare this with your own language.

B Natural disasters

A **disaster** is when something terrible happens, which often results in death, destruction and suffering.

Exercises

37.1 Complete these sentences, as in the example.

Example: The Nile is ...a river........

1 The Atlantic is ....
2 The Alps are ....
3 Greece is ....
4 The Sahara is ....
5 The Amazon is ....
6 The Mediterranean is ....
7 The Bahamas is ....
8 Africa is ....
9 Crete and Corsica are ....
10 Everest is the highest .... in the world.
11 Michigan and Eyrie are two of the Great ....
12 The 'Great Bear' is a group of ....

37.2 Fill the gaps in the text with *the* if necessary.

My journey took me across .... Atlantic Ocean from .... Europe to .... South America.
I travelled through .... Amazon rainforest and down through the interior of .... Brazil as
far as .... Iguacu Falls. From there I headed north again, through Bolivia, round .... Lake
Titikaka and up to Cuzco. Then I crossed .... Andes and finally arrived in Lima. For the last
part of the journey I flew to .... Jamaica in .... West Indies.

37.3 What disaster is being described in each of these sentences?

1 It lifted a car about ten feet off the ground, and then we saw it disappear down the street.
2 It was about two metres deep and we watched as most of our furniture just floated away.
3 The grass turned yellow and most of the crops died.
4 The walls began to move visibly, and large cracks opened up in the ground.
5 We could see the lava slowly advancing towards the town just ten miles away.

37.4 Can you name everything marked
on this map? Write your answers next
to the symbols.

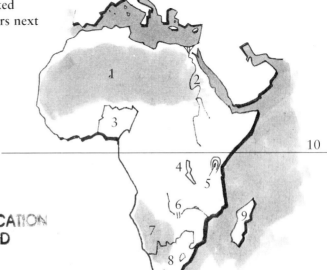

38 Weather

A Weather conditions

Look at this list of common weather words. Notice that it is very common to form adjectives by adding '-y'.

Noun	Adjective	Noun	Adjective
sun	sunny	wind	windy
cloud	cloudy	ice	ic(e)y
fog	foggy	shower	showery
heat	hot	humidity	humid

Note: When it rains for a short period of time, we call it a **shower**, e.g. We had several showers yesterday afternoon.

When it is raining a lot we often say it's **pouring** or it's **pouring with rain.** This phrase is much more common than 'it's raining cats and dogs', which many students seem to learn.

B Temperature

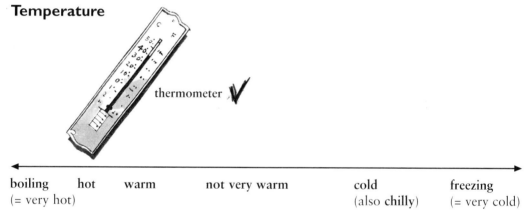

thermometer

boiling   hot   warm   not very warm   cold   freezing
(= very hot)   (also **chilly**)   (= very cold)

People round the world have different ideas about temperature:
5°C (five degrees centigrade) is **freezing** for many Brazilians.
−10°C (minus ten degrees *or* ten degrees below zero) is very cold but quite normal in the mountains in Switzerland during the winter when it usually snows a lot.
30–35°C is **boiling** for England and very unusual, but it is very common in parts of Spain during the summer.

C Wind

The first word here is very gentle; the last is more than 100 km per hour and can be very dangerous.

a **breeze**   a **wind**   a **strong wind**   a **gale**   a **hurricane**

It was a hot day but there was a lovely **breeze.**
The **wind** blew my hat off.
The **hurricane** in Florida destroyed trees and buildings.

D Thunderstorms

A **spell** (= period) of very hot weather often ends with a **thunderstorm.** First it becomes very **humid** (= hot and wet), then you get **thunder and lightning**, and finally, very **heavy rain** (= it pours with rain). Afterwards, it is usually cooler and it feels fresher.

Exercises

38.1 Identify the weather conditions in these pictures.

38.2 *True* or *false*? If a sentence is *false*, write a *true* sentence about the weather conditions in the sentence.

1 It often pours with rain in the desert.
2 It gets quite chilly in the desert in the evening.
3 Thunder makes a noise.
4 Lightning can kill people.
5 A shower is a gentle breeze.
6 A spell of hot weather may end in a thunderstorm.
7 If it is humid, the air will be very dry.
8 Below zero, water turns to ice.
9 Heavy rain means that it is pouring with rain.
10 When it's foggy you need sunglasses.

38.3 Complete these scales.

.... → wind → strong wind → .... → hurricane

.... → hot → warm → not very warm → cold → ....

38.4 Complete this text with suitable words.

The single greatest influence on Japanese weather is the wind. During the summer it (1)............... from the Pacific, causing (2)............... and humid weather, but in winter, the north-westerly (3)............... from Siberia are very cold and it (4)............... heavily on the mountains of the north west. The south-eastern parts receive cold dry air. Between June and mid July, there is a (5)............... of wet weather when the rice fields get the water vital for growth. After that, there is less (6)............... rain, but the air is still (7)............... Autumn, however, is drier, and usually very pleasant.

Write a paragraph about the weather in your own country, or a specific part of your country, e.g. your own region. Try to use as many words as possible from the opposite page.

39 Using the land

A Ground and soil

When we walk, our feet are on the **ground** (= the general word for the surface of the earth). For the top part of the ground where grass and flowers grow, we use the word **soil**.

There were no seats in the park, so we had to sit on the **ground**.
The **ground** is very hard because it hasn't rained for weeks.
Plants don't grow very well here because the **soil** is too dry.

B Above the ground

Some land is used for parks and gardens where we often **grow** trees and **plants** (= living things with **roots** and **leaves**, smaller than trees which grow in the soil). First, you **plant** the tree or plant (= put the tree or plant in the ground), then you must **water** it (= give it water).

tree

leaves

plants

branches

grass

soil

roots

Land in the country is often used for **agriculture/farming**. Some farms concentrate on **dairy produce** such as milk, butter and cheese. Other farms **keep** animals which are **slaughtered** (= killed) and sold for their meat, e.g. cows and lambs. Some farms use the land to **grow** fruit, e.g. apples and pears; vegetables, e.g. potatoes and carrots; and **cereals**, e.g. wheat, maize and barley. When they are ready, farmers **pick the fruit** and **harvest** the other **crops** (= take the other crops from the ground). This period is called the **harvest**. We use the word **crop(s)** as a general word to describe all the things that are grown to be eaten:

In parts of Africa the **crops** failed because of the **drought** (= long period without rain).
We had a wonderful **crop** of barley last year.

C Below the ground

One of the main activities below the ground is **mining**. This is the process of **extracting** (*fml*) (= removing or taking out) different materials, e.g. **coal** or **gold**, from below **the ground**. We call the place a mine, e.g. a coal mine or gold mine.

These are some of the **metals** we take out of the ground:

gold: a valuable yellow metal used to make coins and jewellery
silver: a valuable whitish metal used to make coins and jewellery
iron: usually takes the form of a hard dark-grey metal, and is used in building and to make tools; it is also used to make **steel**
tin: a softer metal often used to cover other metals
copper: a soft reddish metal; it permits heat and electricity to pass through it easily

Exercises

39.1 Which nouns on the right often follow the verbs on the left? (There may be more than one noun for several of the verbs.)

1	plant	coal
2	water	cows
3	pick	wheat
4	extract	apples
5	grow	plants
6	slaughter	trees

39.2 Are these statements *true* or *false*? If *false*, correct them.

1 Plants need roots.
2 Soil is the top part of the ground.
3 Drought is a long period of rain.
4 If you extract something, you remove it.
5 The harvest is the period when we plant the crops.
6 Iron is used to make silver.

39.3 Complete the descriptions of these objects with a suitable 'metal'.

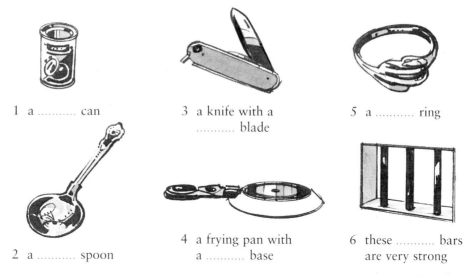

1 a .... can

3 a knife with a .... blade

5 a .... ring

2 a .... spoon

4 a frying pan with a .... base

6 these .... bars are very strong

39.4 Complete these sentences with the correct 'general' word. Look at the example first.

Example: Apples, oranges and bananas are all types of ...*fruit*...........

1 Potatoes, beans and carrots are types of ....
2 Silver, tin and copper are types of ....
3 Milk, butter and cheese are all .... products.
4 .... is the general word for wheat, maize, barley, etc.
5 We use the word .... as a general word for plants which are grown to be eaten.

39.5 Answer these questions about your own country.

1 Which of these are the most important to your economy: agriculture, mining or fishing?
2 Are any **precious** (= valuable e.g. gold or silver) metals found in your country?
3 What are some of the main crops grown in your country?

40 Animals and insects

A Pets and farm animals

Many people keep **pets** (= domestic animals that live with people) in Britain. The most common are dogs and cats, but children in particular sometimes keep **mice** (singular = a **mouse**) and **rabbits**.

rabbit

mouse

goat

Farm animals include: sheep, pigs, cows, horses, chickens and goats.

Note: The word 'sheep' is the singular and plural form i.e. a sheep or some sheep. A young sheep is called a **lamb**.

B Wild animals

In a zoo or **in the wild,** you will find these wild animals.

lion   gorilla

elephant   camel   tiger   monkey   leopard   zebra   giraffe

bear

C Common insects

Here are some common insects.

bee   ant   mosquito   butterfly   fly   spider

D In the water, in the air, and on the ground

Here are some **creatures** (= living things, e.g. animals, birds, fish) that swim, fly, or move along the ground.

snake

snail

eagle

whale   shark

Exercises

40.1 Look at the underlined letters in each pair of words. Is the pronunciation the same or different? Look at the examples first.

Examples: wh<u>a</u>le w<u>a</u>ter (different)   c<u>a</u>t c<u>a</u>mel (same)

1	l<u>i</u>on	t<u>i</u>ger	6	m<u>o</u>nkey	m<u>o</u>squito
2	le<u>o</u>pard	mosquit<u>o</u>	7	c<u>a</u>mel	sn<u>a</u>ke
3	b<u>ea</u>r	<u>ea</u>gle	8	leop<u>ar</u>d	sh<u>ar</u>k
4	g<u>o</u>rilla	g<u>i</u>raffe	9	d<u>o</u>g	w<u>a</u>sp
5	sp<u>i</u>der	w<u>i</u>ld	10	m<u>ouse</u>	c<u>ow</u>

40.2 Divide these words into three groups and give each one a title.

monkey   horse   goat   fly   lion   cow   elephant   pig   mosquito
butterfly   tiger   wasp   sheep   camel   ant   leopard   bear   chicken

40.3 Start each sentence with a suitable creature from the opposite page.

1 .... can fly at a great height.
2 .... can swim very long distances.
3 .... can understand lots of human commands.
4 .... can run very fast.
5 .... can travel through the desert for long distances without water.
6 .... can be 30 metres in length.
7 .... can eat fruit from tall trees.
8 .... change their skin several times a year.
9 .... can pick things up with their trunk.
10 .... provide us with wool.

40.4 Complete the sentences with a suitable word.

1 They've got lots of pets: two dogs, four cats, and a ....
2 Their farm animals include cows, sheep and ....
3 The children love to see the 'big cats' at the zoo such as lions, tigers and ....
4 I hate most insects, but particularly mosquitoes and ....
5 We saw some really large animals at the Safari Park: elephants, giraffes and ....

40.5 Can you match these creatures with their maximum speeds?

lion spider elephant	64 kph 0.05 kph 80 kph
rabbit pig snail	56 kph 40 kph 18 kph
shark golden eagle	270 kph 1.88 kph

41 Countries, nationalities and languages

A Who speaks what where?

Country	Nationality	Language
Germany	German	German
France	French	French
Italy	Italian	Italian
Spain	Spanish	Spanish
Britain	British	English
Portugal	Portuguese	Portuguese
Japan	Japanese	Japanese
Korea	Korean	Korean
China	Chinese	Mandarin (also Cantonese)
Thailand	Thai	Thai
Australia	Australian	English
The United States of America	American	English
Saudi Arabia	Saudi Arabian	Arabic
Brazil	Brazilian	Portuguese
Sweden	Swedish	Swedish
Switzerland	Swiss	Swiss-German, French, Italian
Egypt	Egyptian	Arabic
Holland	Dutch	Dutch
Mexico	Mexican	Spanish
Russia	Russian	Russian
Israel	Israeli	Hebrew
Greece	Greek	Greek
Turkey	Turkish	Turkish
Argentina	Argentinian	Spanish

B The people

When you are talking about people in general from a particular country, there are some nationalities that you can make plural with an 's', but others can only be formed with the definite article (and no plural 's'):

(The)	Brazilians		
	Germans	The British	
	Italians are (usually very ...)	The French	
	Russians	The Swiss are (usually very ...)	
	Israelis	The Dutch	
		The Japanese	

Note:
- With both groups you can also use the word 'people': British people, German people, etc.
- When you talk about one person from these countries, you need to add woman/man/person to the group on the right: a Brazilian but a Japanese person; a German but a Swiss person, etc.

Exercises

41.1 Answer these questions without looking at the opposite page.

1 Write down three countries where the first language is English.
2 What language is spoken in Brazil?
3 What are people from Holland called?
4 Write down three languages spoken in Switzerland.
5 What language is spoken in Saudi Arabia?
6 What nationality are people from Sweden?
7 What language is spoken in Mexico?
8 What are people from Egypt called?
9 What is the first language in Israel?
10 Where do people speak Mandarin?

41.2 Mark the main stress on the words in the box, and practise saying them.

Japan	Japanese	Brazilian	Egyptian	Arabic	Italian
Austria	Australia	Chinese	Portuguese	Saudi Arabia	

What do you notice about the stress on words ending *-ia*, *-ian*, and *-ese*?

41.3 Complete these sentences with the name of the people from the country on the right.

Examples: I've worked a lot with ....Germans.....
I've spent a lot of time with ...the French...

1 We do a lot of business with ....
2 .... are usually hard-working.
3 I have always found .... very friendly.
4 People often say that .... are reserved.
5 .... are very organised.
6 I met a lot of .... on my trip to Athens.

Germany
France
Japan
Israel
Brazil
Britain
Switzerland
Greece

41.4 Complete these sentences.

1 Bangkok is the capital of .... 6 Riyadh is the capital of ....
2 Buenos Aires is the capital of .... 7 Athens is the capital of ....
3 Ankara is the capital of .... 8 Tel Aviv is the capital of ....
4 Seoul is the capital of .... 9 Stockholm is the capital of ....
5 Cairo is the capital of .... 10 Lisbon is the capital of ....

41.5 Can you identify these languages?

1 Здравствуйте   4 今日は   7 goede dag   10 Bonjour

2 안녕하세요   5 Γεια σου   8 Hola   11 Hej!

3 Ciao   6 你好嗎   9 Grüezi

41.6 Have you met someone from each of the countries on the opposite page? Go through the list and tick the ones you have.

42 The body and what it does

A Parts of the body

Learn the parts of the body that you don't already know.

forehead
eyebrows
cheek
lips
chin
neck
shoulders
bust (chest for men)
arm
hips
elbow
waist
bottom
thigh
wrist
hand
thumb
fingers
knee
foot
ankle
toes
heel

B Physical actions

You can **breathe** through your nose or your mouth. Most people **breathe** about 12–15 times a minute.

People **smile** when they're happy, or to be polite; they **laugh** when people say something funny; they may **cry** when they're sad; they **yawn** when they're tired, or bored.

Many people **nod** their head to mean 'yes', and **shake** their head when they mean 'no'.

When you pick up something heavy, you must **bend** your knees and keep your back straight.

C Common expressions

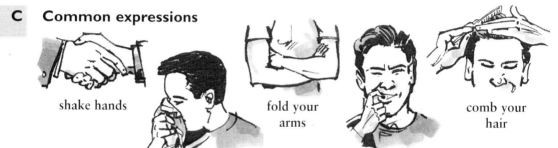

shake hands

blow your nose

fold your arms

bite your nails

comb your hair

Exercises

42.1 How much of the picture can you label without looking at the page opposite?

1 forehead
2 cheek
3 chin
4 chest
5 arm
6 hip
7 knee
8 foot
9 toe
10 finger
11 back
12 shoulder
13 belt
14 elbow
15 wrist
16 hand
17 bottom
18 thigh
19 heel

42.2 Match the verbs on the left with a suitable part of the body on the right to form common expressions. Use each verb and noun once only.

1 blow   your knees
2 shake   your nose
3 comb   your nails
4 fold   your head
5 bend   your arms
6 nod   your hair
7 bite   hands

42.3 What do these actions often mean? (There may be lots of possible answers.)

1 People often smile when ....
2 They often breathe quickly after ....
3 They laugh when ....
4 They may bite their nails ....
5 They blow their nose ....
6 They shake their head ....
7 And nod their head ....
8 They cry ....
9 They yawn when ....

42.4 There are fourteen words describing parts of the body, either across or down, in this word square. Can you find them?

C	E	L	B	O	W	A
H	T	I	A	E	N	R
I	O	P	C	Y	A	M
N	E	C	K	E	I	H
I	H	A	N	K	L	E
K	C	H	E	S	T	E
C	H	E	E	K	A	L

43 Describing people's appearance

A General

Positive: **beautiful** is generally used to describe women; **handsome** is used to describe men; **good-looking** is used for both; **pretty** is another positive word to describe a woman (often a girl) meaning 'attractive and nice to look at'.

Negative: **ugly** is the most negative word to describe someone; **plain** is more polite.

B Height and build

tall and slim   medium height and build   short and fat   medium height and very muscular

Note: Another word for **slim** is **thin**, but **slim** has a more positive meaning, e.g. John is lovely and slim, but his brother is terribly thin. **Skinny** also has the same meaning but is very negative. It is not very polite to say someone is **fat**; **overweight** is more neutral and polite.

C Hair

straight   wavy   curly

fair
blond(e)   light brown

dark
dark brown   black

D Special features

The man on the left has got very **pale skin** (= white skin). He also has **broad shoulders**, with a small **scar** at the top of his left arm. The other man has **dark skin**. He also has a **beard** and **moustache** and quite a **hairy chest** and a **tattoo**.

E Asking questions about a person's appearance

Q: What does she **look like**? A: She's quite tall, with short fair hair.
Q: **How tall** is she? A: About 1 metre 65.
Q: **How much** does she **weigh**? A: I don't know and it may be rude to ask. Probably about 45 kilos.

Exercises

43.1 Complete these sentences in a suitable way. (More than one answer may be possible.)

1 She's got blonde ....
2 He's got very pale ....
3 They've both got curly ....
4 I would say he was medium ....
5 Her brother has got very broad ....
6 She doesn't like men with hairy ....
7 Last time I saw him he had grown a ....
8 He's got very muscular ....
9 Both men were very good-.............................. .
10 All of them have got dark ....

43.2 Replace the underlined word in each sentence with a word which is either more suitable or more polite.

1 He told me he met a <u>handsome</u> girl in the disco last night.
2 She's beautiful but her younger sister is really quite <u>ugly</u>.
3 I think Peter is getting a bit <u>fat</u>, don't you?
4 Most people want to stay slim, but not as <u>skinny</u> as that girl over there.
5 I think she's hoping she'll meet a few <u>beautiful</u> men at the tennis club.

43.3 You want to know about the following:

– someone's general appearance
– their height
– their weight

What questions do you need to ask? Complete these questions.

What .... ?
How .... ?
How much .... ?

Now answer these questions.

1 How tall are you?
2 How would you describe your build?
3 How much do you weigh?
4 What kind of hair have you got?
5 What colour is it?
6 Would you like it to be different? If so, what would you like?
7 Do you think you have any special features?
8 Are there any special features you would like to have?
9 Do you like beards?
10 Can you think of a famous woman you would describe as beautiful, and a famous man you would describe as good-looking?

If possible, ask another person these questions.

44 Describing character

Describing character

A Opposites

Many positive words describing character have clear opposites with a negative meaning.

Positive	Negative
warm and friendly	cold and unfriendly
kind	unkind
nice, pleasant	horrible, unpleasant
generous (= happy to give/share)	mean (= never gives to others)
optimistic (= thinks positively)	pessimistic (= thinks negatively)
cheerful (= happy and smiling)	miserable (= always seems unhappy)
relaxed and easy-going	tense (= nervous; worries a lot; not calm)
strong	weak
sensitive	insensitive (= does not think about others' feelings)
honest (= always tells the truth)	dishonest

Jane is very **tense** at the moment because of her exams, but she's usually quite **relaxed** and **easy-going** about most things.

I think the weather influences me a lot: when it's sunny I feel more **cheerful** and **optimistic**; but when it's cold and raining I get very **miserable**.

He seemed a bit **unfriendly** at first, but now I've got to know him I realise he's very **warm** and **kind**.

The shop assistant told me that the dress I tried on looked better on people younger than me. I thought that was very **insensitive** of her, but at least she was being **honest**, I suppose.

B Character in action

People often talk about qualities of character that you may need in a work situation. Again, some of these words come in pairs of opposites: one positive and one negative.

Positive	Negative
hard-working	lazy (= never does any work)
punctual (=always on time)	not very punctual; always late
reliable	unreliable (= you cannot trust / depend on someone like this)
clever, bright (*infml*)	stupid, thick (*infml*)
flexible	inflexible (= a very fixed way of thinking; unable to change)
ambitious	unambitious (= no desire to be successful and get a better job)

Some pairs of opposites do not have a particularly positive or negative meaning:

He is very **shy** when you first meet him because he finds it difficult to talk to people and make conversation; but when he knows people quite well he's much more **self-confident**.

People often say the British are very **reserved** (= do not show their feelings), but when you get to know them they can be very **emotional** like anyone else.

C Using nouns

Some important qualites are expressed through nouns.

One of her great qualities is that she **uses** her **initiative**. (= she can think for herself and take the necessary action; she does not need to wait for orders all the time)

That boy has got no **common sense** (= he does stupid things and doesn't think what he is doing). His sister, on the other hand, is very **sensible**. (= has lots of **common sense**)

Exercises

44.1 Organise these words into pairs of opposites and put them in the columns below.

mean	clever	nice	lazy	relaxed	hard-working
tense	cheerful	generous	unpleasant	stupid	miserable

Positive   *Negative*

....
....
....
....
....
....

44.2 What prefix forms the opposite of each of these words? (You need three different prefixes.)

kind	flexible	friendly	honest
reliable	sensitive	ambitious	pleasant

44.3 How would you describe the person in each of these descriptions?

1 He never bought me a drink all the time we were together.
2 I have to tell her what to do every minute of the working day. She wouldn't even open a window without someone's permission.
3 He often promises to do things but half the time he forgets.
4 She's always here on time.
5 I don't think he's done any work since he's been here.
6 She finds it difficult to meet people and talk to strangers.
7 He could work in any of the departments, and it doesn't matter to him if he's on his own or part of a team.
8 One of the great things about her is that she is so aware of what other people think or feel.
9 Bob, on the other hand, is the complete opposite. He is always making people angry or upset because he just doesn't consider their feelings.
10 The other thing about Bob is that he really wants to get the supervisor's job and then become boss for the whole department.

44.4 What nouns can be formed from these adjectives? Use a dictionary to help you.

Example: kind *kindness*

punctual	optimistic	reliable	lazy
confident	generous	ambitious	stupid
sensitive	strong	flexible	shy

44.5 Choose three words from the opposite page which describe you. Is there one quality you do not have but would like to have? What, in your opinion, is the worst quality described on the opposite page? If possible, compare your answers with a friend.

45 Human feelings and actions

A Feelings

Noun	Adjective(s)
love (≠ hate)	–
happiness (≠ sadness)	happy (≠ sad)
anger	angry
fear	afraid (of) / frightened (of)
pride	proud (of)
jealousy	jealous (of)
embarrassment	embarrassed/embarrassing (see Unit 30)

Note:
- **Pride** has different meanings, but the most common is the feeling of satisfaction you have because you (or people you are connected with) have done something well.
  He was very **proud** when his wife became the first President of the organisation.
- **Jealousy** is a feeling of anger and unhappiness you may have if (a) someone you love shows a lot of interest in others, or (b) if someone has something you want / don't have.
  a) My boyfriend gets very **jealous** when I talk to other boys.
  b) He's **jealous of** his brother because his brother is more intelligent and makes more money.
- A common adjective is **upset**, which means unhappy, sad, and even angry, because something unpleasant has happened, e.g. He was very **upset** when we didn't invite him.

B Ways of ...

Ways of speaking
whisper (v, n) (= speak very quietly)
shout (v, n) (= speak in a very loud voice)

Ways of looking
stare (v, n) (= look at someone/something in a fixed way for a long time)
glance (at) (v, n) (= look at someone or something very quickly)

Ways of walking
stroll (v, n) (= walk in a slow casual way)
march (v, n) (= walk quickly and with a clear purpose/reason)

C Things we do with our hands

clap

knock (on a door) (v, n)

wave (goodbye)

point (at sth./sb.)

press (a button)

punch someone

Exercises

45.1 **What nouns can be formed from these adjectives?**

angry   sad   happy   proud   jealous   embarrassed

45.2 **Find the logical ending on the right for each of the sentence beginnings on the left.**

1 He was very proud when
2 He was very jealous when
3 He was very embarrassed when
4 He was very angry when
5 He was very sad when
6 He was very frightened when

a someone stole his money.
b his father appeared on TV with the Prime Minister.
c he heard that his aunt had died.
d he saw those big dogs running towards him.
e he bought her a birthday present on the wrong day.
f his best friend went out with the girl he really liked.

45.3 **Answer these questions. If possible, ask someone else the same questions.**

1 Would you feel embarrassed or upset (or both) if you forgot your mother's birthday or your father's birthday?
2 Do you ever feel frightened in a car (as a passenger) because you are going very fast?
3 Do you get angry when other people want you to do things that you don't want to do?
4 If you made a stupid mistake in English, would you feel embarrassed?
5 Is there any one thing that you are very proud of?
6 Are there any common situations where you sometimes feel embarrassed?

45.4 **What are these people doing? Describe their actions using words from the opposite page.**

45.5 **Replace the underlined words with a single verb that has the same meaning.**

1 She stopped working and <u>looked quickly</u> at the clock.
2 As we were in the library, he <u>spoke very quietly</u> in my ear.
3 We <u>walked casually</u> along the beach and then stopped for a drink.
4 He made us all <u>walk quickly</u> up the hill.
5 The man <u>kept looking</u> at Susan, but she didn't seem to notice.
6 Jim doesn't know what happened, except that the man <u>hit</u> him <u>hard</u> on the side of his face.

46 Family and friends

A Relatives (= members of your family)

These are the most important relatives (also called **relations**):

	male	*female*
Your parents' parents	grandfather	grandmother
Your parents' brother and sister	uncle(s)	aunt(s)
Your aunt's/uncle's children	cousin(s)	cousin(s)
The father and mother of the person you marry	father-in-law	mother-in-law
The brother and sister of the person you marry	brother-in-law	sister-in-law
Your brother's/sister's children	nephew(s)	niece(s)
The person you marry dies, so you are a …	widower	widow
Your mother or father remarries, so you have a …	step-father	step-mother

B Family background (= family history)

My grandfather was a market gardener in Ireland. He grew flowers, fruit and vegetables, and sold them in the market every day. He worked hard all his life, and when he died, his son (now my uncle) and daughter (my mother) **inherited** a large house and garden (= received this house and garden from my grandfather when he died). They carried on the business together until my mother met my father. They got married, moved to England, and I was born two years later. They didn't have any more children, so I am an **only child**.

C Family names

When you are born, your family gives you a **first name**, e.g. James, Kate, Sarah and Alex are common first names in Britain. Your **family name** (also called your **surname**) is the one that all the family share e.g. Smith, Brown, Jones, and O'Neill are common surnames in Britain. Some parents give their children a **middle name** (like a first name), but you do not usually say this name. Your **full name** is all the names you have, e.g. Sarah Jane Smith.

D Changing times

Society changes and so do families. In some places, people may decide to live together but do not get married. They are not husband and wife, but call each other their **partner**. There are also many families in some parts of the world where the child or children live(s) with just their mother or father; these are sometimes called **single-parent families**.

E Friends

We can use a number of adjectives before **friend**:

an **old** friend (= someone you have known for a long time)
a **close** friend (= a good friend; someone you like and trust)
your **best** friend (= the one friend you feel closest to)

We use the word **colleagues** to describe the people we work with.

F Ex-

We use this for a husband/wife/boyfriend/girlfriend we had in the past but do not have now:
The children stay with my **ex-husband** at the weekend.
I saw an **ex-girlfriend** of mine at the disco last night.

Exercises

46.1 Look at the family tree and complete the sentences below.

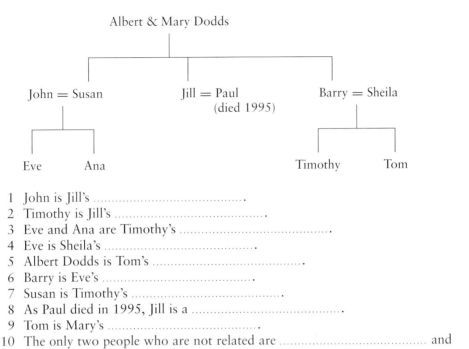

Albert & Mary Dodds

John = Susan   Jill = Paul   Barry = Sheila
                     (died 1995)

Eve   Ana   Timothy   Tom

1   John is Jill's ....
2   Timothy is Jill's ....
3   Eve and Ana are Timothy's ....
4   Eve is Sheila's ....
5   Albert Dodds is Tom's ....
6   Barry is Eve's ....
7   Susan is Timothy's ....
8   As Paul died in 1995, Jill is a ....
9   Tom is Mary's ....
10 The only two people who are not related are .... and
    ....

46.2 Answer these questions about yourself and your country.

1   What's your first name?
2   What's your surname?
3   Is that a common name in your country?
4   Do you have a middle name?
5   Are you an only child?
6   Who is your oldest friend?
7   Do you work? If so, how many of your work colleagues are also your friends?
8   Do you have any ex-boyfriends or ex-girlfriends who speak English very well?
9   Are single-parent families becoming more common in your country?
10 In your country, do more and more people live together without getting married?

46.3 Draw your own family tree. Are there any relationships you cannot describe in English? Can you also write a short summary of your family background (as in B on the opposite page)?

47 Ages and stages

A Growing up

Age	Stage
0–1 approximately	a **baby**
1–2	a **toddler**
2–12 approximately	a child – this period is your **childhood**
13–17 approximately	a **teenager** (14 = early teens)
18+	an **adult**
20–30	**in your twenties** (24–26 = mid twenties)
30–40	**in your thirties** (38 = late thirties)
40+	people are **middle-aged; in middle age**
60 or 65	**retirement** (= when people stop work; they are **retired**)
75+	**old age** (you can also use **elderly**)

Note: For boys, the period between 14–17 approximately (slightly younger for girls) is called **adolescence**, i.e. you are an **adolescent**. In law you are an **adult** at the age of 18, but many people think of you as an adult when you leave school.

B Childhood and adolescence

Sam (on the right) **was born** in Scotland but when he was two, his father got a new job in London and he **grew up** in the south of England. He **went to university** at 18 where he …

C Romance

… where he **met** Anthea. He **went out with** her (= she was his **girlfriend**; he was her **boyfriend**) for three years, but towards the end they had lots of **rows** (= arguments) and they **split up** (= **broke up** / separated). In his **mid twenties** …

D Marriage

… in his mid twenties he met Maureen. They **fell in love** and **got married** within six months. A year later she got **pregnant** and they had their first child, a boy. As you can see, she is now **expecting** their second child (to be pregnant = to be expecting a baby). But sadly Sam met another woman and he left Maureen two months ago to live with the other woman.

Exercises

47.1 **What stage of life are these people at?**

1 Paul isn't 2 yet, so he's still a ....
2 Albert was a bus driver for 40 years but stopped work two years ago, so he is now
....
3 Susan is 25, so she is in her ....
4 Caroline is 50 this year so she is now in her ....
5 Ron is 33 and his wife is 32, so they are both in ....
6 Joan is 75 this year, so she is quite ....
7 Jason was born six weeks ago, so he's a ....
8 Leyla is 13 this year, so she'll soon be a ....
9 Ravi is 18 this year, so legally he becomes ....
10 15 is often a difficult age for boys going through ....

47.2 **Are these sentences *true* or *false* about the people on the opposite page? If the sentences are *false*, write the correct answer below. Try to answer the questions first without looking at the opposite page.**

1 Sam was born in Scotland.
....
2 He grew up in the south of Ireland.
....
3 He went out with Anthea for two years.
....
4 They split up because Sam went to live in Japan.
....
5 Sam fell in love with Maureen.
....
6 They had a baby a year after they got married.
....
7 Maureen is now expecting her third child.
....
8 Maureen left Sam.
....

47.3 **Find the logical ending for each of the sentence beginnings on the left and construct Rebecca's life.**

1 Rebecca was born	a was a boy at her secondary school.
2 She grew up	b in her early thirties.
3 Her first boyfriend	c on a farm with lots of animals.
4 She went out with him	d when she was in her late twenties.
5 She went to university	e in a small local hospital in 1978.
6 She fell in love	f for six months.
7 They got married	g just after the baby was born.
8 She had a baby	h with another student doing medicine.
9 Her father retired	i when she left school.

How many of the sentence beginnings on the left can you answer about your own life?
Answer the ones you can.

48 Daily routines

A Sleep

During the week I usually **wake up** at 6.30 a.m. I sometimes **lie in bed** for five minutes but then I have to **get up** (= get out of bed and get dressed). Most evenings, I **go to bed** at about 11.30 p.m. I'm usually very tired, so I **go to sleep / fall asleep** very quickly. Occasionally though, I can't **get to sleep** (= succeed in sleeping). When that happens, I sometimes manage to **fall asleep** about 3 a.m., then I **oversleep** (= sleep too long) in the morning. If I **have a late night** (= go to bed very late; ≠ an **early night**), I try to **have a nap** (= a short sleep, e.g. 20–25 minutes) in the afternoon. The weekends are different. On Saturday and Sunday I **have a lie-in**. (= stay in bed until later, e.g. 8 a.m. or 8.30 a.m.)

B Food

In the week I **have breakfast** at 7.30 a.m., lunch at 1.00 p.m., and dinner around 7 p.m. I also have one or two **snacks** (= small amounts of food), e.g. cakes, biscuits or fruit, during the day at work. As I live **alone / on my own / by myself** (= without other people), I also have to **make my own breakfast and dinner** (= prepare breakfast and dinner for myself), but during the week I don't **bother** (= make an effort) to cook very much.
I also have to **feed** (= give food to) my two cats twice a day as well.

Note: With **breakfast, lunch** or **dinner** in general, there is no definite article (the).

C Keeping clean

In the summer I **have a shower** in the morning, but in the winter I often **have a bath instead** (= in place of a shower). Sometimes I **have a shave** at the same time, or I shave when I **have a wash** and **clean/brush my teeth** after breakfast. I **wash my hair** two or three times a week.

Note: In some contexts, it is more common in English to use **have + noun** than a single verb, e.g. I'm going to **have a wash**. [NOT ~~I'm going to wash.~~]

D Work

In the morning I **leave home** about 8.15 a.m. and **get to work** (= arrive at work) by 9 a.m. I **have a lunch break** (= stop work for lunch) from 1–2 p.m., and a couple of short **breaks** during the day. I **leave work** around 5.30 p.m. and **get home** about 6.15 p.m.

E Evenings

During the week I usually **stay in** (= stay at home) and **have a rest** (= relax and do nothing). But at the weekend I often **go out** (= leave the house for social reasons, e.g. go to the cinema or disco with friends), but quite often I also **have friends for dinner** (= invite friends to my house and cook dinner for them), or friends just **come round** (= visit me at the house) for a **chat** (*infml*) (= conversation) or we **play cards**, e.g. poker or bridge.

F Housework

I **do the shopping** (= buy the food) on Saturday.
Fortunately (= luckily) I have a **cleaner** (= a person who cleans) and she does most of the housework: she **does my washing** (= washes the clothes), the **washing-up** (= washes the dishes) and **does** most of the **ironing**.

Exercises

48.1 The opposite page includes a number of expressions with 'have + noun', e.g. have breakfast, have a shower. Can you remember six more?

have ....   have ....
have ....   have ....
have ....   have ....

48.2 Now complete some more word partnerships and expressions by matching the verbs on the left with the correct word on the right.

1	fall	a rest
2	do	my teeth
3	have	the dog
4	play	asleep
5	go	cards
6	clean	the ironing
7	feed	early
8	get up	to bed

48.3 Complete this dialogue with suitable words or phrases from the opposite page.

A: Don't (1)....................... to cook a meal this evening.
B: Why not?
A: We could (2)..................... instead.
B: Yeah. Where?
A: Well I'd like to go to that new Korean restaurant. We could ask Karen and Mike to come.
B: That's miles away. No, I think I'd rather (3).................... and have an (4).................... night.
A: But it's Friday. You can have a (5).................... tomorrow if we have a late night.
B: Yes I know but I'm tired. Look, why don't you ask Karen and Mike to (6).................... for a meal. I can order some pizzas from the takeaway and we'll have a nice evening here.
A: Sorry, but if you don't want to come to the restaurant with me, I'll go (7)......................

48.4 Here are some common sentences in English. Translate them into your own language and then decide which of these sentences you often use in your own language.

1 Did you go out last night?
2 I think I'm going to stay in this evening.
3 I overslept this morning.
4 I couldn't get to sleep last night.
5 Do you want to come round this evening?
6 I forgot to do the shopping.
7 What time did you get home?
8 I nearly fell asleep in the lesson today.

48.5 Can you find three facts from the opposite page which are exactly the same in your routine, three which are similar, and three which are completely different? Complete the table below.

	same	*similar*	*completely different*
1	I go to bed around 11.30 p.m.	I leave home at 8.40 a.m.	I never do any ironing.
2	....	....	....
3	....	....	....
4	....	....	....

49 Homes and buildings

A Houses

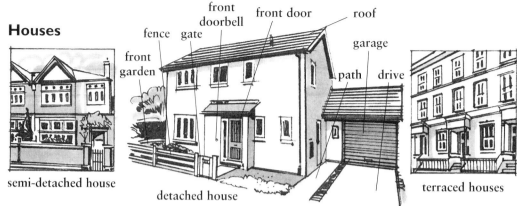

semi-detached house

detached house

terraced houses

B Flats

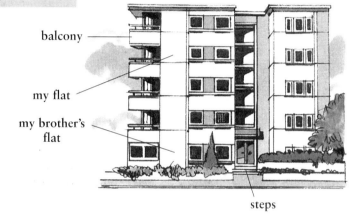

I live in a **block of flats.**
My brother lives **on the ground floor,**
and I have a flat **on the third floor.**
Unfortunately there is no **lift,** so I
have to climb three flights of **stairs** to
reach my flat. But I do have a **balcony**
with a wonderful **view** of the park
opposite the flats.

Note: **Steps** are usually outside a building or inside a public building; they are stone or
wooden. **Stairs** (*pl*) connect floors inside a building and are often covered with a carpet.

C Buying and renting

Some people buy a flat or house (= they **own** it / it **belongs to** them). When they do this in
Britain, people usually borrow money from a bank or an organisation called a Building
Society. This money, which is called a **mortgage,** is often paid back over 25 years.
Other people **rent** a house or flat (= they pay money every week or month to the person
who owns the house). When they do this, the money they pay is called **the rent**, and the
person who owns the house or flat is the **landlord.**

D Describing a flat or house

The rooms on the ground floor are quite **dark** (≠ light) because they don't **get** (= receive)
very much sun. They are also quite **noisy** (≠ quiet) because they are near the roads and the
traffic. The other negative thing is that the rooms are **draughty** (= cold air comes into the
room through the windows and under the doors because they don't fit very well). This
means it is expensive to **heat** the rooms (= to keep the rooms warm). Fortunately I have a
very good **central heating** system. In other ways, it is also very nice: it's **in good condition** (=
in a good state/doesn't need to be repaired; ≠ **in bad condition**), and the rooms are
huge/enormous (= very, very big; ≠ **tiny** / very, very small)

Exercises

49.1 What can you remember about the house and block of flats on the opposite page? Without looking, try to answer these questions. If you think an answer is false, correct it. Finally, check your answers by looking at the opposite page.

1 Does the house have a garage?
2 Does it have a fence around the front garden?
3 Is there a window in the roof?
4 Is the gate open or shut?
5 How many steps are there in front of the entrance to the block of flats?
6 Does each flat have a balcony?
7 Does the brother live on the first floor?
8 Do the flats have a view of the countryside?

49.2 Complete these sentences with a suitable noun or verb.

1 I opened the ...., walked up the .... and rang the ....
2 We had to .... six flights of stairs to get to her flat because the .... wasn't working.
3 I've got a great .... from my balcony.
4 Do you own the flat or do you .... it?
5 I'm living in the house now but it actually .... to my brother. He bought it two years ago. It was in very bad .... then, but he spent a lot of money on it.
6 It costs a lot of money to .... a house when you live in a cold climate. Central .... is usually quite expensive.

49.3 Write down four more positive things and four more negative things you could say about a house/flat or the rooms in a house/flat. When you have finished, compare your answers with section D opposite.

Positive	*Negative*
the rooms are very light	the rooms are very dark
....	....
....	....
....	....
....	....

Now think about your answers again. Which positive features are the most important for you? Which negative features do you hate the most?

49.4 What about your home? Answer these questions.

1 Do you live in a house or flat?
2 If you live in a flat, what floor is it on?
3 If you live in a house, do you have a garden?
4 Does the house/flat belong to you (or your family), or do you rent it?
5 Do you have your own garage or personal parking space?
6 Would you describe your house/flat as dark or light?
7 Is it noisy or quiet?
8 Do you have central heating?

50 Around the home I

A Rooms

The **living room** or **lounge** (= where you sit, relax, talk and watch TV); the **dining room**; the **kitchen**; the **bedroom(s)**; and the **bathroom(s)**.

Some people also have **a study** (= room with a desk where you work), a **utility room** (= a room usually next to the kitchen, where you have a washing machine), a **spare room** (= a room you don't use every day. Often this is a room that guests can use), and possibly **a playroom** for small children.

B The lounge

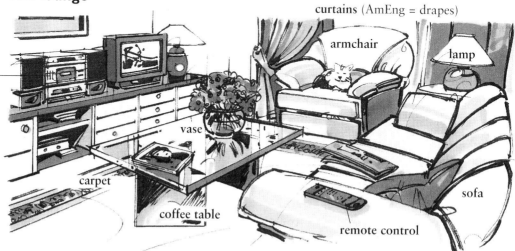

curtains (AmEng = drapes)

CD player / hi-fi / music system

armchair

lamp

vase

carpet

coffee table

remote control

sofa

While the cat was asleep **in the armchair**, I sat **on the sofa** and **had a look** at the paper. Then I **turned on** the TV and went to make a cup of tea.

C The kitchen

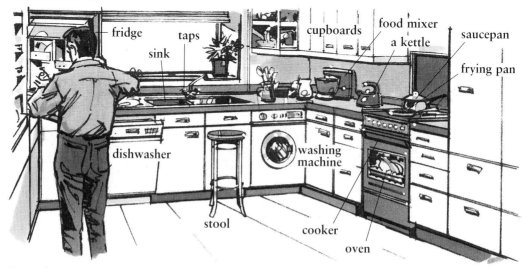

fridge

taps

sink

cupboards

food mixer

a kettle

saucepan

frying pan

dishwasher

washing machine

stool

cooker

oven

I **put** the meat **in the oven**, put my dirty clothes **in the washing machine**, made the coffee and **put** the milk **back** in the fridge.

Exercises

50.1 Complete the descriptions. (There may be more than one possible answer.)

1 The bedroom, that's where you ...sleep......
2 The kitchen, that's where you do the ....
3 The bathroom, that's where you have a .... and ....
4 The lounge, that's where you .... and ....
5 The dining room, that's where you ....
6 A spare room, that's often where ....
7 A study, that's usually where you ....
8 A utility room, that's often where ....

50.2 You are in the kitchen. Where would you put these things?

1 milk
2 meat that you are going to cook
3 dirty clothes
4 dirty cups and saucers
5 clean cups and saucers
6 biscuits and a packet of spaghetti

50.3 Here are some things you find in the lounge or kitchen but the letters are jumbled. What are they, and where do they belong?

skin   nacitusr   rapcet   shadriswhe   teklet
faos   veon   digref   hiamcrar   pobcadru   acepasnu

50.4 Complete these sentences with the correct adverb or preposition.

1 He put the plates .... the cupboard.
2 I took the ham .... of the fridge, made myself a couple of sandwiches, and then I put the rest of the ham .... in the fridge.
3 I usually sit .... the sofa and my husband sits .... an armchair.
4 I was bored, so I turned .... the television.
5 You normally cook it .... the oven for about forty minutes.
6 I took the butter .... of the fridge and put it .... the table.

50.5 Imagine you have just moved into a new flat, and for the first six months you can only have six of the following. Which would you choose?

sofa   carpets   dishwasher   TV   cooker   curtains   fridge   desk
hi-fi   bed   dining table   washing machine   kettle   saucepans
food mixer   armchair

50.6 Write down:

1 three things in the lounge and kitchen you can turn on/off.
2 three things in the kitchen you can wash.
3 three things in the lounge and kitchen you can sit on.
4 two things you can use to boil water.

51 Around the home 2

A The bedroom

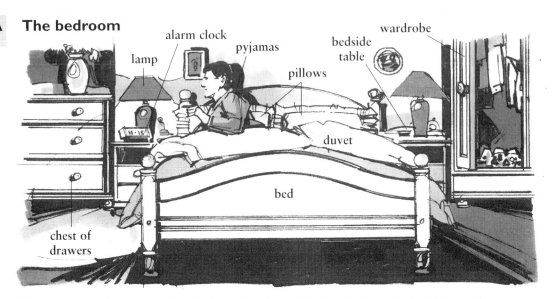

I **put on** my **pyjamas**, **got into bed**, set the **alarm clock**, **switched off** the light, and went to sleep.

B The bathroom

I didn't have time for a bath, but I **had a wash**, cleaned my teeth, and then I went to school.

C Housework (U)

My room is very **clean and tidy** (= everything in order), but my brother is very untidy; he leaves his clothes all over the floor and never makes his bed. What's worse, he doesn't clean his room very often, so most of the time it is quite dirty.

I **do the washing-up** every evening after dinner, and I normally **do the washing and ironing** at the weekend when I have a bit more free time. I also **hoover** the carpets and **polish** the dining room table once a week.

Exercises

51.1 Find the correct ending on the right for each of these sentence beginnings on the left, then put the sentences in the most logical order.

1 I cleaned	the light
2 I went	into bed
3 I set	a wash
4 I switched off	my teeth
5 I had	to sleep
6 I put on	the alarm clock
7 I got	my pyjamas

51.2 The pictures show six things the woman did this morning. Complete the sentences below.

1 She ....
2 She ....
3 She ....
4 She ....
5 She ....
6 She ....

How often do you do these things? Complete these sentences about yourself.

1 I often ....
2 I sometimes ....
3 I occasionally ....
4 I never ....
5 I ....
6 I ....

51.3 Test your memory. Cover the opposite page and answer these questions about the pictures.

1 Does the alarm clock show 11.30?
2 Does he have one pillow or two?
3 Is the wardrobe open?
4 How many drawers does the chest of drawers have?
5 Is the girl in the bathroom holding a towel?
6 Is she looking in the mirror?
7 Is the shower above the bath?
8 Can you see any soap on the washbasin?

How well do you know your own home? Answer these questions as quickly as possible.

1 Have you got a mirror above the washbasin in the bathroom?
2 Have you got a towel rail on the same wall as the washbasin?
3 Is the toilet next to the bath/shower?
4 Have you got a wardrobe and chest of drawers in your bedroom?
5 Have you got a lamp on your bedside table?
6 Have you got an alarm clock?

52 Everyday problems

A ## There's something wrong with ...

If there is a problem with a machine or a thing that you use e.g. TV, light, washing machine, computer, food mixer, pen, etc., we often use these expressions:

There's something wrong with the TV. (= there is a problem with it)
The light's **not working**. (= not functioning / there is no light)
The shower's **not working properly**. (= it is functioning but not very well)
The telephone is **out of order**. (= not in use / not functioning)

Note: The phrase **out of order** is often used when a public machine or piece of equipment isn't working, e.g. public telephone, public toilet, drinks machine at a station, etc.

B In the home

Yesterday morning Paul had a lot of problems.

He **dropped** a cup

and it **broke**

He got another cup, made a coffee, and then **spilt** it.

It **ruined** (= destroyed) his T-shirt because there was a large **stain** on it.

He decided to make some toast, but he **burnt** the first piece (if you **burn** something, you damage it with fire), then realised he'd **run out of** bread (= the bread was finished / there was no more bread). He did not leave home **in a good mood** (= feeling very happy).

C Out and about

After Paul went out, things got worse. He left home with a ten-pound note in his pocket, and walked to the bus stop. Unfortunately he was a bit late and the bus was a bit early, so he **missed the bus**. While he waited for the next one, he got out his walkman, but the **batteries** had **run out** (= the batteries were finished). When the bus arrived, he got on and put his hand in his pocket – no ten-pound note (he had **lost his money**). The driver told him to get off. He didn't want to be late for school, so he started running. Moments later, he saw a dog, but not its lead – and **tripped over** the lead.

He got to his feet, carried on to school, then he realised he had **left** his bag on the bus.

Note: Students often say 'he forgot his bag on the bus' in this situation. In English, we must the verb **leave** if we say where something is. For example:

forgotten my bag; *but* I **left** my bag <u>on the bus</u>.

Exercises

52.1 Complete the past tense and past participle of these verbs.

Infinitive	Past tense	Past participle
burn		
break		
drop		
spill		
trip		
lose		
leave		

52.2 Match the sentence beginnings on the left with the correct ending on the right.

1 I dropped the radio on the floor	a when I lit that cigarette.
2 The batteries have run out	b and had to wait ages for another.
3 I'm afraid I left	c and it made a mess on the carpet.
4 I spilt the drink	d to bring my money.
5 I missed the bus	e my money at home.
6 I burnt myself	f and now I can't get it to work.
7 I forgot	g so I can't listen to my walkman.

52.3 This is what happened when Paul had a party at his house. Write a description of the damage.

1 　　2 　　3

52.4 Write logical answers for each of these questions, using vocabulary from the opposite page.
1 How did you break that glass?
2 Why can't we watch TV?
3 How did you cut your knee like that?
4 I'm cold. What's wrong with the central heating?
5 What happened to the money I gave you?
6 Where's your homework?
7 What's wrong with this radio?
8 Why can't you use the public phone in the station?

52.5 Answer these questions using *often / occasionally / hardly ever / never*.

How often do you:

drop things?	break things?	burn things?
spill things?	lose things?	forget things?
trip over things?	leave things behind?	run out of things?

What sort of things do you drop, burn, run out of, etc.?

53 Money

A Notes and coins

Here are some examples of British money. The **currency** (= the type of money used in a country) is called **sterling**.

banknotes

coins

ten pounds
a **ten-pound note**

fifty pence (we usually say 50p)
a **fifty-pence piece**

B Common verbs

Notice how these common verbs are used.

spend £££ (**on**) sth.	Last week I **spent** £100 **on** food, and £20 **on** books.
pay (**for**) sth.	I **paid** £200 **for** my new desk. (= it cost me £200)
	Where do I have to **pay for** these things?
cost	My new desk **cost** (me) £200. (= I paid £200)
charge	The mechanic **charged** me £100. (= asked me to pay £100 for the service he provided)
lend	Could **you lend me** some money? *or*
borrow	Could **I borrow** some money?
waste	Parents often think that children **waste** their money (= use it badly) on sweets and other things that they don't need.
save (**up**)	I'm **saving** (**up**) (= keeping some of my money when I receive it) for a new bike. I should have enough by the end of the year.

C Adjectives

free	cheap	reasonable	quite expensive	very expensive	incredibly expensive
–	$	$	$	$	$

D Important words and phrases

I **can't afford** (= don't have enough money) to go on holiday this year.
How much is that watch **worth**? (= What is the **value** of that watch?)
It's **worth** about £50. (= the value is £50)
The **cost of living** (= how much people pay for things) is very high in places like Sweden or Norway, but people still have a good **standard of living** (= the level of money and comfort people have).

Exercises

53.1 Fill the gaps using the past tense of verbs from the box. Be careful, most of them are irregular.

buy	spend	lose	pay	cost
sell	win	waste	find	give

1 My car was five years old, so I .... it and .... a new one.
2 I was very sad when I .... my watch in the street. It was a present from my wife and it .... her a lot of money. Fortunately, somebody .... it the next day and took it to a Police Station.
3 I .... over £2,000 for my computer, but it isn't worth very much now.
4 My father .... me £50 last week but I .... most of it on a ticket for a concert on Friday.
5 Last week somebody .... £1m in a game on television. It was incredibly exciting.
6 I'm afraid I .... my money on those CDs because I never play them.

53.2 What can you say in these situations? Complete the sentences but do not use the underlined words and phrases.

Example: You want to tell a friend that a restaurant <u>wasn't cheap</u>.
...*The restaurant was quite expensive.*......

1 You want to know the <u>value</u> of your friend's gold ring.
How much is ....?
2 A friend wants to go to an expensive restaurant but you <u>don't have enough money</u>.
I'm afraid I ....
3 You want to <u>borrow</u> some money from a friend.
Could you ....?
4 You want to know how much a friend <u>paid</u> for her dictionary.
How much ....?

53.3 How quickly can you answer these questions? Write down answers to all of them in one minute, then go back and check. If possible, ask someone else the same questions.

1 Is the currency in America called the dollar?
2 Is a five-pound note worth less than a fifty-pence piece?
3 If you lend something to someone, do they borrow it?
4 If you waste money, do you use it well?
5 Is 'sterling' a currency?
6 If you 'can't afford' something, do you have enough money for it?
7 Does 'cost of living' mean the same as 'standard of living'?
8 If someone tells you a hotel is reasonable, is it very expensive?

53.4 Write down the approximate price of six things in your country, e.g. a daily newspaper, a short bus journey, a cup of coffee in a bar/cafe, a ticket for the cinema, a takeaway hamburger, a pair of jeans, etc. Do you think the price is expensive, reasonable, cheap? Compare your answers with someone from the same town, and if possible, someone from a different country.

54 Health: illness and disease

A Common problems

She's sneezing.

She's coughing.

She's got a sore throat.

She's blowing her nose.

She's got a temperature.

What's the matter?	*How do you know?* (**the symptoms**)	*Cause of illness*
I've got **a cold**	a sore throat, sneezing, a cough	a virus
I've got **flu** (U) (more serious than a cold)	symptoms for a cold + aching muscles and a temperature, e.g. 39.5	a virus
I've got **hay fever** (U)	sneezing, runny nose, sore eyes	allergic reaction to pollen from grass
I've got **diarrhoea** (U)	I keep going to the toilet	often food, or a virus
I **feel sick**	I want to vomit (= be sick)	many e.g. food, alcohol
I've got **a hangover**	headache, feeling sick	too much alcohol

Note: For these **illnesses**, you can either buy something from the **chemist**, or go to your doctor, who may give you a **prescription** (= a piece of paper with an order for some medicine) that you get from the chemist.

B Aches and pains

Nouns: We only use **ache** with the following: I've got **toothache** (U), **a stomach-ache**, **backache** (U), **earache** (U) and **a headache**. For other parts of the body we use **pain**, e.g. I woke up in the night with a **terrible pain** in my chest.

Verbs: You can use **ache** for some things, e.g. my back aches; but **hurt** is more common to describe real pain, and it can be used with or without a direct object:

She **hurt** her foot when she jumped off the bus and fell over. (also **injured** here) *or*
She **hurt herself** when she jumped off the bus and fell over.
I hit my leg against the table and it **really hurts**. (= gives me a terrible pain)

Adjectives: The only common adjective is **painful** (≠ **painless**):

I had an **injection** yesterday and it was very **painful**.
A: Did it hurt when you had your **filling**? (= when the dentist fills a hole/cavity in the tooth)
B: No, it was **painless**.

C Serious illnesses

Doctors believe smoking is the major cause of **lung cancer**.
He had a **heart attack** and died almost immediately.
Hepatitis is a **liver disease**.
Asthma (**chest** illness causing **breathing** problems) has become more common.

Note: **Illness** and **disease** are often used in the same way, but **disease** is used for a serious condition caused by an infection e.g. a liver disease. **Illness** is a more general word.

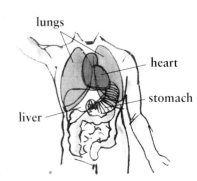

Exercises

54.1 Write down the main symptom or symptoms for these conditions.

1 a cold: ....
2 flu: ....
3 hay fever: ....
4 a hangover: ....
5 diarrhoea: ....
6 asthma: ....

54.2 Look at the underlined letters in these pairs of words. Is the pronunciation the same or different? Look at the examples first.

Examples: <u>a</u>che   p<u>ai</u>n   *same*
            <u>co</u>nstipated   st<u>o</u>mach   *different*

1 <u>di</u>sease   <u>di</u>arrhoea   4 <u>vi</u>rus   <u>i</u>llness
2 <u>ch</u>emist   a<u>ch</u>e   5 f<u>lu</u>   m<u>u</u>scle
3 h<u>ur</u>t   all<u>er</u>gic   6 c<u>ough</u>   en<u>ough</u>

54.3 Look at the pictures and write what happened in the space below. Try to use at least three or four words or phrases from the opposite page.

I had ....
....

54.4 Fill the gaps with a suitable word.

1 I hit my hand on the desk and it really ....
2 They say she died of a heart ....
3 She had some apples that weren't ready to eat and now she's got stomache-..................... .
4 I've got this terrible .... in my neck from sleeping in the wrong position.
5 He died of .... cancer even though he never smoked a cigarette in his life.
6 I went to the doctor, and she gave me a .... for some tablets.
7 Pollution makes her .... worse and it's difficult for her to breathe.
8 There are different forms of hepatitis; one is a more serious .... than the other.
9 I hurt .... when I fell off that chair.
10 My back .... from sitting at that computer all day.

54.5 Look at the opposite page again. Have you had any of these illnesses recently? Have you had any aches and pains recently? Make a list of the ones you have had. Are there any other illnesses you have had or still have? If so, find the name for it/them in English.

55 Health: injuries

A Common injuries

An **injury** is damage to part of your body, usually caused by an accident in the home, on the roads, or during a game, e.g. of football. Here are some common **injuries**:

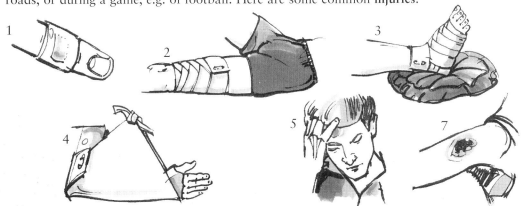

	What's the problem?	*How did it happen?*	*Result*	*Solution*
1	I **cut** (v, n) my finger	using a knife	it's **bleeding** a bit	**a plaster**
2	I cut my leg quite badly	I fell over	it's bleeding quite a lot	**a bandage** (n, v)
3	I **twisted my ankle**	running for a bus	I can't walk on it easily	rest
4	I **broke** my arm	I fell off my bike	I can't use it	**plaster** (U) and a **sling**
5	I've got **concussion**	playing football	I'm confused; don't know where I am	rest
6	I **burnt** my hand	taking something out of a hot oven	it's very **painful**	special cream
7	I've got **a bruise** (n, v) on my arm	I hit it on the side of my desk	it's **swollen** and blue/black in colour	ice pack

B Hospital treatment

Look carefully at the key words in these texts.

John fell off a chair, hit his head on the floor, and **knocked himself unconscious**. His wife called an **ambulance** but John was still **unconscious** when it arrived. He was **rushed** to hospital (= taken very quickly) where they kept him for two days for **blood tests**.

I jumped for the ball and **collided** with another player (= we ran into / hit each other). We both had **cuts** on our head, but I had to go to hospital for eight **stitches**.

C Wounds and injuries

Wound (n, v) and **injury** are both used to describe damage to the body, but a **wound** is generally caused by a **weapon** (e.g. gun or knife) and it is usually intentional.

He **shot** the man in the chest. (= a **bullet wound** in the chest) [from a gun]
He **stabbed** the boy in the back. (= a **knife wound** in the back)
He **got into a fight** and **got beaten up**. He had a **black eye** and two **broken ribs**.

Exercises

55.1 Complete the table with the correct verb forms.

Noun	Verb
cut wound injury shot	

Noun	Verb
blood bandage bruise treatment	

55.2 Look at the pictures and write the story.

Now compare your story with the model answer in the key.

55.3 Complete these conversations in a suitable way.

1 A: ... bleeding quite a bit, so I had to put a plaster on it before I could finish.
   B: How did you do it, anyway?
   A: Oh, I was ....
2 A: ... the next day the eye was really swollen and he had bruises down both his arms.
   B: My goodness. What did he tell his parents?
   A: More or less the truth. He said ....
3 A: ... tried to get up again but I couldn't move. It was incredibly painful, but
     fortunately there were a few pedestrians around to help me.
   B: That's lucky. But what were you doing?
   A: ....
4 A: ... my face was cut and he had a terrible bruise on his head.
   B: Sounds very unpleasant. How did it happen exactly?
   A: ....

55.4 Answer these questions about yourself. If possible, ask another person the same questions.

1 Have you ever broken your arm or leg?
2 Have you ever needed stitches ?
3 Have you ever had concussion?
4 Have you ever been unconscious?
5 Have you ever had a blood test?
6 Have you ever been in an ambulance?

56 Clothes

A Pocket, buttons, collar, sleeves

Note: Some of these words are plural nouns, e.g. **jeans** and **trousers**. See Unit 27.

B Important verbs

Use this text to guess the meaning of the key words.

I got up at 7.30, had a shower, **got dressed**, and had breakfast. It was a cold morning so I **put on** my overcoat and left home about 8.20. When I got to work I **took off** my coat and **hung** it **up** behind the door. It was hot in the office, so I **took** my jacket **off** as well. During my lunchbreak I had a look round the shops. I saw a nice jacket in one shop and **tried** it **on**, but it didn't **fit** me – it was too small and they didn't have a bigger **size**.

Note: Notice the different word order with the verbs put on, take off, hang up, and try on. If you want to know the rule about this, turn to Unit 17 Phrasal verbs: grammar and style.

C Too small and not long enough

The man is wearing a suit, but it doesn't fit him very well: the jacket **is too small** (= **not big enough**); the trousers **are too short** (= **not long enough**).

Exercises

56.1 Finish this sentence with six different items of clothes.

I need a pair of ....

....

....

....

....

....

56.2 Find a logical order for these sentences.

1 He took off his trousers.
2 He put his shoes back on.
3 He tried on the suit.
4 He went into the changing room.
5 He took it off.
6 He paid for the suit.
7 He took off his shoes.
8 He went back to the sales assistant.
9 He put his trousers on again.

56.3 What's missing?
Write down anything
that is missing in the
second picture of
the woman.

...~~earrings~~........

....

....

....

....

....

56.4 Fill the gaps with suitable words. (More than one answer may be possible in some cases.)

1 She decided to wear a .... and a .... instead of a dress.
2 I tried on a ....; the jacket was fine but the .... were too short.
3 It was hot in the office, so I took off my jacket and ...., and rolled up the sleeves of my ....
4 I wanted to buy the jacket, but unfortunately the one I tried on wasn't big .... and they didn't have it in a bigger ....
5 I also wanted a new jumper, but unfortunately the medium size was .... big and the small size wasn't big ....

56.5 Write down:

1 five things usually worn by women only; and five things worn by men and women.
2 a list of clothes you like and don't like wearing.
3 five more items of clothing you have at home in your wardrobe / chest of drawers.

57 Shops and Shopping

A Shops and shopping

shop assistant: person who works in a shop; also called **sales assistant**
shop window: the window at the front of the shop
shopping centre: a place with many shops, outside or indoors
window shopping: to look round the shops but not buy anything
shopping list: a list of things to buy

I **went shopping** yesterday (= I went to the shops to buy food or clothes, etc.)
I **did the shopping** yesterday (= I bought food and household goods)

B Types of shop (and what they sell)

Name of shop	*What it sells*
department store	almost everything (furniture, clothes, electrical appliances, e.g. TV and washing machine, toys, jewellery, etc. and sometimes food)
supermarket	food and household goods, e.g. cleaning products
newsagent('s)	newspapers, cigarettes, sweets, stationery, e.g. writing paper, cards, envelopes, etc.
butcher('s)	meat
greengrocer('s)	fruit and vegetables
boutique	fashionable clothes
chemist('s)	medicine, baby products, shampoo, soap, toothpaste, etc.

Note: Most other shops are just '+ shop', e.g. shoe shop, record shop, camera shop, etc.

C Useful words and expressions

ASSISTANT: Can I help you?   CUSTOMER: Yes, I'm **looking for** (= I want) a blue jumper.

ASSISTANT: Can I help you?   CUSTOMER: No, **I'm just looking**, thanks. (= I don't need help)

ASSISTANT: Can I help you?   CUSTOMER: **I'm being served**, thanks. (= another assistant is already serving/helping me)

ASSISTANT: What **size** are you looking for? (e.g. big? small? medium? 12? 14? 16?)

CUSTOMER: Where's the **changing room**? (= the room where you try on clothes; also called the **fitting room**)

ASSISTANT: It's down there on the right.

CUSTOMER: Yes, **I'll take** this one / these. (= Yes, I want to buy this one / these)

CUSTOMER: No, **I'll leave it** thanks. (= No, I don't want to buy it/them)

CUSTOMER: Excuse me. Where do I pay for these?

ASSISTANT: Over at the **cash desk/till**.

CUSTOMER: And can I **pay by** cheque / credit card?

ASSISTANT: Yes, of course.

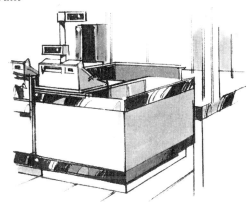

Exercises

57.1 Can you find a 'general' word on the opposite page to describe each group of items below?

Example: ..*fruit*.. e.g. apples, oranges and peaches

1 .... e.g. shoes, a blouse, a jacket
2 .... e.g. a sofa, an armchair, a table
3 .... e.g. a television, a washing machine, a food mixer
4 .... e.g. washing powder, soap, milk, toilet paper
5 .... e.g. teddy bear, plastic gun, lego
6 .... e.g. writing paper, envelopes

57.2 Where would you buy each of the items on the left? Choose from the shops in the box.

newsagent
chemist
department store
butcher
greengrocer
supermarket

Now write down two more things you could buy in each shop.

57.3 What word or phrase is being defined in these sentences?

1 A shop where you can buy fashionable clothes.
2 A place with many shops, either outside or indoors.
3 A person who works in a shop.
4 The place where you can try on clothes in a shop.
5 The place where you pay for things in a shop.
6 To look round the shops without planning to buy anything.
7 The shop where you buy meat.
8 The shop where you buy medicines, baby products, shampoo, etc.

57.4 Complete this shopping dialogue.

ASSISTANT 1: Can I help you?
CUSTOMER: Yes, I'm (1)............................ a blouse like this, but in blue.
ASSISTANT 1: I see. And what (2)............................ are you looking for?
CUSTOMER: Uh, 14 usually.
ASSISTANT 1: Ok, I'll just go and see if we've got any.
CUSTOMER: Thank you.
ASSISTANT 2: Can I help you?
CUSTOMER: No, it's OK, I'm (3)............................ thanks.
ASSISTANT 1: Here we are. The last one in stock.
CUSTOMER: Great. Can I try it on?
ASSISTANT 1: Yes of course. The (4)............................ is just over there.
ASSISTANT 1: How was it?
CUSTOMER: Fine. I'll (5).............................
ASSISTANT: Right. Would you like to pay over there at the (6)............................?

58 Food

A Fruit

apple orange lemon strawberry peach melon
pear banana grapes pineapple cherry

B Vegetables

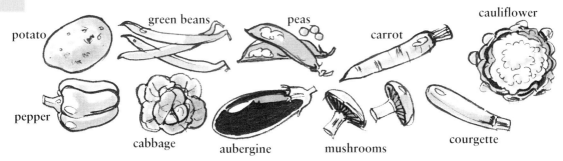

potato green beans peas carrot cauliflower
pepper cabbage aubergine mushrooms courgette

C Salad

A salad is a mixture of uncooked vegetables. The main ingredient in a salad is **lettuce**, but it may also contain **tomato**, **cucumber**, and other things.

lettuce tomato cucumber vinegar oil

D Animals (meat), fish and shellfish

animal:	cow	calf (= young cow)	lamb (= young sheep)	pig
meat:	beef	veal	lamb	pork

Note: A person who does not eat meat is a **vegetarian**.

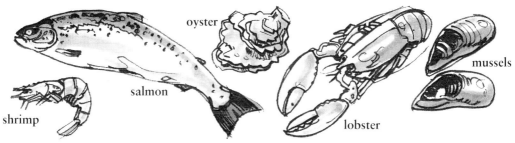

oyster mussels salmon shrimp lobster

Exercises

58.1 Can you write down a vegetable and fruit:

		Vegetable	Fruit
1	beginning with the letter 'p'	potato	
2	beginning with the letter 'b'		
3	beginning with the letter 'm'		
4	beginning with the letter 'c'		
5	beginning with the letter 'a'		

58.2 Find a word in the right-hand box where the underlined letter(s) are pronounced in the same way as the underlined letter(s) in a word in the left-hand box. Be careful: there are two extra words in the right-hand box which you do not need.

lett<u>u</u>ce	<u>o</u>nion
<u>o</u>range	b<u>a</u>nana
<u>au</u>bergine	sa<u>l</u>mon

toma<u>to</u>	mel<u>o</u>n
sa<u>la</u>d	ch<u>i</u>cken
ca<u>l</u>f	l<u>a</u>mb
<u>ca</u>uliflower	m<u>u</u>shroom

58.3 Which is the odd one out in each group, and why?

1 pork   veal   salmon   beef
2 salmon   shrimp   oyster   lobster
3 lettuce   aubergine   tomato   cucumber
4 peach   onion   mushroom   courgette
5 chicken   lamb   beef   mussels

58.4 Do you eat the skin (= the outside) of these fruits – always, usually, or never? Make three lists.

apples	pineapples	cherries	grapes
pears	bananas	peaches	mangoes
oranges	lemons	melons	strawberries

58.5 Using words from the opposite page, complete these sentences about yourself and your country. If possible, compare your answers with someone else who has done this exercise.

1 In my country .... is/are more common than ....
2 In my country .... is/are more expensive than ....
3 In my country a mixed salad usually contains ....
   ....
4 In my country we don't grow ....
5 And we don't often eat ....
6 Personally, I prefer .... to ....
7 I love .... but I don't really like ....
8 My favourite meat is ....

59 Cooking and restaurants

A Ways of cooking food

boil: in water, e.g. carrots
fry: in oil or butter above the heat, e.g. sausages
grill: under the heat, e.g. toast or meat
roast: in the oven using oil, e.g. meat
bake: in the oven without oil, e.g. cakes
Note: Food which is not cooked is **raw**.

boil
fry

grill

roast
bake

B Cooking steak

If you have steak you can eat it **rare** (= cooked very quickly and still red); **medium-rare** (cooked a bit longer and just red in the middle); **medium** (cooked a bit more and just pink); or **well-done** (cooked even longer and not pink at all).

C Describing food

tasty: has lots of taste: a positive word; ≠ **tasteless**: a negative word
bland: without a strong taste; neutral in flavour, e.g. boiled rice
sweet: lots of sugar; ≠ **bitter**
salty: lots of salt
hot/spicy: lots of spice, e.g. curry
fresh: recently produced, e.g. fresh bread; recently picked, e.g. fresh fruit
tender: easy to cut; a positive word used to describe meat; ≠ **tough**
fatty: meat with a lot of fat; ≠ **lean**
fattening: food which makes you **put on weight** / get fat, e.g. cream, biscuits, etc.

D Eating in restaurants

In Britain you often have three **courses**: a **starter** (e.g. soup), **a main course** (e.g. steak or chicken), and a **dessert** (e.g. strawberries or ice cream). You may also have an **aperitif** (= a drink before the meal, e.g. gin and tonic), and coffee after the meal. When you pay the **bill** (= the money for the meal; AmEng = **check**), you sometimes also leave a **tip** (= money) for the waiter if **service is not included** in the price. (10% is a normal tip.) If it is a popular restaurant, you may also need to **book** (= reserve) a table **in advance** (= before you go).

E The menu

⊗ **Starters** ⊗
Broccoli Soup
Home-made Chicken Liver Paté
Tagliatelle with Courgettes, Cream and Bacon

⊗ **Main Courses** ⊗
Baked Salmon with Spinach
Breast of Chicken in a White Wine Sauce with Mushrooms
Grilled Fillet Steak in a Pepper Sauce
Mushroom Risotto

⊗ **Desserts** ⊗
Chocolate Mousse
Fruit Salad
Ice Cream

Exercises

59.1 Do you often eat the following food in your country? If so, do you eat it in the same way?

Example: In Britain, we often eat 'fish' but not usually 'raw fish'.

raw fish	fried rice
fried eggs	grilled sausages
baked potatoes	roast beef
raw spinach	roast peppers
fried bread	boiled eggs
grilled cheese	baked bananas

59.2 Look at the menu on the opposite page again, and answer these questions.

1 Which starter doesn't contain vegetables?
2 Which dish contains pasta?
3 Which dish may be rare or well-done?
4 Which dish is definitely cooked in the oven?
5 Which dish will probably be quite spicy?
6 Which dish contains alcohol?
7 Which meat may be fatty or tough if you are unlucky?
8 Which dessert(s) will be quite sweet?
9 Which dessert must be very fresh?
10 You are on a diet (= you are trying to lose weight) and you do not want to have a fattening meal. Which would probably be the best dish to choose for each course?

59.3 Choose a possible adjective from the opposite page to describe each of these foods.

	Adjective		*Adjective*
lemon	....	ice cream	....
chicken	....	fillet steak	....
honey	....	chillies	....
bacon	....	avocado	....

59.4 What about restaurants in your country, and your own taste in food? Answer these questions about yourself and your country.

1 Do you normally need to book a restaurant in advance?
2 Is it common to give the waiter a tip? If so, how much?
3 Do you normally eat three courses in a restaurant? If not, how many courses do you normally have?
4 How many of these do you normally find on the table in a restaurant in your country?
   salt   *yes/no*   pepper   *yes/no*   oil   *yes/no*
   vinegar   *yes/no*   napkins   *yes/no*
5 Generally, do you add more salt to your food when you eat in restaurants?
6 Do you like steak? If so, how do you like it cooked?
7 Would you say that food in your country is very spicy?
8 Would you say that food in your country is generally quite fattening?

If possible, ask another person the same questions.

60 Town and country

Town and country

A Towns

Here are some of the things you will find in most big towns.

a **commercial centre**: an area with lots of banks and company offices
shopping centres: places with many shops, either indoors or outdoors
car parks: places to leave many cars
factories: buildings where you make/manufacture things, e.g. cars
suburbs: areas outside the centre of town where people live
libraries: places where you can borrow books
pollution: dirty air because of smoke and petrol fumes
night-life: places to go at night, e.g. bars, restaurants, cinemas, theatres, discos, etc.

B The country

Here are some of the things you will find **in the countryside**.

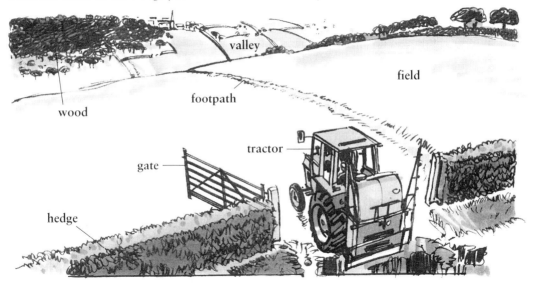

C Advantages and disadvantages

People who prefer the countryside to big towns, often say this:

Towns:	*The countryside:*
are noisy	is quiet and peaceful
are dirty and polluted	is clean
are stressful	is calm and relaxing
are crowded (= full of people)	has lots of open space
are dangerous	is safe

People who prefer big towns have a different point of view:

In towns:	*In the countryside:*
there are plenty (= lots) of things to do	there's nothing to do
it's exciting	it's boring
there's a **wide range of shops** (= many different shops)	there are only a few shops
there's lots of night-life, e.g. bars, cinemas, discos	there's no night-life

Exercises

60.1 Complete this table of opposites.

Big towns and cities	Village life and the countryside
....	quiet and peaceful
....	clean air
exciting	....
stressful	....
....	lots of open space
....	nothing to do in the evening
dangerous	....

Do you agree with everything in the table above? Put a tick (✔) beside each answer you do, and a (✘) beside each answer you don't. If possible compare and discuss your answers with someone else.

60.2 Organise the words in the box into three groups: things that you usually find in towns (in your country), things you usually find in the country, and things you often find in both town and country.

fields	factories	gates	car parks
libraries	tractors	suburbs	villages
traffic	Town Hall	shopping centres	footpaths
pollution	valleys	night-life	woods

Town	Country	Town and country

60.3 Look at the picture on the opposite page for one minute, then cover it and complete this text based on the picture.

We opened the (1)........................, said 'hello' to the man on the (2)........................, and then followed the (3)........................ across the (4)........................ and down into the (5)......................... We stopped and had a picnic by the river and then walked up through the (6)........................ on the other side of the (7)......................... A bit later we came to a (8)........................ where we stopped and bought some bread.

60.4 Think of your journey to school, college or work. How many of these things do you see or pass?

| a car park | factories | woods | a library | a museum | parking meters |
| lots of traffic | commuters | a night club | fields | suburbs | a railway station |

61 On the road

A Road features

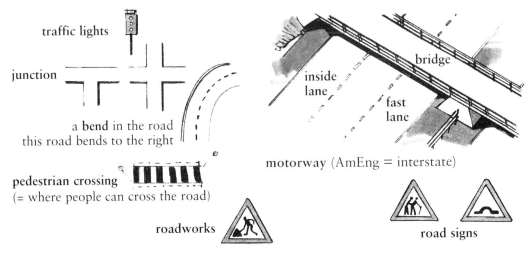

traffic lights

junction

a **bend** in the road
this road bends to the right

pedestrian crossing
(= where people can cross the road)

roadworks

bridge

inside lane

fast lane

motorway (AmEng = interstate)

road signs

B An accident

Read the text and use the context and the diagram to help you with the key words.

There was a serious **accident** on one of the **main roads** into Stuttgart this morning. An old lorry (AmEng = truck) **broke down** in the middle of the road, and the driver couldn't move it. It was eight o'clock, the middle of the **rush hour**, so it soon created a terrible **traffic jam**. Drivers got very angry and a man in a Mercedes tried to go round the lorry. Unfortunately another car **was coming in the opposite direction**. The driver **braked** hard and tried to stop, but he couldn't **prevent** the accident – the Mercedes **crashed into** the front of his car. The driver of the Mercedes was OK, but the other driver was **badly injured** and both cars were very **badly damaged**.

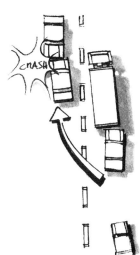

C Giving directions

Go **along** here, **turn** right **into** the main road, then **take the first turning on your left**. Keep going, and then turn left again when you **get to** the bank.

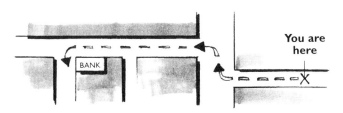

BANK

You are here

D Important words and phrases

Taxis (AmEng = cab) use the road; **pedestrians** use the **pavement** (AmEng = sidewalk).
The **speed limit** on motorways in Great Britain is 70 mph (120 kph).
Most **petrol stations** (AmEng = gas station) in Great Britain are self-service.
Get in the car and remember to **fasten your seat belt**.
The other car was going very slowly, so I decided to **overtake** (= pass it on the outside lane).

Exercises

61.1 Complete the text for directions to the bank using the map to help you.

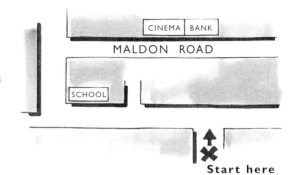

Go .... and .... at the junction. Then you .... and .... right when you .... the .... Then .... again .... Road, and the bank is .... just .... cinema.

61.2 Fill the gaps with the correct words.

1 Don't forget to .... your .... belt when you .... the car.
2 There was a bad accident this morning. One driver died, the other driver was badly ...., and both cars were badly ....
3 In the morning, the .... starts at about 7 o'clock and goes on until at least 9.30. Then it starts again about 4.30 in the afternoon.
4 It was raining, so when I .... the car didn't stop quickly enough, and I .... into the back of the car in front.
5 The bicycle hit me just as I stepped off the .... to cross the road.
6 The car ...., so I phoned a garage and they sent someone to repair it.
7 There was a terrible ...., and that's why it took me two hours to get home in the car.
8 I was doing about 65 mph on the inside .... of the motorway, and suddenly a car .... me doing about 90 mph.

61.3 Many road signs are international. Do you know or can you guess what these mean?

1 You can't ....   4 There's only one ....   7 traffic ....

2 50 mph* is the ....   5 end of ....   8 a low ....

3 you can't ....   6 a car ....   9 ....

(*mph = miles per hour; 50 mph = 80 kph approximately)

61.4 Answer these questions about your own country.

1 Do you have a speed limit on motorways? If so, what is it?
2 How many lanes do motorways usually have?
3 Do drivers usually stop for pedestrians at pedestrian crossings?
4 Are most petrol stations self-service, or do people serve you?

62 Transport

A Vehicles

Vehicle is the general word for all types of road transport.

A: How did you get here?
B: I came by bus.
A: And the others?
B: Sue and John came by car.
A: And Paul?
B: He missed the bus, so he had to take a taxi.

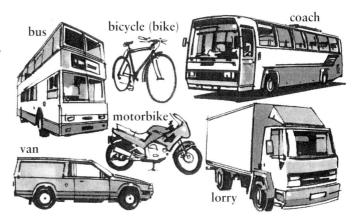

bus   bicycle (bike)   coach
motorbike
van   lorry

B Catch a bus, take a taxi

Bus	Train	Plane	Taxi	Bicycle	Car
driver	driver	pilot	driver	cyclist	driver
drives	drives	flies	drives	rides	drives
(£) fare	fare	air fare	fare	–	–
catch/take	catch/take	take	take	go on (my)	go by
get on/off	get on/off	get on/off	get in/out	get on/off	get in/out
bus station	railway station	airport	taxi rank	–	–

C Railway stations

You may hear these announcements.

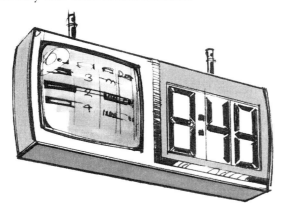

The train now arriving at **platform** 3 is the 8.48 **to** London Paddington, calling at Swindon and Reading. **Passengers** for Didcot **change** (= change trains) at Swindon.
We apologise to passengers for the **late arrival** of the 8.52 **to** Oxford. This train will now arrive at platform 6 in approximately 20 minutes.
The next train **due to** (= timetabled to) arrive at platform 4 is the 9.06 to Birmingham.

D Buses

Sometimes buses are not very **punctual** (= they don't arrive at the correct time). Where I live buses should **run** (= come) every ten minutes, but sometimes I wait at the **bus stop** for half an hour with a long **queue** (AmEng = line) of people, and then three buses come together, and they're all **full up** (= full of people, and no more people can get on). On other occasions the bus is early and I **miss** it (= I don't catch it. NOT ~~I lost the bus.~~).

Exercises

62.1 Cross out the incorrect word in these sentences.

1 You mustn't <u>ride/drive</u> a motorbike without a crash helmet.
2 She told him to <u>get in / get on</u> the car and fasten his seat belt.
3 Bus <u>fares/tickets</u> are getting more expensive.
4 Trains to the airport <u>travel/run</u> every half hour.
5 The pilot couldn't <u>drive/fly</u> the plane in such bad weather.
6 Have a look at the train <u>schedule/timetable</u> to find out when the next one arrives.
7 We were late, so we had to <u>take/catch</u> a taxi.
8 I left my house a bit late and I <u>lost/missed</u> the bus.

62.2 Write down two different words that can combine with each of the words below.

Example: miss ...*the bus*......
...*the train*....

1	3	5 ....
fare	station	get in
....	....	....

2	4	6 ....
get on	driver	journey
....	....	....

62.3 Identify these means of transport without looking at the opposite page.

1 .... 2 .... 3 .... 4 .... 5 ....

62.4 Fill the gaps with the correct word.

1 Our train leaves from .... 7.
2 I waited at the .... for ten minutes, and then two buses arrived.
3 I couldn't get on the first bus because it was ....
4 The train was half an hour late. I think the reason for the late .... was bad weather.
5 Buses are not very .... Sometimes they come every five minutes, then other times you have to wait for forty minutes.
6 When I got to the bus stop there was a long .... of people.
7 The flight was fine but we had a terrible .... from the airport to our hotel.
8 I think the next train is .... to arrive in about ten minutes.

62.5 Are these statements *true* or *false* in your experience?

1 Trains are more reliable than buses.
2 Train fares are more expensive than bus fares.
3 Train journeys are more interesting than bus journeys.
4 Railway stations are nicer places than bus stations.
5 You get to the place you are going faster by taxi than by car.

63 Work: duties, conditions and pay

A What do you do?

People may ask you about your job. They can ask and you can answer in different ways:

What do you do?   I'm (+ job) e.g. a banker / an engineer / a teacher / a builder
What's your job?   I work in (+ place or general area) e.g. a bank / marketing
What do you do for a living?   I work for (+ name of company) e.g. Union Bank, ICI, Fiat

Note: 'Work' is usually an uncountable noun, so you cannot say 'a work'. If you want to use the indefinite article you must say 'a job', e.g. She hasn't got a job at the moment.

B What does that involve? (= What do you do in your job?)

When people ask you to explain your work/job, they may want to know your main **responsibilities** (= your duties / what you have to do), or something about your daily **routine** (= what you do every day/week). They can ask like this: What does that (i.e. your job) **involve**?

Main responsibilities
I'm **in charge of** (= **responsible for**) all deliveries out of the factory.
I have to **deal with** any complaints (= take all necessary action if there are complaints).
I **run** the coffee bar and restaurant in the museum (= I am in control of it / I manage it).

Note: We often use **responsible for** / **in charge of** for part of something, e.g. a department or some of the workers; and **run** for control of <u>all</u> of something, e.g. a company or a shop.

Daily duties/routines
I have to **go to** / **attend** (*fml*) a lot of **meetings**.
I visit/see/meet **clients** (= people I do business with or for).
I **advise** clients (= give them help and my opinion).
It involves **doing** quite a lot of **paperwork** (a general word we use for routine work that involves paper e.g. writing letters, filling in forms, etc.). Note the **-ing** form after **involve**.

C Pay

Most workers are **paid** (= receive money) every month and this **pay** goes directly into their bank account. It is called a **salary**. We can express the same idea using the verb **to earn**:

My **salary** is $60,000 a year. (= I **earn** $60,000 a year.)

With many jobs you **get** (= receive) **holiday pay** and **sick pay** (when you are ill). If you want to ask about holidays, you can say:

How **much holiday** do you get? *or* How **many weeks' holiday** do you get?

The total amount of money you receive in a year is called your **income**. This could be your salary from one job, or the salary from two different jobs you have. And on this income you have to **pay** part to the government – called **income tax**.

D Working hours

For many people in Britain, these are 8.30–9.00 a.m. to 5.00–5.30 p.m. Consequently people often talk about a **nine-to-five job** (= regular working hours). Some people have **flexi-time** (= they can start an hour or so earlier or finish later); and some have to **do shiftwork** (= working at different times, e.g. days one week and nights the next week). Some people also **work overtime** (= work extra hours). Some people are paid to **do/work overtime**, others are not paid.

Exercises

63.1 Match the verbs on the left with the nouns or phrases on the right. Use each word once only.

1	earn	overtime
2	work	meetings
3	pay	a shop
4	go to	clients
5	deal with	£500
6	run	income tax

63.2 Starting with the words you are given, rewrite each of these sentences using vocabulary from the opposite page. The basic meaning must stay the same.

Example: I'm a banker.
I work *in banking*.

1 What do you do?
What's ....
2 I earn $50,000 dollars.
My ....
3 I get £20,000 from my teaching job and another £10,000 from writing.
My total ....
4 I am a chemist.
I work for ....
5 In my job I have to look after and maintain all the computers in the building.
My job involves ....
6 I'm responsible for one of the smaller departments.
I'm in ....

63.3 This is part of a conversation with a teacher about her job. Can you supply the missing questions?

A: ....?
B: I usually start at nine and finish at four.
A: ....?
B: Yes a bit. On certain courses I work until five o'clock, and then I get paid extra.
A: ....?
B: Twelve weeks. That's one of the good things about being a teacher.
A: ....?
B: No we don't, I'm afraid. That's one of the disadvantages of being a teacher. But I suppose money isn't everything.

63.4 Can you answer these general knowledge questions about work?

1 What are normal working hours for most office jobs in your country?
2 Can you name three jobs that get very high salaries in your country?
3 When you start paying income tax in your country, what is the minimum amount you have to pay?
4 What jobs often involve shiftwork? (Give at least two examples.)
5 Is flexi-time common in your company or your country?

63.5 Think about your own job. How many of the things on the opposite page do you do? How is your work different? Can you explain your responsibilities and daily duties in English?

64 Jobs

A The medical profession

These people **treat** (= give medical treatment and try to solve a medical problem) and **look after** (= care for / take care of) others: **doctor, nurse, surgeon** (= a specialist doctor who works in a hospital and **operates on** people), **dentist**, and **vet** (= animal doctor). The word 'vet' is a short form for 'veterinary surgeon'.

B Manual jobs

These are jobs where you work with your hands, and all the examples below are **skilled** jobs (= they need a lot of training).

bricklayer (builds walls)

carpenter (makes things using wood)

plumber (fits and repairs water pipes, bathrooms, etc.)

electrician (fits and repairs electrical things)

mechanic (repairs cars)

C Professional people

Job	Definition
architect	designs buildings
lawyer	represents people with legal problems
engineer	plans the building of roads, bridges, machines, etc.
accountant	controls the financial situation of people and companies
university lecturer	teaches in a university
broker (stock market)	buys and sells stocks and shares

D The armed forces and the emergency services

soldier (in the army)

sailor (in the navy)

pilot (in the air force)

police officer (in the police force)

firefighter (in the fire brigade)

Exercises

64.1 Write down at least one job from the opposite page that would probably be impossible for these people.

1 Someone who didn't go to university.
2 Someone with very bad eyesight (= cannot see very well).
3 Someone who is always seasick on a boat.
4 Someone who understands nothing about cars.
5 Someone who will not work in the evening or at weekends.
6 Someone who is afraid of dogs.
7 Someone who is afraid of heights and high places.
8 Someone who is terrible at numbers and figures.
9 Someone who can't stand the sight of blood.
10 Someone who is a pacifist, who is anti-war.

64.2 Complete these definitions.

1 An architect _designs buildings._
2 A university lecturer ....
3 An accountant ....
4 A vet ....
5 A lawyer ....
6 An engineer ....
7 A bricklayer ....
8 A stock broker ....
9 A mechanic ....
10 A surgeon ....

64.3 Respond to the statements below, as in the example.

Example: A: He's a policeman.
            B: _Really? When did he join the police force?_

1 A: He's a soldier.
  B: .... ?
2 A: He's a sailor.
  B: .... ?
3 A: He's a fighter pilot.
  B: .... ?
4 A: He's a firefighter.
  B: .... ?

64.4 You have just bought a piece of land and you are planning to build a house on it. Write down at least six people from the opposite page that you may need to help you. What would you need their help for?

Example: a bricklayer to build the walls

64.5 Write a list of friends, relatives and neighbours (just choose people who have jobs). Can you write down what each person does? Use a bilingual dictionary to help you if necessary.

Example: My uncle Jim is an engineer. His wife is an accountant.

65 The career ladder

A Getting a job

When Paul left school he **applied for** (= wrote an official request for) a job in the accounts department of a local engineering company. They gave him a job as a **trainee** (= a very junior person in a company). He didn't earn very much but they gave him a lot of **training** (= organised help and advice with learning the job), and sent him on **training courses**.

Note: **Training** is an uncountable noun, so you cannot say 'a training'. You can only talk about **training** (in general), or a **training course** (if you want to refer to just one). Here you can use the verbs **do** or **go on**: I did / **went on** several training courses last year.

B Moving up

Paul worked hard at the company and his **prospects** (= future possibilities in the job) looked good. After his first year he got a good **pay rise** (= more money), and after two years he was **promoted** (= given a higher position with more money and responsibility). After six years he was **in charge of** (= **responsible for** / the boss of) the accounts department with five other **employees** (= workers in the company) **under him** (= under his responsibility/authority).

C Leaving the company

By the time Paul was 30, however, he decided he wanted a **fresh challenge** (= a new exciting situation). He was keen to work abroad, so he **resigned** from his company (= officially told the company he was leaving his job; you can also say 'he **quit** the company') and started looking for a new job with a bigger company. After a couple of months he managed to find a job with an international company which **involved** (= included) a lot of foreign travel. He was very excited about the new job and at first he really enjoyed the travelling, but ...

D Hard times

After about six months, Paul started to dislike the constant moving around, and after a year he hated it; he hated living in hotels, and he never really made any friends in the new company. Unfortunately his work was not satisfactory either and finally he was **sacked** (= told to leave the company / **dismissed** / **given the sack**) a year later.

After that, Paul found things much more difficult. He was **unemployed** (= **out of work** / without a job) for over a year. He had to sell his car and move out of his new house. Things were looking bad and in the end Paul had to accept a **part-time** job (= working only some of the day or some of the week) on a fruit and vegetable stall in a market.

E Happier times

To his surprise, Paul loved the market. He made lots of friends and enjoyed working out in the open air. After two years, he **took over** (= took control of) the stall. Two years later he opened a second stall, and after ten years he had fifteen stalls. Last year Paul **retired** (= stopped working completely) at the age of 55, a very rich man.

Exercises

65.1 Write a single word synonym for each of these words/phrases.

1 given the sack = ...
2 out of work = ...
3 left the company = ...
4 was given a better position in the company = ...
5 future possibilities in a job = ...
6 stopped working for ever = ...
7 workers in a company = ...

65.2 Find the logical answer on the right for each of the questions on the left.

1 Why did they sack him?   a Because he was nearly 65.
2 Why did they promote him?   b Because he was late for work every day.
3 Why did he apply for the job?   c Because he needed more training.
4 Why did he retire?   d Because he was out of work.
5 Why did he resign?   e Because he was the best person in the department.
6 Why did he go on the course?   f Because he didn't like his boss.

65.3 Complete these sentences with a suitable word or phrase.

1 I don't want a full-time job. I'd prefer to work ....
2 She'd like to go on another training ....
3 I'm bored in my job. I need a fresh ....
4 He works on a stall in the ....
5 At the end of this year we should get a good pay ....
6 She's got more than a hundred workers under ....
7 I didn't know he was the new manager. When did he take .... ?
8 It's a boring job and the pay is awful. Why did he .... ?

65.4 Complete this word-building table. Use a dictionary to help you.

Verb	General noun	Personal noun(s)
promote	....	–
employ	....	....
resign	....	–
retire	....	–
train	....	....

65.5 Have you got a job in a company? If so, answer these questions as quickly as you can.

1 What does your job involve?
2 Are you responsible for anything or anyone?
3 Have you had much training from the company?
4 Have the company sent you on any training courses?
5 Have you been promoted since you started in the company?
6 Do you normally get a good pay rise at the end of each year?
7 How do you feel about your future prospects in the company?
8 Are you happy in the job or do you feel it is time for a fresh challenge in another company?

If possible, ask another person the same questions.

66 In the office and in the factory

A The office

B Office work

Brenda works for a company which produces furniture. She works in an office, which is just opposite the factory where the furniture is made. This is how she spends her day:

She **works at a computer** most of the time, where she writes letters and reports.
She answers phone calls, mostly from **retailers**. (= shops selling the factory's furniture)
She makes phone calls to retailers, and the factory making the furniture.
She **sends invoices** to customers. (= paper showing products sold and the money to pay)
She **shows visitors around** the factory.
She **does general paperwork**, e.g. filing reports, writing memos, answering letters.
She **arranges meetings** for her boss and other managers in the company.

C The 'shop floor' of the factory

This is where products are **manufactured** (= made). Modern factories have fewer workers than in the past – this is because of **automation** (= machines do most of the work), and most factories use an **assembly line** (= an arrangement in which each worker makes a part of the product and then passes it on to the next person or machine). On an assembly line, workers **fit/assemble** the different parts, and **supervisors** (= people in charge/control) **check/inspect/examine** each stage to make sure the product **meets the required standard** (= is good enough).

D Finished goods

Goods (*pl*) is the general word used for things that are made to be sold. When the product, e.g. a radio, is finished, it is **packaged** (= put in plastic and then in a box) and **stored** (= kept) in a **warehouse**. When a customer, e.g. an electrical shop, **orders** some of these **goods**, they are **delivered** to the shop (= taken to the shop) using road or rail.

Exercises

66.1 Write down three nouns that could follow each of these verbs. You can use the same noun more than once. Not all of them are on the left-hand page.

1 write ...a letter............... 3 make ....
....
....
2 send .... 4 arrange ....
....
....

66.2 Fill the gaps with the correct word to form a compound noun in each case.

1 I told him to put the details on the notice..............................
2 She has to check the goods when they come off the assembly ....
3 I'm sure I took the reports out of the filing .... and put them in my brief..............................
4 It's a very boring job and I spend most of my time doing general paper..............................
5 I threw all that stuff in the wastepaper ....

66.3 What words from the opposite page are being defined here?

1 The place where you store finished products before they are sold.
2 The process of using machines to do work that used to be done by men and women.
3 A plural noun for things that are made to be sold.
4 A thing you often hang on the wall, which tells you the date.
5 A book where you often write down all your appointments and things you have to do.
6 A piece of paper which shows the products that a customer bought and the money they have to pay.
7 A person or business that sells goods to the public.
8 A part of a desk where you often keep pens, paper, notes, etc.

66.4 Replace the underlined verb using a different verb with the same meaning (in this context).

1 This particular machine is <u>made</u> in Germany.
2 I help them to <u>assemble</u> the different parts.
3 The supervisor always <u>inspects</u> our work carefully
4 When the books are printed they are <u>kept</u> in the warehouse.
5 The factory said they'll be able to <u>take</u> the furniture to the shops next Monday.

66.5 Have you got a job? If so, how many of these statements are true for you in your job? (If you haven't got a job, how many of these things would you like to do?)

1 I work at a computer a lot of the time.
2 I do quite a lot of general paperwork.
3 I make a lot of phone calls.
4 I send faxes occasionally.
5 I show people around my workplace.
6 I arrange meetings.
7 I attend (= go to) quite a lot of meetings.
8 I have to write letters and reports.
9 I go to conferences.

67 Business and finance

Banks and businesses

Most businesses need to borrow money to **finance** (= pay for) **investments** (= things they need to buy in order to help the company, e.g. machines). The money they borrow from the bank is called **a loan**, and on this loan they have to **pay interest**, e.g. if you borrow £1,000 and the **interest rate** is 10%, then you have to **pay back** £1,000, plus £100 in interest.

B Businesses and profit

One of the main **aims/objectives** (= the things that you hope to do/achieve) of a company is to **make a profit** (= earn/receive more money than it spends) (≠ **make a loss**). If a company does not make a profit or a loss, it **breaks even**.

Most companies are happy if they can **break even** in their first year of business.

Companies receive money from selling their products – this money is called the **turnover**. The money that they spend is called the **expenditure** (*fml*). They spend money on these things: **raw materials** (= materials in their natural state used to make something else, e.g. coal and oil are important **raw materials** used to make plastics); **labour** (= employees); **overheads** (= necessary costs for a company, e.g. rent for buildings, electricity, telephone)

C Rise and fall

Business people often need to talk about the movement of sales, prices, interest rates, profit and loss, etc. Here are some of the words used to describe these **trends** (= movements):

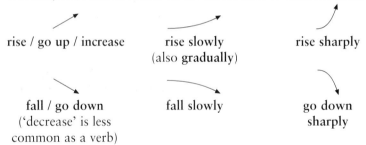

rise / go up / increase   rise slowly   rise sharply
(also **gradually**)

fall / go down   fall slowly   go down
('decrease' is less   sharply
common as a verb)

Note: rise, increase, and fall are also used as nouns: a **slow rise** in interest rates, a **steady increase** in sales, a **sharp fall** in profits, a **dramatic** (= sharp) **rise** in inflation. We can also use **be up/down**: prices are **up** by 10%; profits **are down** by £2m.

D Businesses and the economy

In order to **grow/expand** (= get bigger) and **thrive/prosper** (= do well / be successful), many companies want or need the following:

low inflation, so prices do not go up
low interest rates, so the company can borrow money without paying a lot of interest
economic and **political stability** (= things remain steady and stable and there are no sudden changes in the economic and political situation)
a **healthy/strong** economy (= in good condition), and not an economy **in recession** (= in a period of reduced and slow business activity)
tax cuts (= tax reductions / lower taxes), so they can keep more of their profit. This often depends on government expenditure, e.g. The government will not be able to **reduce taxes** if **public expenditure** continues to rise.

Exercises

67.1 What single word or phrase is being defined in each of these sentences?

1 Money you borrow from a bank for your business.
2 What you must pay the bank if you borrow money.
3 The continuous increase in the price of things.
4 The things you hope to do/achieve within a period of time.
5 When a company does not make a profit or a loss.
6 When an economy is in a period of reduced and slow business activity.

67.2 Replace the underlined word(s) in each sentence with another word that has the same meaning.

1 There has been a <u>slow</u> rise in sales.
2 This comes after a <u>dramatic</u> fall last year.
3 Fortunately the company is <u>doing well</u> now.
4 And it's <u>growing</u> very quickly.
5 This is one of their main <u>objectives</u>.
6 Profits have <u>risen</u> considerably.

67.3 Look at the graph and complete the sentences on the left with one word for each gap.

1 In 1993 sales ....
2 In the following year they
   ....
3 In 1995 there was a ....
   .... in sales.
4 In 1996 business improved and there
   was a ....
5 And in 1997 sales ....
   ....
6 In the five-year period sales
   .... by 40,000.

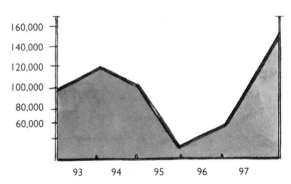

67.4 Fill the gaps to form compound words or common phrases.

1 .... expenditure   3 tax ....   5 raw ....
2 .... stability   4 .... rate   6 profit and ....

67.5 Can you answer these questions about your own country?

1 What is the current inflation rate?
2 If you borrowed $10,000 from your bank, what would the interest rate be approximately?
3 What is the state of the economy at the moment? Is it strong? Is it in recession?
4 Do you think businesses are optimistic about the future?
5 Has the government reduced company taxes or personal taxes in the last twelve months?
6 Has public expenditure risen or fallen in the last twelve months?

68 Sales and marketing

A What is marketing?

People talk about the **marketing mix**. This **consists of** (= it is formed from and includes):

choosing the right **product** (= what a company produces/makes or offers)
selling it at the right **price** (= what it costs to the buyer/consumer)
using the right kind of **promotion** (= the ways to make the product popular and well-known; this includes **advertising**.)
making it available in the right **place** (= where you sell the product and how it reaches the **consumer**; also known as **distribution**)

This 'mix' is often referred to as the four **Ps**, and marketing people have the job of matching these things to the needs of **consumers** (= the people who buy and use products). People who buy the products of a particular company are that company's **customers/clients**.

B 'Sales' and 'market'

There are a number of words which combine with **sales** and **market** to form compound nouns and word partnerships which are very common in marketing.

sales figures: the amount you have sold
sales target: the amount you <u>would like</u> to sell in a future period
sales forecast: the amount you <u>think you will</u> sell in a future period, e.g. next year
sales representative: a person who sells a company's products; abbreviated to **sales rep**
sales/marketing manager: the person who runs the **sales/marketing department**
market research: collecting and studying information about what people want and need
market share: the % of a market that a company has, e.g. a 20% market share
market leader: the company or product with the biggest market share

C Competition

Ford Motors is the **market leader** in the UK car industry. Its **main competitors** (= the most important companies in the same market) are Vauxhall and Rover, and it has had to work very hard in recent years to maintain its **market share**. Every time a competitor **launches** a new product (= introduces a new car onto the market), it is harder for Ford to stay in front.

D A company's image

The **image** of a product/company (= the picture or idea that people have of the product/company) is very important in sales and marketing. Some companies want a **fashionable** image (= modern and up-to-date), others do not. For example:

mass-produced (= made in large numbers), **reliable** (= you can trust it), **good value** (= good for the money) functional but boring.

young; **exciting, glamorous** (= exciting + attractive); often fashionable, dangerous; not very practical.

high quality (= high standard/ very good), **luxury** (= expensive and giving great comfort), **high status/prestige** (= important; driven by important people).

Exercises

68.1 The 'marketing mix' consists of the four Ps. Can you remember what they are? Write them down and then check on the opposite page.

68.2 See how many different compound words and word partnerships you can form from the words in the box (you can use a word more than once), then complete the definitions below.

sales	market	manager	share	figures
marketing	leader	research	department	forecast

1 A sales .... is what you think you are going to sell during a future period.
2 The marketing .... will be responsible for all the activities in the marketing ....
3 Sales .... tell you how much you have sold of a product.
4 The market .... is the company with the largest market .... in a particular market.
5 Market .... gives you information about what people want, need and buy.

68.3 What knowledge is necessary to be a good sales rep? Complete this text and then try to add a further sentence of your own.

First of all a good sales (1)........................... needs to have an excellent knowledge of their company's (2)........................... . Secondly, he or she needs to know all about the (3)........................... of their main (4)........................... . Thirdly, a sales representative should be familiar with the needs of (5)........................... in their particular market, and should obviously be very familiar with the needs of their company's most important (6)........................... .

68.4 Complete this word-building table. Use a dictionary to help you.

Noun	Adjective	Noun	Adjective
....	exciting	prestige	....
....	glamourous	luxury	....
competition	....	....	reliable
fashion	....	....	dangerous

68.5 Which nouns or adjectives from the last exercise (or any others from section D on the opposite page), do you associate with these companies and products?

Rolex ....   Benetton ....
Coca Cola ....   Sony ....
Ferrari ....   Levis ....
Swatch ....   mobile phones ....

68.6 Can you answer these questions about your own country? If possible, compare your answers with someone else.

1 Which company is the market leader in the motor car industry in your country?
2 Do you know its approximate market share?
3 Which companies are its main competitors?
4 Write down the names of at least two cars that have been launched in the last six months.

69 Hobbies

Hobbies are activities that we do in our **spare time** (= free time).

A Things people play

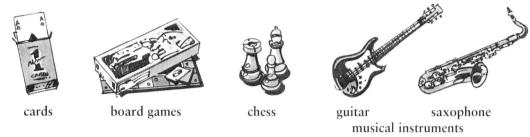

cards   board games   chess   guitar   saxophone
                                                    musical instruments

Note: People **join clubs** (= become members of clubs) where they can **play** cards and chess.

B Things people collect

stamps   coins   antiques

C Outdoor activities

hiking   camping   rock climbing   hunting   jogging

With these hobbies we can use two different verbs, **go** and **do**:
We often **go camping** in the summer. *or* I **do** a bit of / a lot of **rock climbing** in the summer.

D Creative hobbies

Caroline **makes her own clothes**. (= she makes clothes for herself; she doesn't buy them)

Barbara likes **photography**.

Brigit is **mad about** (= really likes) **DIY**. (DIY = do-it-yourself)

Note: When we start a hobby for the first time we often use the phrasal verb **take up**, and when we stop doing the hobby for the final time, we often use the phrasal verb **give up**.
I **took up** golf when I was fifteen, but I **gave** it **up** last year.

Exercises

69.1 Without looking at the opposite page, write down:

1 three things that people often play
2 three things that people often collect
3 five outdoor hobbies which include some physical exercise

69.2 Here are some people talking about their hobbies. Can you guess what the hobby is in each case?

1 I usually use colour, but sometimes you get a better effect with black and white. It really depends on the subject.
2 I really enjoy going round the shops and markets looking for a bargain.
3 I try to practise every day, but sometimes it's difficult because I don't like to disturb my neighbours too much. And one neighbour gets very angry if I play the same thing over and over again.
4 The great thing is you can do it when you like. I usually do it three or four times a week – either early in the morning, or after school. I only go for about 25 minutes but it really keeps me fit.
5 Obviously it saves me a lot of money; and in any case, I hate buying things in boutiques because so many things are badly made.
6 I joined a club because I wanted to get better, and I now play twice a week in the evenings. It has helped me a lot and I have a much better memory for all the different moves and strategies.
7 I think this is a very common hobby for people like me, who have a house but don't have much money. That's why I started, but now I think I do a better job than many professionals.

69.3 Complete these sentences with a suitable verb.

1 How often do you .... jogging?
2 She .... hiking because she wanted to get more exercise. Unfortunately, she didn't like it and she .... it .... about six months later.
3 She has always .... her own clothes; it's much cheaper than buying them.
4 He .... old coins.
5 I .... quite a lot of rock climbing when I'm on holiday.
6 I learnt to .... the piano when I was at school.
7 I wanted to improve my chess, so I .... a chess club.
8 I don't really .... anything in my spare time.

69.4 Answer these questions.

1 Have you got a hobby? If so, what is it?
2 How long have you had this hobby?
3 Is it an expensive hobby?
4 Why do you like it?
5 How much time do you spend on your hobby?
6 Is it a common hobby in your country?
7 Write down three other common hobbies in your country.

If possible, ask another person these questions.

70 Sport 1: games, people, and places

In English you normally **play a game** but **do a lot of / a bit of sport**:
In the winter I **do** quite a lot of **skiing**; in the summer I **play tennis** and **cricket**.

A Ball games and equipment

football (AmEng = soccer)   rugby   volleyball

basketball   golf   baseball

tennis   table tennis   cricket

squash   badminton   hockey

For most ball games you need **boots** or **training shoes** (trainers).
For tennis, squash and badminton you need a **racket**.
For baseball and table tennis you need a **bat**. For golf you need **clubs**.
In tennis, volleyball and badminton there is a **net** across the middle of the
court. There is also a **net** around each **goal** in football.

B Things you can do with a ball

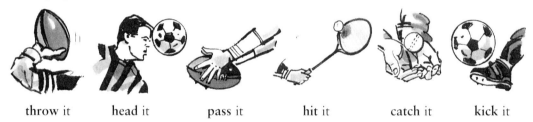

throw it   **head** it   **pass** it   **hit** it   **catch** it   **kick** it

C Places and people

The playing area for football, rugby, hockey and cricket is called a **pitch**; for tennis,
volleyball, basketball, squash and badminton it is a **court**; for golf it is a **course**.

Note: When you describe the playing area for football and the area around for the **crowd** (=
the people who watch, also called **spectators**), it is called a **stadium**, e.g. Wembley Stadium.

Players: Some games are played by individuals, others are **team** games. In a team, one
player is the **captain**, and there is a **manager** (e.g. in football) or a **coach** (e.g. in basketball).

Officials: Football, rugby and hockey have a **referee** but tennis, cricket and baseball have an
umpire. In football the referee has a whistle to control the game and two **linesmen**. In tennis
there are **line judges** to decide if the ball is 'in' or 'out'.

D Other sports

Name	Place	Equipment
athletics	track	vest, shorts, running shoes or spikes (pic)
motor racing	track	crash helmet
swimming	pool	swimming costume (women); trunks (men)
boxing	ring	vest, shorts, gloves, boots
skiing	slopes (piste)	sticks, ski suit, ski boots

Exercises

70.1 Write down six things you can do with a ball. Cover the opposite page first.

.... it   .... it   .... it

.... it   .... it   .... it

70.2 Write down:

1 five games where you can hit the ball (with various kinds of equipment).
2 four games where you can pass the ball.
3 three games where you can catch the ball.
4 two games where you can kick the ball.
5 one game where you can head the ball.

70.3 Organise these words and put them in the correct columns below? (You can put a word in more than one column if you wish.)

swimming   gloves   crash helmet   course   football   racket   track
ring   boots   pool   motor racing   clubs   tennis   net   court   golf
pitch   track   trunks   boxing   goals   costume   shorts   whistle   vest

Sport	Place	Equipment

70.4 *True* or *false*? If *false*, correct the sentence to make it *true*.

1 The people who watch a football match are the audience.
2 The official who gives the score in tennis is the umpire.
3 Athletes wear shorts.
4 You need a stick to play hockey.
5 Boxers wear gloves.
6 Tennis is played on a pitch.
7 The referee in football has a whistle.
8 Women wear trunks for swimming.

70.5 Answer these questions. If possible, ask a friend the same questions.

1 Are there any games or sports on the opposite page that you watch but don't play? If so, what are they and where do you watch them?
2 Are there any games or sports on the opposite page you play/do yourself? If so, which?
3 Are there any that you are good at?
4 Are there any that you hate?
5 Are there any that are not played much in your country?
6 Which game or sport is the most popular in your country?
7 Which game or sport on the opposite page is the most dangerous in your opinion?
8 Which game or sport requires the most strength?
9 Which one has the biggest crowds?
10 Can you write down at least three more games/sports not included opposite.

71 Sport 2: winning, losing, and scoring

A Winning and losing

Notice how these key words are used:

Spain **beat** Switzerland 3–2. (= Switzerland **lost to** Spain 3–2) In other words:
Spain **won** the match. (= Switzerland **lost** the match)
Spain **defeated** Switzerland. (= Switzerland **were defeated** by Spain)
Spain were the **winners**. (= Switzerland were the **losers**)

If both teams or players have the same **score** (= number of goals or points), it is a **draw** (e.g. 2–2 is a **draw**). We can also use **draw** as a verb, e.g. we **drew** yesterday's **match/game** 2–2.

Note: A **match** is used for an organised game: We had a **game** of football with a few friends in the park, but we've got an important **match** against a very good team next week.

When the game is still in progress, we often use the verb **lead** to describe the position of the teams and players, or **latest** to describe the score:

HALF-TIME SCORE: SPAIN 2 SWITZERLAND 1
At half-time, Spain **are leading** Switzerland two–one. (= the **latest score** is two–one to Spain)
Sampras is **leading** three–two in the first set. (= the **latest score** is three–two to Sampras)

B What's the score?

In most games you score **goals** (e.g. football, hockey) or **points** (e.g. table tennis, basketball). At the end of the game there is a **result** (= players/teams win, lose, or draw). However, the scoring system – and the way we describe it – is different from game to game.

Football
Spain 0–0 Italy (we say nil–nil)
Spain 1–0 Italy (one–nil to Spain)
Spain 1–1 Italy (one–all)
Spain 1–2 Italy (two–one to Italy)
Spain 2–2 Italy (two–all)

If the **final score** is 2–2 in a cup match, you may have to play **extra time**. And if the score is still 2–2 at the end of extra time, there is a **penalty shoot-out**.

Tennis
15–0 (fifteen–love)
30–0 (thirty–love)
30–30 (thirty–all)
40–40 (deuce) [pronounced like 'juice']
Advantage X
Game X

Game and set to X (e.g. 6–3 or 7–5)
If the **score** reaches 6–6 you have a **tie-break** to decide the set.

C Competitions

In many sports, players and teams **play** every week in a **league** (the player/team that wins the most games in a **season** is the winner of the **league championship**). In most sports, there is also a **cup** competition, which is usually a **knock-out** competition.

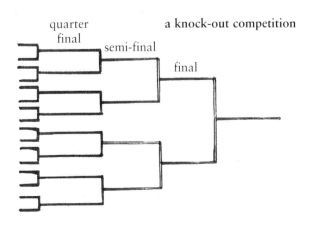

a knock-out competition

quarter final
semi-final
final

Exercises

These exercises also revise some vocabulary from the previous unit.

71.1 **Complete the table with the correct forms.**

Infinitive	Past tense	Past participle	Infinitive	Past tense	Past participle
win lose beat			lead catch draw		

71.2 **How do we say these scores?**

1 *Football:*   0–0   2–1   4–4
2 *Tennis:*   15–0   40–30   40–40

71.3 **Fill the gaps in these texts with suitable words or phrases.**

In the World Cup Final of 1994, Brazil (1).................... Italy 3–2 in a (2).................... shoot-out. After ninety minutes the (3).................... was 0–0; and it remained the same after thirty minutes of (4)...................., but then Italy (5).................... 3–2 in the penalty shoot-out after Baresi and Baggio both missed. This was the fourth time that Brazil had (6).................... the World Cup.

Ivanisevic (7).................... to Sampras in the second round. He (8).................... the first (9).................... 6–4, but then (10).................... the second (11).................... on a (12).................... . After that, Sampras dominated the rest of the (13).................... and won easily. The final (14).................... was 4–6, 7–6, 6–1, 6–2.

71.4 *True* or *false*? **Check your answers by looking back at this unit and the previous unit.**

1 Brazil won the football World Cup in 1994.
2 Football has an umpire.
3 A set in tennis is always decided on a tie-break.
4 If two teams have the same score at the end of the game, it is a draw.
5 Golf is played on a course.
6 If someone gives you the latest score, the game has finished.
7 Sticks are used in skiing and hockey.
8 In a knock-out competition, you can lose one or two games but still win the competition.

71.5 **Which sport is being described in each sentence? (The underlined words are key words and you can look them up to increase your vocabulary in different sports.)**

1 The referee gave the <u>try</u> although many people thought it was a <u>forward pass</u>.
2 He scored the winner with a beautiful <u>free kick</u> from just outside the <u>penalty area</u>.
3 He <u>served</u> fifteen <u>aces</u> and not one <u>double fault</u>.
4 The <u>coach</u> called a <u>time out</u> with just 45 seconds left and two points between the teams.
5 He <u>crashed into</u> the car in front with just two <u>laps</u> remaining.
6 First he was <u>booked</u> (= the yellow card) for a bad <u>tackle</u>, and then he <u>handled the ball</u> inside the <u>penalty area</u>, so the referee had to <u>send him off</u> (= the red card).
7 In the <u>200 metres freestyle</u>, he overtook the Russian on the final <u>length</u> to win the race.
8 She <u>sprinted</u> away from the rest of <u>the field</u> on the <u>final lap</u> and won easily.

72 Cinema and theatre

box
curtains
stage
rows
aisle
stalls
circle

A Theatre

At the theatre you can see **plays**, e.g. *Hamlet* by Shakespeare, or **musicals**, e.g. *Phantom of the Opera* by Andrew Lloyd Webber. In a play the **cast** (= the total number of actors) is usually quite small, but musicals often have a very large cast.

One difference between the theatre and cinema is that you usually **book** (= reserve) tickets **in advance** (= some time before the actual performance) if you are going to the theatre. Another difference is that the **audience** (= the people watching the play/musical) **clap** at the end of the **performance**. This does not usually happen (in Britain) at the end of a film.

B Cinema

Plays are **performed** on **stage**, films are **shown** on **screen**. In your country, films in English are either shown with **subtitles** (= there is a translation across the bottom of the screen), or they are **dubbed** (= the English is removed and replaced by actors speaking in your own language).

Films **are set** (= take place) in many different periods and places, e.g. *Room with a View* is set in the early part of the 20th century; *Blade Runner* is set in the future. And when people talk about films, they often talk about the **director**, e.g. Spielberg, Bertolucci; and the **stars**, the most important actors and actresses, e.g. Tom Hanks and Jodie Foster.

C Types of film

western: a film about America in the 19th century; often with cowboys and indians
war film, e.g. *Born on the 4th of July*   **action film**, e.g. *Indiana Jones*
horror film, e.g. *Dracula*; *Frankenstein*   **comedy**: a funny film that makes you laugh
science fiction film: about the future   **thriller**: an exciting story often about a crime

D Describing plays and films

Journalists write articles in which they give their opinion of new films and plays. They are called **critics**, and their articles are called **reviews**. These are some words they may use:

moving: producing strong emotions, often of sadness; a positive word
violent: includes lots of scenes with fighting and death
powerful: has a big effect on our emotions
gripping: exciting and very interesting
good fun: used to describe a film that may not be very serious or important but is enjoyable
slow: boring

Exercises

72.1 Look at the picture of your visit to the theatre and answer these questions.

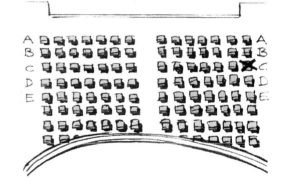

1 Did you sit in the stalls or circle?
2 Which row were you in?
3 Were you next to an aisle?
4 Did you have a good view of the stage?

72.2 What word or phrase is being defined?

1 A play or film in which part of the story is sung to music.
2 The total number of actors in a play or film.
3 The people who watch a play at the theatre.
4 What these people do with their hands at the end of a play.
5 The person who makes a film.
6 Journalists who write articles about films and plays.
7 The name of the articles they write.
8 The translation of the story of a film across the bottom of the screen.
9 To reserve tickets before the performance.
10 The most important actors or actresses in a film.

72.3 Have you seen these famous films made in English over the last twenty years? If so, try to complete the rest of the table using words from the opposite page. Then write in the titles of three more films you have seen and complete the rest of the table for it.

Film	Type of film	Subtitles or dubbed?	Description of film (adjectives)
1 *Dirty Harry* with Clint Eastwood			
2 *Blade Runner* with Harrison Ford			
3 *Four Weddings and a Funeral* with Hugh Grant			
4 *Schindler's List* with Liam Neeson			
5 *Dances with Wolves* with Kevin Costner			
6			
7			
8			

73 Music, art and literature

A Forms and people

	Forms	Person	
Music	classical pop/rock	composer songwriter	
Art	painting sculpture	painter sculptor }	artist (general)
Literature	the novel short stories poetry plays	novelist short story writer poet dramatist/playwright }	writer (general)

B Music

Classical music: e.g Beethoven's piano concertos, Schubert's symphonies. Beethoven and
Schubert are both **composers** (= people who write classical music) and most of their
music is played by an **orchestra** (= large group of musicians including violins, cellos, etc.)
which is led by a **conductor**, e.g. Georg Solti or Loren Maazel, as leader.

Opera (= a play in which the words are sung): e.g. *La Bohème* by Puccini, *Carmen* by Bizet.

Rock and **pop music:** e.g. U2, Bon Jovi, Maria Carey. This music is played by **groups/bands**,
e.g. Bon Jovi, Simply Red; or **solo artists**, e.g. Madonna. Many solo artists, e.g. Phil
Collins, are **singer-songwriters** (= they **write** and **perform/play** their own songs).

Jazz: e.g. Duke Ellington, Miles Davis, Stan Getz.

C Musical instruments and musicians

cellist · violin · pianist · guitar · saxophonist · drummer · flute
cello · violinist · piano · guitarist · saxophone · drums · flautist (= person who plays flute)

D Art

If you want to see the paintings of a famous artist, you need to go to an **art gallery** or
museum. There you can see individual paintings and sometimes an **exhibition** (= a collection
of paintings by one painter or **school of painters,** e.g. the Impressionists), e.g.

There's a Monet **exhibition** at the National **Gallery** next week.

There are many different types and styles of painting:

a **portrait** (= a painting of a person)
a **self-portrait** (= a painting of the artist by himself/herself)
a **landscape** (= a painting of part of the countryside)
an **abstract painting** (= a painting that is not realistic)

Exercises

73.1 What are or were these people? (painter? sculptor? novelist? poet? dramatist? songwriter? composer? conductor? rock star? pop star? musician? singer? pianist? etc.) Some of them may be more than one of these things.

1 Leo Tolstoy
2 William Wordsworth
3 Henrik Ibsen
4 Yukio Mishima
5 Anton Chekhov
6 Wolfgang Amadeus Mozart

7 Giuseppe Verdi
8 Mick Jagger
9 Milton Nascimento
10 Paul Tortelier
11 Paul Simon
12 Mark Knopfler

13 Henry Moore
14 Jorge Luis Borges
15 Pablo Picasso
16 Saki
17 Leonard Bernstein
18 Alberto Giacometti

73.2 What do you call the people who play the following instruments?

piano   guitar   drums   violin   cello   flute

73.3 What types of painting are these?

1

2

3

73.4 Use the context and your own knowledge to fill the gaps in these sentences and dialogues.

1 He used to be conductor of the Berlin Philharmonic ....
2 Phil Collins was in a famous .... called *Genesis* before he became a
....
3 A: Do you like .... music?
B: Yes, very much.
A: And who's your favourite .... ?
B: It's hard to say, but I love Bach and Vivaldi.
4 There's going to be an .... of his paintings at the new art ....
5 She used to .... her own songs but now she mainly .... material written by other people.
6 I haven't been to the .... since I saw *The Marriage of Figaro* last year.
7 I think *The Great Gatsby* is Scott Fitzgerald's best ....
8 His first .... was performed in a very small theatre.

74 Newspapers

A Background

In Britain, most newspapers are **daily** (= they **come out** / **are published** every day); a few only come out on Sundays. Magazines are usually **weekly** (= they come out every week), or **monthly** (= published every month).

Some newspapers are **tabloids** (= small in size) e.g. *The Mirror*; others are called **broadsheets** (= larger in size) e.g. *The Times*. In general, the tabloids represent the **popular press** (short articles and lots of pictures) and the broadsheets represent the **quality press** (longer articles and more 'serious'). The largest **circulation** (= number of readers) is *The Sun*.

B Contents

Most British papers contain the following:

home news (= news about Britain)
foreign/international news (= news about other countries)
business news
sports news
features (= longer articles about special subjects, e.g. a famous person or a political issue)
radio and TV programmes
weather forecast (= tells you what the weather will be like)
reviews (= when film, theatre and music **critics** write about new films, plays and records, and give their opinion of them)

C People

Editor: the person in control of the daily production.
Reporters/journalists: people who report news and write articles; many journalists are **freelance** (= they work for themselves and are not employed by the newspaper).

D Headlines

Certain words (usually very short) are often used in newspaper headlines. Here are some:

row (pronounced like 'cow') (= an argument)   **back** (= to support)
quit (= to leave a job)   **hit** (= to affect badly)
bid (n, v) (= an effort / a try / an attempt)   **talks** (= discussions)
cut (v, n) (= to reduce / make less)   **key** (= very important)

E 'It said in the paper that ...'

When we refer to something in a newspaper we can use the verb **say** (NOT ~~write~~), or the expression **according to**:

It **says** in *The Times* that they've found the missing girl.
According to *The Guardian*, the missing girl was found last night.

Exercises

74.1 Think about newspapers in your own country. Answer these questions.

1 How many daily national newspapers are there?
2 How many are tabloids?
3 Are any of the 'quality' papers in tabloid form?
4 How many broadsheets are there?
5 How many newspapers *only* come out on Sunday in your country?
6 Which newspaper has the largest circulation?
7 Can you name at least one editor of a daily paper; and two or three famous journalists who write for daily or weekly papers?
8 How often do you read the newspaper? How often do you buy a newspaper?

74.2 Explain these headlines in your own words. Do not use the underlined words.

1 **Minister to quit**

2 **Government cuts spending on new hospitals**

3 **New bid to cut teenage smoking**

4 **Bad weather hits farmers**

5 **Germany backs US plan**

6 **Ministers in tax row**

7 **POLICE DISCOVER KEY WITNESS**

8 **Japan and US enter fresh talks**

74.3 Buy two different newspapers (in English or your own language) and complete this table.

	Paper 1 (no. of pages)	*Paper 2* (no. of pages)
home news foreign/international news feature articles business news sports news		

For the same two papers complete this table.

	Paper 1 (yes/no)	*Paper 2* (yes/no)
weather forecast cartoons crossword radio and TV programmes reviews		

How many pages are left? What are they about? If possible, compare answers with a friend.

75 Television

A Operating a television

| plug it in | turn it on (≠ turn it off) | remote control |

You may also want to **turn** it **up** (= increase the volume because you can't hear) (≠ **turn** it **down**); and **turn over** (= change to a different **channel**, e.g. from 1 to 3)

Note: You can also say **switch on, switch off,** or **switch over** (but *not* switch it up/down).

B Types of programme

Here are some types of TV programme:

Soap opera: a programme often on two or three times a week, which follows the lives of a group/community of people; the stories are often exciting, dramatic and hard to believe.

Quiz show or **Game show:** individuals, teams or families who answer questions or play different games against each other. The winner gets a **prize,** e.g. a car, a holiday, money.

Chat show: a programme where a presenter talks to famous people about their lives and careers; sometimes there is music as well.

Documentary: a film with factual information, often analysing a problem in society.

A series: a number of programmes about the same situation or the same characters in different situations. This may be a **comedy series** (the programmes are intended to be funny), or a **drama series** (the programmes are intended to be exciting, with interesting characters and situations).

Current affairs programme: a programme about a current social/political problem. **Current** means that it is happening 'now / at the present time'.

C TV in Great Britain

At the moment there are five 'terrestrial' **channels** (or **stations**) on TV (BBC 1, BBC 2, ITV, Channel 4, and Channel 5). If you pay extra, you can have a **satellite dish** and receive **satellite TV;** or pay to have **cable TV** – there are many channels available.

D Talking TV

Here are some useful words and phrases connected with television:

What's **on** TV tonight? (= what programmes are showing on TV tonight?)
What time's the film **on?** (= what time does it start?)
How long do the **commercials last?** (= the advertisements between programmes)
What's your **favourite** programme? (= the programme you like most/best)
Are they showing the game **live** (= as it happens) or just **recorded highlights?** (= parts of the game after it has been played, e.g. later in the day/evening)
How much is a TV **licence?** (= money you have to pay the government if you have a TV)

Exercises

75.1 You are watching TV with a friend. What could you say in each of the situations below? Look at the example first.

Example: You want to watch a programme on TV.   Could you ..*turn the TV on?*...

1 You can't hear the programme very well.   Could you ....?
2 You want to watch a different programme.   Could you ....?
3 Now it's too loud for you.   Could you ....?
4 You don't want to watch any more.   Could you ....?

75.2 Here is part of an evening from three British TV channels. Can you find at least one example of: a documentary, a quiz show, a game show, a drama series, and a current affairs programme? There is also one example of a comedy series and two soap operas. Can you guess which programmes they might be?

7.00 Telly Addicts
Noel Edmonds hosts the quiz in which teams have their television knowledge put to the test.

7.30 Watchdog
Anne Robinson presents the stories that affect consumers in the 1990s. With Alice Beer and reporters Chris Choi and Johnathan Maitland.

8.00 EastEnders
Kathy tries to come to terms with Ted's revelations. Michelle receives a letter that could change her life.
For cast see Tuesday
Stereo   Subtitled 5500

8.30 2 Point 4 Children
The Deep. There's something fishy going on when Bill and Ben are asked to look after their neighbour's house.

9.00 Nine O'Clock News
With Peter Sissons.
Subtitled
Regional News
Weather Rob McElwee 3245

7.00 The Krypton Factor
Four new contestants compete for a place in the November final.
Director Tony Prescott; Producer Wayne Garvie   *Stereo   Subtitled* 9448

7.30 Coronation Street
It's farewell time at the Rovers.
Episode written by Stephen Mallatratt
For cast see Wednesday. Repeated on Wednesday at 1.25pm   Subtitled *239*
◆ **Bet's off:** page 22

8.00 Bruce's Price Is Right
Game show testing knowledge of the price of consumer goods.
Director Bill Morton; Producer Howard Huntridge   *Stereo   Subtitled* 2968

8.30 World in Action
In a classroom fitted with cameras, World in Action reveals what is really going on in Britain's overcrowded schools and asks who is to blame.

9.00 New series Cracker
Brotherly Love (part 1). In the first of this three-part thriller, a prostitute is found raped and murdered, opening old wounds at the station. See today's choices.

7.00 Channel 4 News
Presented by Jon Snow and Cathy Smith. Including **Weather**
Subtitled *829535*

7.55 The Slot
The daily soapbox offering viewers the chance to air their opinions.
Stereo *141603*

8.00 New series Desperately Seeking Something
A four-part series in which Pete McCarthy explores the strange universe of alternative beliefs.

8.30 Baby It's You
Continuing the six-part series which uses natural history filming techniques to observe the first two years of a baby's life.

9.00 Cutting Edge
The Trouble with Money
Strange though it seems to some, not everyone enjoys winning the lottery. This documentary explores the joys and pitfalls of getting rich quick.

75.3 Answer these questions about TV in your own country.

1 How many 'terrestrial 'channels are there?
2 Do you watch satellite TV and/or cable TV?
3 In total, how much TV do you watch every week?
4 What are your favourite programmes on TV at the moment?
5 What night are they on?
6 Do you enjoy watching the commercials?
7 Do you often watch football matches live on TV? If not, do you watch the highlights?
8 Do you need a TV licence in your country? If so, how much is it?

76 On the phone

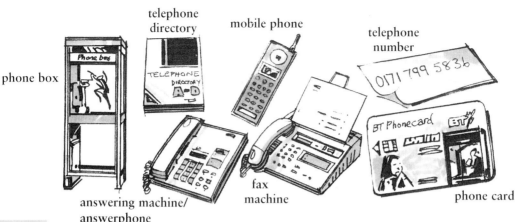

phone box · telephone directory · mobile phone · telephone number · 0171 799 5836 · BT Phonecard BT · fax machine · answering machine/ answerphone · phone card

A Starting a phone conversation

The first example is an informal situation; the second example is a more formal call.

A: Hello.
B: **Is that** Mary? [NOT ~~Are you Mary?~~ or ~~Is it Mary?~~]
A: Yeah.
B: Hi. **It's** Ruth. [NOT ~~I am Ruth~~, or ~~Here is Ruth~~]

Note: When British people answer the phone at home they usually just say 'hello' and sometimes they also give their number. They do not give their name.

C: Good morning. Chalfont Electronics.
D: Oh good morning. **Could I speak to** Mrs Gordon, please?
C: Yes. **Who's calling**, please?
D: **My name is** Paul Scott. (This is usually how you introduce yourself in a formal situation.)
C: Right, Mr Scott. I'll **put you through**. (= I will connect you with Mrs Gordon)

B Telephone problems

4.20 p.m   You try to phone your sister Susan but the **line is engaged** (= the line is busy). In other words, someone is already **on the phone** (= using the phone).

4.30 p.m.   You phone your sister again but it's the **wrong number** (= you have **dialled** another number, e.g. 637 424 and not 627 424, and a stranger answers).

4.35 p.m.   You **get through to** your sister's number (= make contact) but she's **out** (= not at home). Her husband answers and says that Susan **won't be back** (= will not return) for a couple of hours, so you **leave a message**, e.g. Could you ask Susan to ring me when she gets back? The husband agrees to give Susan the message.

7.30 p.m.   Susan **phones** you **back** but you are out. She leaves a message on your answerphone. Her message is: Jean, this is Susan. I'm just returning your **call** (= phone call). I'll **give you a ring** (= phone you) tomorrow.

C Useful vocabulary

A **reverse charge call** (AmEng = **collect call**). This is when the person you ring agrees to pay for the phone call. If you **make a reverse charge call**, you must go through the **operator**. If you have someone's name and address, you can call **Directory Enquiries** to get their phone number. If you phone another town or city, you need to know the **code**, e.g. the code for Cambridge is 01223. This type of call is a **long distance call** (≠ a **local call**).

Exercises

76.1 Write down five words or expressions including the word 'phone' or 'telephone'.

76.2 Fill the gaps in these phone conversations with suitable words or phrases.

A A: Good morning. Boulding Limited. Can I help you?

    B: Yes. (1)............................ Paul Mathews and I'm trying to contact Mr Patterson. He actually left a (2)............................ on my answerphone yesterday afternoon.

    A: I see. Well, I'm afraid Mr Patterson's (3)............................ at the moment. Can I ask him to (4)............................ later?

    B: Yes please. I shall be here until lunchtime. My (5)............................ is 748 7267.

B A: Hello.

    B: Hi. (6)............................ Sandra?

    A: No, sorry. I'm (7)............................ Sandra's not here at the moment.

    B: Oh. Do you know when she'll (8)............................?

    A: No, I've no idea.

    B: OK. Well in that case, could I (9)............................ a .... for her?

    A: Yes, of course.

    B: Could you ask her to (10)............................ this evening, please?

    A: Sure. What's your name?

    B: Catherine. I'm a colleague from work. She's got my number.

    A: Right. I'll tell her.

    B: Thanks very much. Bye bye.

    A: Bye.

C A: Hello?

    B: (11)............................ Carlos?

    A: Yeah, speaking.

    B: Hi Carlos. (12)............................ Serena.

    A: Oh hello. I was expecting you to ring yesterday.

    B: I did – or at least I tried. I (13)............................ your number about six times last night but I couldn't (14)............................. It was (15)............................ all the time.

    A: Oh yes, I'm sorry about that. I was (16)............................ the phone to my brother for about an hour and then someone from school rang me about the table tennis tournament next week.

    B: Oh well, never mind. Anyway I'm phoning about …

76.3 Can you answer these questions?

1 In your country, what is the emergency number for the police, fire brigade or ambulance?
2 Is there a Directory Enquiries? What number is it?
3 From your country, what's the dialling code for the United Kingdom?
4 How much does it cost to make a local call?
5 How often do you have to pay your phone bill?
6 Is it cheaper to phone during the night?
7 What's the phone number of your English school?
8 Have you ever made a reverse charge call? If so, who was it to?

If possible, compare and discuss your answers with someone from the same country.

77 Computers

A Hardware

VDU (monitor)

laser printer

screen

central processing
unit (= the heart
of the computer)

keyboard

mouse

laptop

As well as the **hardware** (= the machines), you also need **software** (= the programs needed to work the machines). These programs are on **disks**, e.g. the **hard disk** inside the computer, or **floppy disks** or on CD-ROMs (= Compact Disc Read Only Memory, a CD on which you can put a large amount of information).

B Operating a computer

Using the **mouse**, you can do a number of things by **clicking on** different **icons** (= moving the mouse to point at different pictures at the top of the screen).

open a new
document

open an existing
document

save the data
in this document

print   cut   copy   paste

C What do people use computers for?

A **word processor** is a computer used to prepare documents or letters, or the software that is used for this purpose. Many people use their computers for **word processing**, e.g. writing letters and reports. A lot of business people use **spreadsheets** (= a program used to enter and arrange numbers and financial information) and **databases** (= programs which allow you to store, look at or change a large amount of information quickly and easily). Some people also use **graphics** (= the pictures and symbols a computer program can produce).

D Important vocabulary

More and more people are becoming **computer-literate** (= have experience of working with computers and know how to use them) as many programs and machines are so **user-friendly** (= easy to use). You can now connect your computer to computers all over the world using the **Internet** (= a system that allows computers to connect using telephone lines). People send each other **e-mail** (electronic mail) messages using this system or **network**.
If your computer is slow it may need more **memory**. It may **crash** (= stop working) if there is not enough memory or if it has a **bug** (= a software problem; also a **virus**). Make sure you make a **back-up copy** of your work (= an extra copy on a floppy disk).

Exercises

77.1 Add another word, abbreviation, or part of a word, to complete common 'computer' words and phrases.

1 soft..........
2 a word ....
3 floppy ....
4 ....-friendly
5 ....-literate
6 key..........

7 a computer ....
8 ....-ROM
9 laser ....
10 lap..........
11 spread..........
12 ....-mail

77.2 Can you remember what these symbols mean?

77.3 Complete this text about using a computer for word processing.

I wrote a report on the (1)_____ this morning. When I finished, I (2)_____ out two copies – one for me and one for my boss. Then, without any warning, the computer went (3)_____, and I'm afraid I lost the whole document. This is very unusual because normally I (4)_____ the data while I'm writing and then make a (5)_____ copy when I have finished; this morning I forgot.

Anyway, I gave the report to my boss, hoping that she would not ask me to change it in any way. She did. She thought it was a bit long and said it would be better if I used more (6)_____ to illustrate some of the written information. She also thought it would make the report look more attractive.

I went back and rewrote most of the report when the computer was OK, only I (7)_____ part of the middle section which was rather repetitive, and I added extra (8)_____ as my boss advised. It did look better by the time I'd finished, and this time I remembered to (9)_____ it and make a (10)_____ copy.

77.4 Answer these questions. If possible, ask someone else the same questions.

1 Do you have a computer at home? If so, what is it?
2 Do you use computers at school/college/university/work? If so, what type?
3 What do you use them for?
4 Would you say you are computer-literate?
5 Do you find most computers user-friendly?
6 What software programs are you familiar with?
7 Do you use e-mail?
8 Have you used CD-ROM? If so, what programs did you use and why?
9 Do you think 'The Internet' will have an important influence on our daily lives? Do you think it will be important in helping people from different countries to learn English?

78 Education: school

A The system

Most children in England and Wales follow this route in the **state system** (= free education).

Age

3   some go to **nursery school**

5   everyone starts **primary school**

11 pupils go to a **secondary** school (AmEng = **high** school). This may be a **comprehensive** (= mixed ability) or a **grammar school** (= children selected for their **academic ability**)

16 they **leave school** and get a job, or go to a college for **vocational** (= job) training, e.g. hotel management, secretarial courses; or **stay at school** for two more years

18 they leave school and get a job or ⟋ **go to university** ⟍ **go to a college** for further education/training, e.g. teaching, business studies.

Note:
- You **go to school** (as a pupil to study) and **go to university** (as a student to study). You don't use the definite article 'the' here. Other expressions like this are **go to bed** (to sleep); **go into hospital** (when you are ill); **go to church** (to pray / to worship).
- In some areas of the UK there are not many grammar schools.
- There are also **public schools**. In fact, these are private, and parents pay to send their children there. Some are expensive. About 5% of the population go to public schools.

B A school timetable

	MON	TUES	WED	THURS	FRI
Lesson 1	Religious Education	Maths	Social Education	English	Visual Art
(break)					
Lesson 2	History	Science	Music	Science	Geography
Lesson 3	English		French	Physical Education (PE)	Maths
(lunch)					
Lesson 4	Maths*	History	Information Technology	Maths	Physical Education
Lesson 5	Geography	Visual Art		French	English

* Maths is an abbreviation of mathematics.

As you can see, the **pupils** have five **lessons** every day, and altogether they do (= study) eleven **subjects** a week plus Physical Education (PE). Every morning they have a twenty-minute **break**. There are three **terms** (= periods of continuous work) in a school year, and the timetable changes every year.

Note: Some words in English which end in 's' look plural, but in fact they are singular:

Maths **isn't** my favourite subject, and physics **is** very difficult.

Most nouns of this type refer to subjects; other examples are **economics** and **politics**.

Exercises

78.1   Here are some school subjects but the letters are mixed up. What are the subjects?

Example: MGREAN   *German*

1 TAHMS ....
2 IRTHOSY ....
3 CNECSEI ....
4 NISGEHL ....
5 HOGTCEYNLO ....
6 EHGORAGPY ....
7 RAT ....
8 SIMCU ....
9 EHNFCR ....
10 NEOCCIOSM ....

78.2   How much can you remember? Try to answer these questions or complete the sentences without looking at the opposite page.

1 At what age do children go to nursery school?
2 At what age do they start primary school?
3 When they go to secondary school it is either a grammar school or a ....
4 At what age can English and Welsh children leave school?
5 According to the timetable the foreign languages studied is ....
6 Not including PE, how many subjects do the children do?
7 What happens if children fail all the exams they take at the age of 16?
8 What can they do if they pass all their exams at the age of 18?

78.3   What about you and your country? Answer these questions.

1 Did you go to nursery school?
2 Do most children start primary school at the age of five?
3 Is the secondary school system similar or different?
4 How many subjects did/do you study at secondary school?
5 Did/do you study any subjects which are not included opposite?
6 What was/is your favourite subject?
7 How many lessons did/do you have every day?
8 Is/was your school a state school or public school?
9 At what age can you leave school?
10 How many terms are there in a school year?

78.4   Complete these sentences with the correct expression.

1 When she was a child she went .... in a small village with only fifty other pupils.
2 He didn't go to school last term because he was very ill and he had to go ....
3 I was very tired, so after I finished my homework I went ....
4 When I left school I went .... and studied medicine.
5 It was a religious school, so we had to go .... quite a lot.

78.5   The next unit is about university and further education. Can you think of six subjects you can study at university which you do not usually study at school? Write down your answers, then turn to the next page.

79 Education: university

A Subjects

You can normally **do/study** these **subjects** at university but not always at school:

medicine   law   philosophy   engineering
psychology   sociology   architecture   politics
business studies   agriculture   history of art

Note: The underlined letters in some of the words above show the syllable with the main stress. Also note that the first syllable of **psychology** is pronounced /saɪ/ like 'my'.

B Studying at university (in England and Wales)

If you want to **go to** (= **enter** *fml*) university, you must first **pass examinations** that most students take at the age of eighteen (called 'A' levels). Most students take three 'A' levels (three examinations in three different subjects) and they must do well in order to **get/obtain** a place at university because the places are limited. At the moment, approximately 30% of young adults go to university in Britain.

If you get a place at university, the **tuition** (= the teaching) is free, and some students also **get** (= receive) a **grant** (= money to pay for living expenses, e.g. food and accommodation) as well. Students at university are called **undergraduates** while they are studying for their first degree.

Most university courses **last** (= go on for / continue for) three years, some courses last four years, and one or two courses, e.g. medicine, may be even longer. During this period students can say that they are **doing/studying** history, or **doing / studying for** a degree in history, for example. When they finish the course and pass their examinations, they receive **a degree** (the qualification when you complete a university course successfully). This can be a **BA** (= Bachelor of Arts) or a **BSc** (= Bachelor of Science), e.g. I have a friend who has a BA in history, and another who has a BSc in chemistry.

C Postgraduate courses

When you complete your first degree, you are a **graduate**. (In the US, students also use this word as a verb and say, they 'graduated in history' or 'graduated in chemistry', for example.) Some students then go on to do a second course or degree (**postgraduate course / postgraduate degree**). These students are then **postgraduates**. There are usually three possible degrees:

MA (Master of Arts) or MSc (Master of Science); usually one year
MPhil (Master of Philosophy); usually two years
PhD (Doctor of Philosophy); at least three years

When people study one subject in great detail (often to find new information), we say they are **conducting / doing / carrying out research** (U); e.g.

I'm **doing** some **research into/on** the languages of different African tribes.

D School vs. university

At school, you have **teachers** and **lessons**, at university, you have **lecturers** and **lectures**. When a lecturer **gives/does** a lecture, the students listen and **take/make notes** (= write down the important information), but do not usually say much, except to ask occasional questions.

Exercises

79.1 Read these sentences spoken by university students. What is each person studying?

1 We have to know every bone in a person's body.
2 I'm concentrating on the modernist style and the work of Le Corbusier and Frank Lloyd Wright.
3 The way we use fertilizers is much more precise than twenty years ago.
4 We're going to concentrate on Freud and Jung this term.
5 I've been reading some books on time management.
6 Expressionism was really a reaction to the work of the Impressionists.
7 We 've spent a lot of time on American foreign policy and how it has been affected by various domestic problems.
8 You must know this case – it's one of the most famous in legal history.

Now mark the stress on each of your answers, check with the answer key, and practise saying the words.

79.2 What do you call:

1 the money some students receive if they get a place at university?
2 the qualification you get at the end of university?
3 the name we give students during this period at university?
4 teachers at university?
5 students when they have completed their first degree?
6 students studying for a second degree?
7 the study of one subject in great depth and detail, often to get new information?
8 the talks that students go to while they are at university?

79.3 Replace the underlined verbs with different verbs that have the same meaning in the context.

1 Who is <u>giving</u> the lecture today?
2 Did she <u>receive</u> a grant for her course?
3 Is it more difficult to <u>obtain</u> a place at university?
4 You have to pass the exams before you can <u>enter</u> university.
5 He's <u>studying</u> physics, I think.
6 I think they're <u>carrying out</u> some research into the cause of asthma.
7 I didn't <u>take</u> any notes in the lecture yesterday.
8 The course <u>goes on</u> for three years.

79.4 How similar is university education in your own country? Answer these questions. If possible, compare your answers with someone else from your own country and/or someone from a different country.

1 Do you need to pass examinations before you can go to university?
2 Do some students get a grant to study at university?
3 Is the tuition free if you go to university?
4 Do most students go to university at the age of 18 or 19?
5 Do more students go to university in your country than in Britain?
6 Do most degree courses last three years?
7 What is your equivalent of the British BA or BSc?
8 Do you have similar postgraduate degrees in your country?

80 Law and order

A The police

They do a number of things. When someone **commits a crime** (= **breaks the law** and does something **wrong / illegal / against the law**) the police must **investigate** (= try to find out what happened / who is responsible). If they find the person responsible for the crime, they **arrest** them (= take them to the police station). At the police station, they **question** them (= ask them questions to find out what they know) and if they are sure the person committed the crime, the person is **charged with** the crime (= the police make an official statement that they believe the person committed the crime). The person must then go to **court** for **trial**.

B The court

court

judge

barrister
(AmEng
= attorney)

jury

defendant

In **court,** the person charged with the crime (now called the **defendant** or **accused**) must try to **prove** (= provide facts to show something is true) that they did not commit the crime; in other words prove that they are **innocent** (≠ **guilty**). The **jury** listens to all the **evidence** (= information about the crime, for and against the defendant) and then makes their decision.

C Punishment

If the defendant is **convicted of** the crime (= the jury decides that the defendant is guilty), the judge will give the **sentence** (= the punishment). For example, if a person is convicted of murder, the sentence will be many years in **prison**. The person then becomes a **prisoner**, and the room they live in is called a **cell**.

For crimes that are not serious (often called **minor offences**, e.g. illegal parking), the punishment is usually **a fine** (= money you have to pay).

Exercises

80.1 Put this story in the correct order.

1 they found both men guilty.
2 and charged them with the robbery.
3 £10,000 was stolen from a bank in the High Street.
4 After the jury had listened to all the evidence
5 They were sent to prison for seven years.
6 The trial took place two months later.
7 and they finally arrested two men.
8 They questioned them at the police station
9 The police questioned a number of people about the crime

80.2 Answer the questions.

1 Who investigates crimes?
2 Who sentences people?
3 Who live in cells?
4 Who decides if someone is innocent or guilty?
5 Who defend people and present evidence?
6 Who commit crimes?

80.3 Fill the gaps with suitable words.

1 I have never .... the law and .... a crime.
2 In Britain it is .... the law to drive a car without insurance.
3 If you park illegally you will have to pay a ....
4 The police were fairly sure the man committed the crime, but they knew it would be
   difficult to .... it in court.
5 The jury must decide if the accused is innocent or ....
6 In order to reach their decision, the jury must listen carefully to the ....
7 If the accused is .... of murder, the .... may be at least ten years in
   prison.
8 He has been in trouble with the police once before, but it was only a minor ....

80.4 Read this short story, then write down your response to the questions below, based on your
knowledge of the law in your own country.

> Two fifteen-year-old boys broke into a house in the middle
> of the day when the owner was out, and took money and
> jewellery worth about £900. The owner reported the crime
> to the police when she returned home at 6 p.m.

1 Will the police investigate this crime?
2 How will they investigate? What will they do?
3 Do you think the police will catch the two boys?
4 If they do, what crime will they be charged with?
5 Can the boys be sent to prison?
6 What do you think the sentence would be? Do you think this is the correct sentence?

**Compare your answers with the answer key (based on the situation in the United Kingdom).
If possible, discuss your answers with someone else.**

81 Crime

A Against the law

If you do something **illegal** (= wrong / **against the law**), then you have **committed a crime**. Most people commit a crime at some time in their lives, e.g. driving above the speed limit, parking illegally, stealing sweets from a shop when they were children, etc.

B Crimes

Crime	Criminal (= person)	Verb
theft (= general word for stealing)	thief	steal (also **take**)
robbery (= steal from people or places)	robber	rob
burglary (= **break into** a shop/house and steal things)	burglar	burgle / break into
shoplifting (= steal from shops when open)	shoplifter	shoplift
murder (= kill someone by intention)	murderer	murder
manslaughter (= kill someone by accident)	–	–
rape (= force someone to have sex)	rapist	rape

C Crime prevention

What can governments do to **fight** crime (= take action to stop crime)? These things happen in some countries, although many people may think they are not a good idea.

Police **carry** (= have) guns.
Police **are allowed to** (= are permitted to) stop anyone in the street and question them.
The courts give **tougher punishments** for crimes committed than in the past (e.g. bigger fines or longer prison sentences than in the past).
There is **capital punishment** (= death, e.g. by electric chair or hanging) for some crimes.

What can individuals do to **prevent** a crime **from** happening (= stop a crime happening)?
Here are things some people do to **protect themselves** and their **property** (= home and land), although you may not think they are all a good idea.

Don't walk along dark streets **late at night** (e.g. midnight) **on your own** (= alone).
Lock all doors and windows when you go out.
Don't wear expensive jewellery.
Leave lights **on** at home when you go out.
Fit (= install) a **burglar alarm** (= a machine which makes a noise if someone enters your home).

Make sure your money is safe, e.g. wear a **money belt**.

Carry a mace **spray**. (This is a chemical and if you spray it in someone's face, it is very unpleasant. In some countries you are allowed to carry this type of spray.)

Put money and **valuables** (= valuable possessions) in a **safe** (= a strong metal box, which is very difficult to open or break).

Keep a gun in your house for **self-defence** (= to protect yourself if someone attacks you).

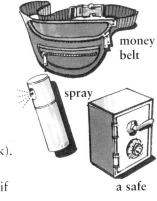

money belt

spray

a safe

Exercises

These exercises also revise some vocabulary from Unit 80.

81.1 Organise the words in the box into three groups: crimes, people, and places.

murder	thief	prison	barrister	robbery
burglar	cell	criminal	court	rape	shoplifting
manslaughter	judge	prisoner	jury	police station

81.2 Respond to these statements or questions confirming the crime in each one.

1 A: He broke into the house, didn't he?
   B: Yes, he's been charged with ....
2 A: He killed his wife?
   B: Yes, he's been charged ....
3 A: She stole clothes and jewellery from that department store, didn't she?
   B: Yes, and she's been ....
4 A: The man on the motorbike didn't mean to kill the boy.
   B: No, but he's been charged ....
5 A: He took the money from her bag?
   B: Yes, but they caught him and he's been ....

81.3 How safe and secure are you? Answer these questions, *yes* or *no*.

1 Do you often walk in areas which are not very safe? *yes* = 1 *no* = 0
2 Do you often walk on your own in these areas late at night? *yes* = 2 *no* = 0
3 Do you wear a money belt when you go out? *yes* = 0 *no* = 1
4 Do you wear an expensive watch or expensive jewellery? *yes* = 1 *no* = 0
5 Do you check doors and windows before you go out when your home is empty? *yes* = 0 *no* = 2
6 Do you have a burglar alarm? *yes* = 0 *no* = 1
7 Do you leave lights on when you go out? *yes* = 0 *no* = 1
8 Is there someone who protects the building while you are out? *yes* = 0 *no* = 2
9 Do you have a safe in your home? *yes* = 0 *no* = 1

Now add up your score: less than 3 = very, very safe; 3–5 = quite safe; 6–8 = you could take a lot more care; more than 8 = you are a dangerous person to know!

81.4 Fill the gaps in these questions with a suitable word.

1 Do you think the police should ...carry... guns?
2 Do you think the police should be ...take... to stop and question people without a special reason?
3 Do you agree with capital .... for certain crimes such as murder?
4 Do you think it should be legal for people to carry a mace ....?
5 Do you think people should be allowed to use a gun or knife in self-.....................?
6 Do you think tougher punishments will help to .... crime?

What is your opinion on these questions? Discuss them with another person if possible.

82 Politics

A Types of government

Monarchy: a state ruled by a king or queen. There are also countries that have a monarchy, but the monarch is not the ruler, e.g. The United Kingdom.

Republic: a state governed by **representatives** (= men or women chosen by the people) and a president, e.g. USA or France. People who believe in this system are **republicans**.

Democracy: a system of government in which leaders are chosen by the people, e.g. France or the UK. People who believe in this system are **democrats**.

Dictatorship: a system of government in which one person rules the country (= one person has total power). This person is called a **dictator**.

B Political beliefs

Abstract noun	*Personal noun/adjective*
conservatism	conservative
socialism	socialist
social democracy	social democrat
liberalism	liberal
communism	communist
fascism	fascist

People who believe in **social democracy** are **social democrats**.

C Political positions

What does it mean to be a **socialist** or a **conservative**? Often, it means different things in different countries, but in Britain we often talk about someone's political position like this:

left-wing / on the left   **middle of the road /**   **right-wing / on the right**
(= socialist)   **in the centre** (= liberal)   (= conservative)

D Elections

In a democracy, people **vote for** (= they choose in a formal way / **elect**) the **political party** (e.g. conservatives, liberals or socialists) that they want to **form** (= make) the government. They do this in an **election**, and in many countries elections **take place / are held** (= they happen) every four or five years.

42% **voted for** the socialists in the last **election** (= the socialists got 42% of the **votes**). The president **was elected** two years ago.

E Government

Political systems are different all over the world. In the UK, when a political party wins a **majority** (= 51% or more) of **seats** (= official positions in parliament) in an election, they become the government of the country, their **leader** (= the head of the party / person in control) becomes **Prime Minister** and they are **in power**.

The government must have **policies** (= programmes of action) to **run** (= manage) the country. This means, for example, an **economic policy** (for the economy), and a **foreign policy** (for actions taken by the country in other parts of the world).

Exercises

82.1 Complete this word-building table. Use a dictionary to help you if necessary.

Abstract noun	Person	Adjective
politics democracy dictatorship socialism conservatism liberalism		

82.2 Fill the gaps to complete this text about the political system in the United Kingdom. One word in each gap.

In the UK (1) _election_ are held every five years. (The (2) _Prime_ Minister may decide to hold one after four years, but five years is the maximum.)
Some countries have a system of proportional representation: this means in theory, that a political party with 30% of the (3)_____ should get 30% of the seats in (4)_____ . In the UK, the political (5)_____ is different: here the winner takes all. This means that the person with the most votes in each political area (called a constituency) wins the seat; and the political (6)_____ which wins a (7)_____ of the seats will (8)_____ the government on their own. As a result of this system, it is possible for a party to be in (9)_____ with only 40% of the total vote. Some people think this system is unfair.

What do you think? What possible reasons could there be to justify (= support) this system? Think about your answer, then compare it with the ideas suggested in the key.

82.3 Answer these questions about your own country. If possible, ask someone else the same questions.

1 Which party is in power at the moment?
2 When were they elected?
3 Who is the leader of this party?
4 Is this person the President or Prime Minister of your country?
5 Do you agree with most of their policies?
6 Would you describe yourself as left-wing, right-wing, or in the centre?
7 Do you think your political views have changed much during your lifetime?
8 How many major (= important) political parties are there?
9 Who did you vote for in the last election?
10 Do you think this party will win the next election? Will you vote for them again?

82.4 You can increase your English vocabulary in politics quite easily:

Buy three newspapers (in English if you are in an English speaking country, or your own language if you are in your own country), and find the same political story in each one. Read the articles and underline any words that appear in all of them, and any other words you think are important. If you are reading a newspaper in English, try to guess the meaning of these words and then use a dictionary to check.

This exercise is equally useful if you read articles in your own language. You use a bilingual dictionary to find the English translation/explanation for your underlined words, and you can then look up these words in a monolingual dictionary as well.

83 Bureaucracy

A What is it?

Bureaucracy refers to the official rules and procedures used by officials (= **bureaucrats**) to control an organisation or country. For many people it is a negative word as it often means unnecessary rules, long waits, and lots of documents and forms.

B Documents

When you need to **obtain** (= get) or show documents, it is important that you know the names of them. Here are some important ones:

passport

identity card: a card with your name, date of birth and photo to show who you are. Great Britain is one of the few countries where people still do not have identity cards.

driving licence: the official document which permits you to drive on public roads.

visa: this gives you permission to enter, pass through or leave a country.

certificates: official pieces of paper stating certain facts, e.g. a **birth certificate** gives facts about your birth, and **exam certificates** state you have passed certain exams.

Officials often **check** (= look at and examine) your documents, e.g. the police may check your driving licence; passport officials may check your identity card.

Some of these documents are for a fixed period of time, e.g. a visa may be for six months. At the end of that time, your visa **runs out** (*infml*) / **expires** (*fml*) (= it finishes / comes to an end). If you want to stay in the country you must **renew** it (= have a new one for a further period of time). You can renew a visa, a passport, a membership card for a club, etc.

C Forms

There are also situations where you need to **fill in** (= complete) forms. Here are some:

landing card: a form you may have to fill in when you enter another country.

enrolment form: a form you often fill in when you do a course, go to a school or college, etc. It may also be called a **registration form**.

application form: a form to write details of yourself, often when applying for a job.

With almost all forms, you will need to **sign** them (= write your **signature**), e.g:

signed *Judy Allingham*

D Formal language

Here are some formal written expressions and their spoken English meanings.

Written	*Spoken*
date of birth	= When were you born?
country of origin	= Where do you come from?
marital status	= Are you single or married?
date of arrival	= When did you arrive?
date of departure	= When are you leaving?(*or* when did you leave?)

E Bureaucratic problems

We often associate bureaucracy with problems. For example, you may have to **queue** (v, n) (= wait in a line) to get an official piece of paper or have it **stamped**.

Exercises

83.1 Write down at least two words which can be used before these nouns.

1 .... card

3 .... licence

....

2 .... certificate

4 .... form

....

83.2 Complete these sentences with a suitable word.

1 Will you need to ...*have*..... a visa if you go to the United States?
2 I was surprised that nobody .... my passport when we arrived in France.
3 Could you .... this form, please?
4 They sent the form back to me because I had forgotten to .... it at the bottom.
5 I'm afraid my visa .... next week, so if I want to stay here I will have to .... it. But I don't think it'll be a problem.
6 You should get there early because there are always long ...., and you may have to wait quite a long time.
7 I want to do an English course in London, so I wrote to a few schools and asked them to send me an .... form.

83.3 How many of these documents do you have?

a passport	an identity card
a driving licence	a TV licence
a birth certificate	a degree certificate (from a university)
a marriage certificate	an exam certificate for an English exam, e.g. Cambridge, Oxford or ARELS

83.4 Complete these sentences with a suitable paraphrase.

1 What's your date of birth? In other words, when ....?
2 What's your country of origin? ....?
3 What's your marital status? ....?
4 What was your date of arrival? ....?
5 When's your date of departure? ....?

83.5 I asked some English people what they felt about bureaucracy and also about problems they had had with bureaucracy. What about you? How do you feel? Have you had any problems? Write down your thoughts and problems, then compare them with the replies from British people in the answer key.

1 ....
2 ....
3 ....

84 War and peace

A The outbreak (= start) of war

Wars often start because of a **conflict** (= strong disagreement) between countries or groups of people, about **territory** (= land that belongs to one group or country). Look at the diagram on the right and read the text on the left.

Country A **invades** country B (= A enters B by force and in large numbers), and **captures** (also **takes** / **takes control of**) the city of X. Soldiers from country B have to **retreat** (= go backwards; ≠ to advance) to the city of Y. A's army and air force continue to **attack** the city of Y (= take violent action to damage it), but B's soldiers **defend** it (= take action to protect it) successfully.

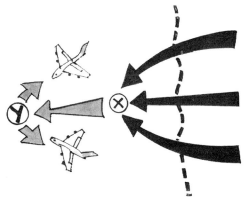

B A war zone

The area around the city of Y is now the main **war zone** (= the area where the fighting is happening). Country B has asked for help from its **allies** (= countries who are friends with country B). The allies send **aid** (= help) in the form of extra **troops** (= large groups of soldiers) and **supplies** (= food and other things that are needed every day, e.g. blankets and medicine) to help. There is **shelling** (= **firing** of **guns** and explosives) of the city every day and hundreds of soldiers are either killed or **wounded** (= injured while fighting). Many **civilians** (= ordinary people who are not in the army) are killed as well.

C Peace talks

For the civilians who are still **alive** (≠ dead), the situation gets worse. As winter approaches, food supplies **run out** (= they are almost gone/finished) and there is no electricity. The soldiers get tired, and both sides begin to see that neither side can win the war; they agree to meet for **peace talks** (*pl*) (= talks to try to negotiate a **peace settlement** / an end to the war). After some time they agree to a **ceasefire** (= a period of no fighting).

D Terrorism

This is violent action for political reasons. People who do this are **terrorists**, and a common terrorist crime is **hijacking** (= to take control of a bus, train, ship or plane; the people on board then become prisoners). The main purpose of hijacking is to use the prisoners (called **hostages**) in order to **bargain** for something (= to demand something in exchange for the hostages). The terrorists may agree to **release** (v, n) the hostages (= permit the hostages to go free) if a government agrees to give the terrorists money or release other terrorists.

Exercises

84.1 Match the words on the left with the correct definition on the right.

1	ally	a	land controlled by a country
2	release	b	stop fighting
3	conflict	c	permit to go free
4	troops	d	injure while fighting
5	invade	e	large groups of soldiers
6	wound	f	friendly country
7	territory	g	strong disagreement
8	ceasefire	h	enter another country by force and in large numbers

84.2 Use opposites to contradict what the speaker says in the sentences below. Look at the example first.

Example: A: Is the soldier <u>dead</u>?
B: No, he's ...*still alive.*...............

1 A: Will they agree to a <u>ceasefire</u>?
   B: No, they'll ....
2 A: Do you think the army will try to <u>advance</u> when the weather improves?
   B: No, I think ....
3 A: Do the people still <u>have lots of</u> food?
   B: No, they're beginning to ....
4 A: Is the town mostly full of <u>soldiers</u>?
   B: No, they're ....
5 A: Do you think they'll <u>keep</u> the hostages for a long time?
   B: No, I'm sure they'll ....

84.3 When we repeat an idea in a text we often try to avoid using the same word twice. Read this text and find examples of words being used as synonyms for previous ideas. The first one has been done for you (food and medicine = supplies).

THERE is a desperate need for <u>food and medicine</u>, but with the town surrounded, the lorries are unable to bring in essential <u>supplies</u>. We have seen ordinary people in the street giving some of their meagre rations of food to the soldiers who are defending them, but very soon the troops will be just as hungry as the civilians if the situation gets any worse.

Meanwhile, the centre of the town is being slowly destroyed. There is almost daily shelling of the buildings that still stand, and this morning we witnessed gunmen firing at almost anyone who dared to go out into the streets. One old woman was hit in the leg and we saw at least two others who were quite badly wounded as well.

Aid agencies have appealed to the soldiers to allow them to enter the town, but so far the General in command has even refused to let anyone in, including doctors and nurses. Many fear it is now only a matter of days before the town is captured, and if this happens, the army could take control of the whole region within weeks.

84.4 Can you answer these questions with two reasons for each one? If possible, discuss your answers with someone else before checking with the key.

1 Why do terrorists take hostages?
2 Why do some governments always refuse to agree to terrorist demands?

85 Pollution and the environment

A Important definitions

People are more worried about the **environment** (= the air, water, and land around us) as a result of the **harmful** (= dangerous/damaging) effects of human activity. Some of these activities cause **pollution** (= dirty air, land and water) and some are **destroying** the environment (= damaging it so badly that soon parts will not exist). Here are some of the problems:

the ozone layer: a layer of gases which stop harmful radiation from the sun reaching the earth; recent research shows that there is now a hole in parts of the ozone layer.
global warming: an increase in world temperature caused by an increase in carbon dioxide.
acid rain: rain that contains dangerous chemicals; this is caused by smoke from factories.

B The 'greens'

Because of these problems, there are many groups of people whose aim is **conservation** (= the **protection** of natural things, e.g. plants and animals). They are often referred to as **greens**, e.g. 'Greenpeace' and 'Friends of the Earth'.

C Common causes of damage

smoke from **factories**

car **exhaust fumes**

dumping (= throwing away) industrial **waste** (= unwanted material) in seas and rivers

aerosol cans (usually called **sprays**). Some of these contain CFCs (= a chemical) which can damage the ozone layer.

cutting down tropical rainforests (e.g. The Amazon). This increases carbon dioxide in the atmosphere.

D How can we help?

- Don't **throw away** bottles, newspapers, etc. Take them to a **bottle bank** or newspaper bank, and then they can be **recycled** (= used again).
- **Plant** more trees.
- Don't **waste** (= use badly) **resources**, e.g. water, gas. Try to **save** (≠ waste) them.

Note: a **resource** is a valuable possession. There are **natural resources**, e.g. water or gold; and **human resources**, e.g. knowledge and skills. The word is usually plural.

Exercises

85.1 Fill the gaps to form a compound noun or phrase from the opposite page.

1 the .... layer
2 .... rain
3 .... waste
4 a bottle ....

5 .... warming
6 .... fumes
7 .... rainforests
8 natural or human ....

85.2 Complete these word-building tables. If necessary, use a dictionary to help you.

Noun	Verb
waste	....
....	protect
....	destroy
pollution	....
damage	....

Noun	Adjective
damage	....
environment	....
harm	....
danger	....
....	safe

85.3 Complete the definitions.

1 Conservation is the protection of natural things, e.g. .... and ....
2 Acid rain is rain that contains dangerous chemicals. It is caused by ....
3 The ozone layer is a layer of gases that stop dangerous radiation from the sun from reaching ....
4 Global warming is an increase in world temperature caused by an increase in ....
  ....
5 CFC (chlorofluorocarbon) is a chemical which ....
  ....

85.4 If we want to look after the environment, there are certain things we should and shouldn't do. Complete these two lists in suitable ways.

We should:
.... paper, bottles and clothes.
.... tropical rainforests.
.... more trees.
.... water and energy.

We shouldn't:
.... paper, bottles and clothes.
.... the ozone layer.
.... water and energy.
.... tropical rainforests.

85.5 Test your knowledge of words from the opposite page and 'green' issues. Are these statements *true* or *false*?

1 CFCs protect the ozone layer.
2 'Greens' believe in conservation.
3 A hole in the ozone layer could increase skin cancer.
4 Cutting down tropical rainforests increases the amount of carbon dioxide in the atmosphere.
5 Plastic cannot be recycled.

86 Air travel

A Departures

This is the usual sequence of activities when you get to the airport.

First you go to the **check-in desk** where they **weigh your luggage**. Usually you are permitted 20 kilos, but if your bags weigh more, you may have to pay **excess baggage** (= you pay extra). The airline representative checks your ticket and gives you a **boarding card** for the plane with your seat number on it. Then you go through **passport control** where an official **checks** [NOT ~~controls~~] your passport, and into the **departure lounge**. Here, you can also buy things in the **duty-free**, e.g. perfume, alcohol and cigarettes. About half an hour or forty minutes before **take-off**, you are told to go to a gate number, e.g. gate 14, where you wait before you **get on** the plane. When you **board** (= get on) the plane, you find your seat. If you have **hand luggage**, you can put it under your seat or in the **overhead locker** above your seat.

The plane then **taxis** (= moves slowly) towards the **runway**, and when it has permission to **take off**, it accelerates along the runway and takes off.

Note: The verb **to taxi** is generally only used in this context.

B The flight

You may want or need to understand certain announcements; these come from the **captain** (= the pilot) or from an **air steward** or **stewardess / cabin crew / flight attendants** (= people who look after the passengers):

Please **fasten your seat belt** and put your seat in the **upright position**.

We are now **cruising** (= flying comfortably) at an **altitude** (= height) of 10,000 metres.

May we **remind** passengers (= ask passengers to remember) that there is no smoking until you are inside the **terminal building** (= where passengers arrive and depart).

The **cabin crew** (= air stewards) are now coming round with **landing cards**. (These are cards you sometimes have to fill in when you enter certain countries.)

C Arrival

When the plane **lands** (= arrives on the ground), you have to wait for it to stop / come to a halt. When the doors are open, you **get off** the plane and walk through the **terminal building** and go to the **baggage reclaim** where you collect your luggage. You then **pass through customs** (green = nothing to declare; red = goods to declare; blue = European Union citizens). If you are lucky, you can then get a bus, taxi or train to the centre of town without waiting too long. You can also **hire** a car (= **rent** a car) at most airports.

Note: In British English you normally **hire** something for a short period, e.g. hire a room for a party, and **rent** something for a long period, e.g. a flat; for a car, you can use both words.

Exercises

86.1 Complete the words or phrases below using words from the box.

off	control	free	card	baggage
in	lounge	luggage	reclaim	locker

1 boarding ....
2 baggage ....
3 excess ....
4 passport ....
5 hand ....

6 duty ....
7 overhead ....
8 take- ....
9 departure ....
10 check- ....

86.2 What do you call:

1 The place where you go when you arrive at the airport with your luggage?
2 The card they give you with the seat number on it?
3 The money you have to pay if your luggage is very heavy?
4 The place where you sit and have a drink when you are waiting for your flight to be called?
5 The bags you carry onto the plane with you?
6 The place above your head where you can put your hand luggage?
7 The part of the airport where the plane accelerates and takes off?
8 The people who look after you on the plane?
9 The part of the airport you walk through when you arrive or depart?
10 The place where you collect your luggage after you land?

86.3 Complete this part of a letter about an unpleasant flight.

Dear Tom

I've just arrived in Rome but I'm still recovering from a really terrible flight.
We (1) _____ two hours late because of bad weather, and then over the
channel we hit more bad weather. The (2) _____ announced that we had to
(3) _____ our seat belts, which was a bit worrying, and for half an hour we
(4) _____ through a terrible storm. It was still raining and very windy when we
(5) _____ in Rome and I was really glad to (6) _____ the plane and get into
the airport building.

Fortunately things have improved since then but I really hope the return
(7) _____ is a lot better.

86.4 Think about the whole experience of flying (from check-in to the time you leave the airport at your destination) and answer these questions. If possible, discuss your answers with someone else.

1 What is the most interesting part, and what is the most boring part?
2 Where do you often have delays, and why?
3 Is there any part that frightens or worries you?
4 What do you usually do during most flights?
5 Do you always eat the food they give you?
6 Is there one thing which would improve flying and make the experience more interesting?

87 Hotels

A Types of hotel

Hotels in Britain are graded with stars from one-star to five-star (**five-star hotels** are the best and most expensive). You can also stay in a **Bed & Breakfast** (B&B) (also called **Guest Houses**) where you pay for a bedroom, possibly an **ensuite** (= room with private bathroom) and breakfast.

B Types of hotel accommodation

a single room: for one person with a single bed
a double room: for two people with one large double bed
a twin room: for two people with two single beds
full board: includes breakfast, lunch and dinner
half board: includes breakfast and dinner
B & B: just the room and breakfast

C A visit to a hotel

We stayed in the Carlton Hotel for three nights in July, but I **booked** (= reserved) our room three months **in advance** (= before; in other words, in April) because it was the middle of the tourist **season.** When we arrived we **checked in at reception**, then the **porter** carried our suitcases up to our room. I gave him a small **tip** (n, v) – about 50p, I think. The staff were very friendly – we had a very nice **chambermaid** (= the woman who cleans the room) – and the room was very comfortable. The only problem we had, in fact, was with the shower which didn't **work** (= function) very well. (You could also say 'There was **something wrong with** the shower'.)

D Useful words and expressions

Could I **book** (= reserve) a room for next Thursday?
Could I have **an early morning call** at 7 a.m. please? (= Could you wake me at 7 a.m.?)
Could you **put it on my bill**, please? (= add the cost to the bill, e.g. for a drink you have in the hotel bar)
Could I **pay my bill**, please? (= pay for everything)
Could you **order** (= call) a taxi for me to go to the airport?
Are you **fully booked** (= completely full) next week?
Is breakfast/dinner **included**? (= Does the price include breakfast/dinner?)
Where's the **lift**? (= the machine which takes you up or down a floor) [AmEng = **elevator**]
Excuse me. **How do I get to** the underground station from here?

Exercises

87.1 **Put these sentences in a logical order.**

1 I paid my bill.
2 I checked in at reception.
3 I left the hotel.
4 I went up to my room.
5 I spent the night in the hotel.
6 I had an early morning call at seven o'clock.
7 I booked a room at the hotel.
8 I went out for dinner in a local restaurant.
9 I arrived at the hotel.
10 I got up and had a shower.
11 I had breakfast.
12 I tipped the porter who carried my luggage upstairs.

87.2 **What would you say in these situations?**

1 You want to stay in a hotel for two nights next week with your husband/wife. You phone the hotel. What do you ask or say?

....

2 You are at the hotel reception and you are planning to leave in about 15 minutes. What could you ask the receptionist?

....

3 You want to wake up at 7 a.m. but you don't have an alarm clock. What do you ask at reception?

....

4 You have a drink in the hotel bar. The barman asks how you want to pay. What's your reply?

....

5 When you turn on the shower in your room, the water comes out very very slowly. What could you say at reception?

....

6 You want to go to the nearest bank but don't know where it is. What do you ask at reception?

....

87.3 **You are staying in quite a good hotel (e.g. two-star or three-star) in your country. Would you expect to have the following?**

1 a room without a private bathroom
2 a hairdryer in the bathroom
3 a colour television in the room
4 a telephone in the room
5 writing paper in the room
6 a machine for making tea and coffee in the room
7 an electric trouser press (= a machine which presses/irons your trousers for you) in the room
8 air conditioning in the room

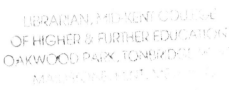

If possible, compare your answers with someone from a different country.

88 A sightseeing holiday

A Sightseeing

You may **do a bit of sightseeing** on holiday, or you may **do a lot of sightseeing**, but you will probably go to a museum or art gallery, and see or visit some of these things:

temple   castle   cathedral

market   fountain   statue   palace

Many people **go on a sightseeing tour** of a town (usually in a bus); they can also **go on a tour of the castle / the cathedral / the art gallery**, etc. When you are sightseeing, it helps to buy a **guidebook** (= a book of information for tourists) and a **map** of the town you are in.

B Things that tourists often do on holiday

look round the shops / **have a look round** the shops
take photographs
spend a lot of / lots of **money**
buy **souvenirs** (= typical products from the country)
get lost (= lose their way)
go out most evenings (= go to different places for social reasons, e.g. restaurant or disco)
have a good/great time (= enjoy themselves)

C Describing 'places'

The word **place** is very common and can describe a building, an area, a town, or country:

Bruges is a lovely **place** (= town) and we found a really nice **place** (= hotel) to stay.
The town is full of interesting **places** (= areas/buildings).

These words are often used when we describe places:

Venice is beautiful but it's always **packed** (= very crowded/full) with tourists in the summer.
New York is very **cosmopolitan**. (= full of people from different countries and cultures)
Vienna has lots of **historical monuments**. (= places, e.g. castles, built a long time ago)
Many beautiful cities have become very **touristy**. (= a negative word: 'too much tourism')
Sao Paolo is a really **lively** place (= full of life and activity) and the **night-life** is fantastic.

Note: If you want to ask if it is 'a good idea' to visit a place, you can use **worth** + -ing:

A: If I go to Scotland, is it **worth** spending a few days in Glasgow?
B: Yes definitely. And if you want to travel round a bit, it's **worth** renting a car.

Exercises

88.1 Complete this postcard that John sent to his family while he was on holiday. You may need a word or phrase in each space.

Hi everyone, I've been in Paris for almost a week now and I'm having a (1) _____. I spent the first few days (2) _____ — The Eiffel Tower, Notre Dame, and all the usual tourist attractions. Most places are absolutely (3) _____ with tourists (it's the time of the year I suppose), so yesterday I decided to have (4) _____ round the shops and I bought a few (5) _____. Today I've been to a couple of very interesting art (6) _____. I got (7) _____ on my way back to the hotel but it didn't matter because I discovered a really fascinating (8) _____ with lots of little stalls selling just about everything from apples to antiques. I ate in the hotel the first night but usually I (9) _____ and have dinner in a restaurant — the food is fantastic. I'm afraid I've (10) _____ a lot of money, but it's a great place and I've (11) _____ lots of photographs so you'll be able to see for yourself when I get back home on the 24th. See you then, John

88.2 Which of these places do you usually visit or go to when you are on holiday?

museums   art galleries   churches/cathedrals   tourist shops   concerts
discos / night clubs   castles/palaces/temples   the cinema   markets   restaurants
bars   the theatre

88.3 Confirm the information in the questions without repeating the same words and phrases. Use words and phrases from the opposite page.

Example: A: You've got quite a few pictures, haven't you?
B: ..Yes, we took lots of photos...................

1 A: Is it a nice city?
  B: Yes, it's a ....
2 A: There's a big mix of people in New York, isn't there?
  B: Yes, it's very ....
3 A: Was it very crowded?
  B: Yes, it was ....
4 A: There's a lot to do in the evenings, isn't there?
  B: Yes, the ....
5 A: Did you enjoy yourselves?
  B: Yes, we ....

88.4 Without using one town more than twice, name a town or city in your country which is:

lively?   packed with tourists in the summer?
cosmopolitan?   famous for its historical monuments?
very touristy?   really worth visiting if you are interested in architecture?
not worth visiting?

89 On the beach and in the country

A Places to stay

When people **go on holiday** they stay in **various** places
(= a number of different places): some go to hotels; others
rent **an apartment** (a 'holiday' flat) or **villa** (= a house by
the sea or in the countryside; often in the Mediterranean /
southern Europe); some prefer sleeping in a **tent** at a
campsite.

B At the beach

Many people spend their holiday in **seaside resorts** (= towns by the sea for tourists, e.g.
Malaga, St. Tropez, Okinawa) where they can spend most of their time on the beach. Some
people enjoy swimming, others love **sunbathing** (= **lying on the beach** in order to **get a
suntan**). If you like sunbathing, you should use **suntan lotion** to help you get **a tan** <u>and
protect your skin</u>. If you don't have any protection, you may get **sunburn**, which is painful
and can be dangerous. And if you want total protection you should use **sunblock**, or sit
under a **beach umbrella**.
Swimming can also be dangerous if there are **rocks** under the water or if the sea is **rough**,
e.g. with big **waves**.

C In the country

People who live in large towns often like to **get away** (= leave the place where they live) at
weekends or in the summer, and enjoy the **peace and quiet** (= calm and tranquillity) of the
country (also called the **countryside**). Some people just like to **put their feet up** (= relax and
do nothing) and occasionally go for **a stroll** (= a slow casual walk); while others enjoy
hiking (= long walks, often hill walking) across hills and valleys. And the countryside is a
great place to have a **picnic** (= eating a prepared meal of cold food outside).

Note: Learners sometimes say 'I love to be in the nature'. This is usually a translation from
their first language and it is not correct in English. The nearest we can say is probably 'I
love being in the countryside'.

Exercises

89.1 Write down at least five words beginning with 'sun'. You can check your answers on the opposite page and in the index.

sun.....................   sun.....................   sun.....................

sun.....................   sun.....................

89.2 Match a word from the left with a word from the right to form eight words or phrases.

1	sandy	waves
2	suntan	bathe
3	beach	beach
4	rough	lotion
5	sun	sea
6	sea	cliff
7	big	side
8	steep	umbrella

Now write answers to these questions.

1 Why do most people go to seaside resorts?
2 Why do people sunbathe?
3 Why do they use sunblock?
4 Why do they use suntan lotion?
5 How does it feel if you get sunburn?
6 What sport requires big waves?
7 Have you been in a boat when the sea was very rough? Were you seasick?

89.3 Complete this short text with a suitable word or phrase in each gap.

> I live and work in Milan but I like to (1).................. at the weekend if possible. My parents have a small house in the (2).................., about 100 kilometres from Milan, and it's a great place to go if you want a bit of peace and (3).................. In the summer you can just (4).................. by the pool during the hottest part of the day, then in the evening go for a (5).................. through the village or over the fields. Sometimes we go out for the whole day and have a (6).................. somewhere, by the lake or next to one of the many vineyards.

89.4 Fill the gaps with a suitable word. (One word only for each gap.)

1 Would you prefer a holiday in a seaside .... or a holiday in the country?
2 Would you prefer to stay in one place, or would you **rather** (= prefer to) go to .... places?
3 Would you prefer to spend your time .... on a beach or would you rather go for long walks?
4 Would you prefer to stay in a hotel or .... an apartment?
5 Would you prefer to eat in a restaurant or have a .... in the open air?
6 Would you prefer somewhere that was quite lively, or would you rather go to a place where there was peace and ....?

Look at the questions again. Which would you prefer? If possible, discuss your answers with someone else.

90 Time

A Prepositions: at, on, in

at a specific time   e.g. at 8 o'clock, at 3.30, at midnight
on a day   e.g. on Monday, on July 14, on the second day
in a period   e.g. in the morning, in April, in 1995

Important exceptions are: **at Christmas, at Easter, at the weekend, at night**

B Words often confused

Some time prepositions are easily confused. These are common problems:

I will stay here **until** she phones. (= I will go after she has phoned)
I will be in the office **until** 4 o'clock. (= I will leave the office at 4 o'clock)
I will be in the office **by** 4 o'clock. (= I will arrive at the office <u>not later than</u> 4 o'clock)
I'll be back home **by** lunchtime. (= I will arrive home <u>not later than</u> lunchtime)

I've worked in this office **for** six months. (for + a period of time)
I've worked in this office **since** May. (since + a point in time)

I worked for a newspaper **during** the war / 1990 / the summer. (this tells you 'when')
I worked for a newspaper **for** four years / six months. (this tells you 'how long')
[NOT I worked for the newspaper ~~during four years~~.]

Note: **During** a period may mean a part of that period or the whole period, e.g. 'during the war' can mean part of the war or the whole war. The context usually makes it clear, but if we want to stress or emphasise that an action occupied the whole period, we often use **throughout**, e.g. It rained throughout the night. (= it didn't stop raining)

I'm going back to Spain **in** ten days' time. (= ten days from now)
We arranged our next meeting **for** April 7th. (= to be on April 7th)

C Approximate times: past and future

I've known my dentist **for ages** (= for a long time), but I haven't been for a check-up **recently/lately** (= e.g. in the last few months).
I haven't seen Tom **recently/lately** (= e.g. in the last few weeks).
I used to go to an Australian dentist but that was **a long time ago** (e.g. 5–10 years ago).
My sister went to the dentist **the other day** (= a few days ago).
This dictionary will be OK **for the time being** (= for now / until I need a better one).

D Periods of time

There are 60 **seconds** in a minute; 60 minutes in an hour, 24 hours in a day, 7 days in a week, 2 weeks in a **fortnight**, 52 weeks in a year, 10 years in a **decade**; 100 years in a **century**.

E Time passing: take and last

My English course **lasts** ten weeks. (= it continues for ten weeks)
How long does the film **last**? (= How long is it from the beginning to the end?)
It **takes** me (= I need) half an hour to get to school.
We can walk but it'll **take** (= we'll need) a long time.

Exercises

90.1 Complete the text with *at*, *on*, or *in*.

There's one bus from London which gets here (1)......... ten o'clock (2)......... the morning and then another which gets in (3)......... four o'clock (4)......... the afternoon. That's (5)......... weekdays, but (6)......... the weekend the timetable is a bit different. (7)......... Saturday there are still two buses but the second one arrives (8)......... five thirty; (9)......... Sunday there is just the one bus (10)......... two o'clock. And (11)......... the winter, the service doesn't run at all (12)......... Sundays.

90.2 Cross out the incorrect answers.

1 The teacher told us to finish our homework <u>by/until</u> Monday.
2 We can't leave <u>by/until</u> the others get back.
3 I've been in the army <u>for/since</u> I was eighteen.
4 They've worked here <u>for/since/during</u> six months.
5 I visit my uncle every week <u>for/since/during</u> the winter.
6 I was at university <u>for/since/during</u> four years.
7 She's going back to France <u>in/after</u> three months' time.
8 He left the office <u>during/throughout</u> the lunch break.
9 It was hot <u>during/throughout</u> August; we didn't have one day under 30 degrees.
10 I booked a table in the restaurant <u>by/for</u> next Saturday. I hope that's OK.

90.3 Can you complete these sentences with the correct number?

1 The Olympic Games usually lasts about .... weeks.
2 Rembrandt was born in the ....th century.
3 President Kennedy died in .... That's .... years ago.
4 It takes approximately .... hours to fly from Tokyo to New York.
5 Some athletes can run 100 metres in less than .... seconds.
6 The .... was the decade in which the USA and USSR (at that time) were both trying to be the first country to put a man on the moon.

90.4 Replace the underlined time expressions with more 'approximate' time expressions.

1 I went to the library <u>three days ago</u>.
2 This dictionary isn't great but it'll be OK <u>until I'm more advanced</u>.
3 I haven't been to the cinema <u>for the last three weeks</u>.
4 And I haven't been to a concert <u>for three or four years</u>.
5 I went to Egypt with my parents but that was <u>ten years ago</u>.

90.5 Complete these sentences about yourself and your country.

1 On weekdays I usually get up at .... and leave home at ....
2 I always clean my teeth in ....
3 I don't go to school/college/work on ....
4 I usually have a holiday in ....
5 I have been in my present school/college/job for ....
6 I have been studying English since ....
7 I haven't spoken English since ....
8 It takes me .... to get to school/college/work.
9 You can't get a driving licence until ....
10 It rains quite a lot during ....

A Cardinal numbers

379 = three **hundred** <u>and</u> seventy nine   2,860 = two **thousand** eight hundred <u>and</u> sixty
5,084 = five thousand <u>and</u> eighty-four   470,000 = four hundred <u>and</u> seventy thousand
2,550,000 = two **million**, five hundred <u>and</u> fifty thousand
3,000,000,000 = three **billion**

Note: There is no plural 's' after hundred, thousand, million and billion when they are part of a number. On their own, they can be plural, e.g. **thousands** of people; **millions** of insects.

B Ordinal numbers and dates

One of the problems with dates is that we write them and say them in a different way:

We write **4 January** (or 4th January), but say **the fourth of January** *or* **January the fourth**.
We write **21 May** (or 21st May), but say **the twenty-first of May** *or* **May the twenty-first**.
1997 = nineteen ninety seven
1905 = nineteen hundred and five *or* nineteen oh five

C Fractions and decimals

$1\frac{1}{4}$ = one and **a quarter** $1\frac{1}{3}$ = one and **a third**   1.75 = one point seven five
$1\frac{1}{2}$ = one and **a half**   1.25 = one **point** two five   1.33 = one point three three
$1\frac{3}{4}$ = one and **three quarters**   1.5 = one point five

D Percentages

26% = twenty-six **per cent**
More than 50% is the **majority**; less than 50% is the **minority**.

E Arithmetic

There are four basic processes for **working out** (= calculating) a problem:

+ = **addition**	e.g. 6 + 4 = 10 (six **plus/and** four **equals/is** ten)
− = **subtraction**	e.g. 6 − 4 = 2 (six **minus** four equals/is two)
× = **multiplication**	e.g. 6 × 4 = 24 (six **times** / **multiplied by** four equals/is twenty-four)
÷ = **division**	e.g. 4 ÷ 2 = 2 (four **divided by** two equals/is two)

F Saying '0'

This can be spoken in different ways in different contexts.

telephone number: 603 724 = six **oh** three, seven two four (AmEng = six **zero** three)
mathematics: 0.7 = **nought** point seven, 6.02 = six point **oh** two
temperature: −10 degrees = ten degrees below **zero** / minus ten degrees
football: 2–0 = two **nil**   tennis: 40–0 = forty **love**

G Talking numbers

Here are several useful words and expressions connected with numbers:

The streets have got **odd** numbers (e.g. 3, 5, 7) on the left and **even** numbers (e.g. 4, 6, 8) on the right.
I got 16 **out of** 20 in our last test.   16/20

Exercises

91.1 How do you say these numbers in English? Write your answers after each one.

  1 462 ....
  2 2½ ....
  3 2,345 ....
  4 6.75 ....
  5 0.25 ....
  6 3⅓ ....
  7 1,250,000 ....
  8 10.04 ....
  9 47% ....
10 10 September ....
11 3 July ....
12 602 8477 (phone number) ....
13 −5 centigrade ....
14 In 1903 ....
15 In 1876 ....

Now practise saying them. If possible, record yourself saying them and then record a native speaker of English saying them or someone from your country who speaks English very well. Listen to both. How do you sound?

91.2 Correct the mistakes in these sentences.

1 After the game I heard the crowd was over twenty thousands.
2 We arrived on the ten September.
3 There were two hundred twenty altogether.
4 I got twenty-five from forty in my test.
5 My birthday is thirty-one August.
6 My phone number is seven twenty three, six nought nine.

91.3 Write answers to these problems.

1 23 and 36 is ....
2 24 times 8 is ....
3 80 minus 20 is ....
4 65 divided by 13 is ....
5 Add 10 and 6, multiply by 8, then subtract 40 and divide by 11. What have you got left?
6 Divide 33 by 11, multiply by 7, add 10, and subtract 16. What number is left?

91.4 Answer these questions. Write your answers in words.

1 When were you born?
2 How much do you weigh?
3 What is the number of the flat or house where you live?
4 Is that an odd or an even number?
5 What is the approximate population of your town?
6 What is the approximate population of your country?
7 What is the normal temperature of a healthy person?
8 How many kilometres are there in a mile?

92 Distance, size and dimension

Distance

The most common way of asking about distance is probably: **How far is it**? Here are two more common questions, and some expressions often used in the reply.

Is it **a long way**?	No, **just round the corner**. / **a couple of minutes' walk** (= very near).
Is it **very far**?	No, **not far**. / No, about **five or ten minutes' walk** (= quite near).
Is it a long way?	Yeah **quite a long way**. / Yeah, over a mile.
Is it very far?	Yes it's **a long way**. / Yes it's miles. / Yes it's **too far to walk**.

Note: We can use **far** in a question or negative but not in a positive statement on its own, e.g. we don't say 'it's far', we say 'it's a long way'. But we can say 'it's too far to walk'.

B
Size and dimension

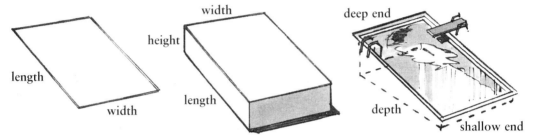

We can describe size using the nouns above or the adjectives formed from them, like this:

What's the **length/width/height/depth/size** of ...? *or* How **long/wide/high/tall/deep/big** is ...?

Note:
- We generally use **tall** to describe people, trees and buildings; and **high** to describe mountains. We also say **high-rise buildings**.
- Notice also that in the answer to these questions, an adjective follows the measurement:

  The garden is about ten metres **wide**. (= The **width** is about ten metres.)

C
Size in people and things

We use different words to describe the size of people and things:

a **tall** girl (≠ a **short** girl)
a **fat** person (≠ a **thin** person) See Unit 43 for more details.
a **long** book (= many pages) (≠ a **short** book)
a **deep** lake (= many metres) (≠ a **shallow** lake)

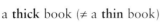

a **thick** book (≠ a **thin** book)　　　　a **wide** road (≠ a **narrow** road)

Note: We can use **big** or **large** to describe size in English, but not **great**. For English speaking people, **great** (*infml*) = fantastic. But we can use **great** before **big** to say that something is very big, e.g. I saw a **great big** dog in the park.

If you want to ask about size in clothes, you say: **What size are you?** *or* **What size (shoes) do you take?** If you don't know, then you need someone to **measure** you.

Exercises

92.1 Think about the room/place you are in now and answer these questions, using some of the expressions from the opposite page.

1 How far is it to the nearest shop?
2 How far is it to a bank?
3 Is it very far to the nearest bus stop?
4 Is it very far to a post office?
5 Is it a long way to the nearest swimming pool?
6 Is it a long way to the next big town?
7 How far is the nearest railway station?
8 Is it far to the centre of town?

If possible, ask someone else the same questions and compare your answers.

92.2 Write down eight different questions you could ask about the distance, size or dimensions of the things in the pictures.

92.3 Contradict the speaker in the sentences below. Look at the example first.

Example: A: Is it a long film?
            B: _No, it's quite short._

1 A: Is he a bit fat?
  B: No, he's ....
2 A: The water's quite deep, isn't it?
  B: No, ...
3 A: Their office is in quite a low building, isn't it?
  B: No, ...
4 A: Is the road very wide at that point?
  B: No, ...
5 A: It's a fairly boring place, isn't it?
  B: No, ...
6 A: He's quite tall, isn't he?
  B: No, ...
7 A: They only live in a small place, don't they?
  B: No, it's ....

93 Shapes, colours and patterns

A Shapes

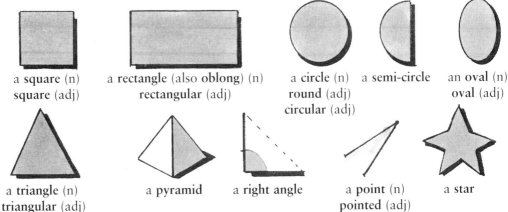

a **square** (n)
square (adj)

a **rectangle** (also **oblong**) (n)
rectangular (adj)

a **circle** (n)
round (adj)
circular (adj)

a **semi-circle**

an **oval** (n)
oval (adj)

a **triangle** (n)
triangular (adj)

a **pyramid**

a **right angle**

a **point** (n)
pointed (adj)

a **star**

a **square** box, a **round** table, a **pointed** end, a **rectangular** field, an **oval** shape

Note: We can also form adjectives to describe shapes in this way:

The ball was **egg-shaped**; a **heart-shaped** wedding cake; a **diamond-shaped** bag.

B Colours

You will already know most of the common colours. Here are some that are less common:

Mix black and white to form **grey**.   Mix red and blue to form **purple**.
Mix green and blue to form **turquoise**.   **Pink** is a colour between red and white.
Beige is a very light brown with some yellow in it.

C Shades of colour (= degrees and variation of colour)

She bought a **dark** green skirt.
He was wearing **light** blue jeans.
My new shirt is **pale** yellow.

shades of grey

dark grey

light/pale grey

Note: With some colours, we use **pale** rather than **light**, e.g. pale yellow, pale pink.

D Patterns (also called 'designs')

striped shirt

tartan skirt

floral tie

check dress

E Use of the suffix -ish

When we want to say that a shape is almost round or a colour nearly green, we can express this idea by adding the suffix **-ish**: a roundish face; a greenish tie; a yellowish colour.

Exercises

93.1 Describe these pictures using the correct noun and a suitable adjective.

93.2 What object is being described in each of these sentences?

1 It's got a point at one end and that's the end you use to write with.
2 It's greyish on the outside, pink on the inside, it swims and you eat it.
3 The shape is rectangular and it's usually green. There are lots of other lines on it, and people play on it.
4 It's a reddish-orange in colour, quite long and usually pointed at one end, and you eat it.
5 At certain times of the month it's completely round; at other times, it's closer to a semi-circle but not quite.
6 It can look pale blue, more often dark blue, and sometimes a greenish blue. It really depends where it is and whether the sun is shining on it.
7 It's oval-shaped, white or beige or light brown in colour, hard on the outside, and you eat it usually when it is cooked.
8 It is triangular, and in some countries you have to carry one in the boot of your car.
9 The bottom part is triangular, and at the top there is another bit in the shape of a semi-circle. You put things on the triangular part and hang them using the semi-circular part.
10 It has four sides and four right angles.

93.3 What are you wearing? Write down a detailed description of what you are wearing, including the exact colour of everything. If there is a colour or design you cannot describe, try to find it using a bilingual dictionary.

94 Partitives

There are many different words used to describe a particular quantity of something. Usually the word is joined to the noun it describes with 'of'.

A Containers (e.g. a bag) and contents (e.g. of shopping)

a **bag** of shopping

a **box** of chocolates

a **carton** of orange juice

a **can** of cola

a **cup** of coffee

a **tube** of toothpaste

a **tin** of fruit

a **bowl** of sugar

a **glass** of water

a **packet** of cigarettes

a **jug** of milk

a **bottle** of wine

a **jar** of marmalade

a **vase** of flowers

B With uncountable nouns

When we use uncountable nouns (e.g. advice), we sometimes want to talk about <u>one</u> of something. We cannot say ~~an advice~~ or ~~one advice~~, but we can use certain words to make these nouns singular: a **sheet of paper** (= one piece of paper) or a **slice of bread** (= one piece of bread). We can actually use the word **piece** with many nouns:

a **piece** of cake

a **piece** of wood

You can use **piece** with some abstract nouns, e.g. a **piece of information**, a **piece of luck**.

The most common partitive is **a bit**, which is informal and used with many nouns. It usually means a small amount but can be quite general. It can be used with the examples above, and more: a **bit of butter**, a **bit of time**, etc.

C A pair of ...

Some nouns have two parts, e.g. trousers (two legs) and shoes (left and right). You can use a **pair of** to specify the number, e.g. a pair of skis, two pairs of shoes, three pairs of tights.

D Groups of things

a **bunch** of flowers

a **gang** of youths/ kids/teenagers

a **herd** of cows

a **group** of people

a **bunch** of grapes

Gang has a negative meaning: it suggests a group of young people who may cause trouble.

Exercises

94.1 Some of these containers do not look exactly the same as the ones on the opposite page, but the names are the same. Can you decide what the missing words are?

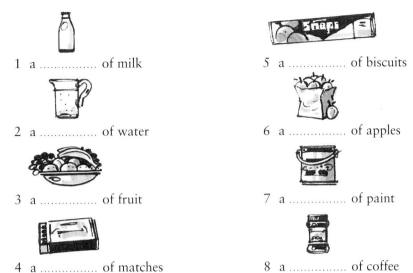

1 a .... of milk

2 a .... of water

3 a .... of fruit

4 a .... of matches

5 a .... of biscuits

6 a .... of apples

7 a .... of paint

8 a .... of coffee

94.2 Contents come in different containers. Would you be surprised to see any of the following?

a glass of soup   a vase of coffee   a bowl of milk

a jug of wine   a tube of cigarettes   a tin of tomatoes

a jar of mustard   a bag of salt   a carton of toothpaste

94.3 Complete these sentences with a suitable noun.

1 They gave her a big .... of flowers for her birthday.
2 They're looking for a .... of youths who may be responsible for the damage.
3 I cut about six .... of ham and put them on a plate.
4 They own a large .... of land on the coast.
5 I did a .... of homework last night, then went out.
6 She told us to take out a blank .... of paper, then write our names at the top.
7 A small .... of people gathered outside the embassy.
8 I need at least two .... of socks inside these shoes.
9 I asked him for a .... of advice.
10 I like to put a .... of cream in my coffee.
11 Have you seen that old .... of boots I use for gardening?
12 I've got a .... of time, so I can help you now if you like.

94.4 Cross out any answers which are wrong in these sentences.

1 I asked her for a <u>bit/piece</u> of advice.
2 I ordered a <u>piece/sheet</u> of cake.
3 There was a <u>group/gang</u> of journalists outside her house.
4 My lunch consisted of two <u>slices/pieces</u> of bread and a small <u>bunch/group</u> of grapes.
5 She hit me over the head with a small <u>piece/bit</u> of wood.
6 I'm in a hurry but I've still got a <u>bit/piece</u> of time.
7 We had a <u>piece/bit</u> of luck this morning: we won some money!
8 Could I have a <u>piece/bit/drop</u> of milk in my coffee?

95 The senses

A The five basic senses

These are: **sight, hearing, taste, touch** and **smell**. For each one we use a basic verb, which can be followed by an adjective or noun in these constructions:

It **looks** terrible. (from what I could see)   It **looks like** a wedding cake.
He **sounds** German. (from what I heard)   It **sounds like** a good idea.
It **tastes** strange. (from tasting it)   This **tastes like** bread.
It **feels** soft. (from touching it)   It **feels like** a blanket.
It **smells** wonderful. (from smelling it)   This **smells like** garlic.

We can also use the verbs as nouns. These are very common:

I didn't like **the look of** the fish.   I really like **the sound of** church bells.
I don't like **the taste of** olives.   I hate **the smell of** petrol.

B See, look (at) and watch

See is the ability to use your eyes (the verb is not normally used in the progressive); **look (at)** often means to look carefully / pay attention to something that is not moving; and **watch** often means to pay attention to something that is moving:

I can't **see** a thing without my glasses. (= I'm not able to see / I am blind)
I can't find my keys and I've **looked** (= searched / looked carefully) everywhere.
I want the doctor to **look at** (= look carefully and examine) my knee.
The police have been **watching** that man for weeks.
I **watched** the match and then went for a drink with friends.
Look (= look carefully) in the corner of my eye; you can **see** (= are able to see) the mark.
He ran into me because he wasn't **looking**. (= paying attention; the speaker seems angry)
He ran into me because he didn't **see** me. (= wasn't able to see me; the speaker is not angry)

Sometimes two verbs are possible in one context; sometimes only one:

I **saw** a great film last night. (= at the cinema; we cannot use **watch** here)
I **saw/watched** a great programme last night. (= on TV; we can use either verb here)

C Hear and listen (to)

Hear means <u>able</u> to hear; **listen (to)** means to <u>pay attention</u> to things you hear:

I couldn't **hear** what she said. (= I was physically unable to hear)
I can sometimes **hear** the trains from my bedroom. (= I am able to hear without trying)
I don't know what she said because I wasn't **listening**. (= I wasn't paying attention)
I often **listen to** the early evening news on the television. (= I make an effort to listen)
I was **listening to** the radio when I **heard** a strange noise outside.

Sometimes it is possible to use **hear** (but not in the progressive form) to mean 'listen to':

I know he's dead – I **heard** it on the radio last night. (= I heard it when I was listening)

D Touch

Don't **touch** those wires – they're dangerous.
You have to **press** that button to start the machine.
I don't feel safe up here. Could you **hold** my hand?

Exercises

95.1 Complete the sentences using words from the box. Use a dictionary to help you.

water	sore	cod	donkey	photo	silk	fresh
new	washing powder	ripe	door bell	horrible		

1 I don't think I'll eat this peach; it doesn't feel ....
2 Those shoes look .... When did you buy them?
3 This milk smells .... I'll open another bottle.
4 This coffee tastes like .... Who made it?
5 My feet are feeling .... after that run.
6 I love the smell of .... bread.
7 That painting looks like a ....
8 I know it's a horse but it looks like a ....
9 British people eat a lot of haddock. It's a white fish and tastes like ....
10 I'm sure it is expensive perfume, but to me it smells like ....
11 Your telephone sounds just like a ....
12 This blouse was very cheap but it feels like ....

95.2 Complete the sentences below the pictures using *looks/tastes/feels* + adjective.

1 This man .... 2 This pillow .... 3 This apple ....

95.3 Cross out any answers which are wrong.

1 I was <u>listening to / hearing</u> the radio when I <u>listened to / heard</u> a terrible noise outside.
2 The government is going to introduce new laws about noisy neighbours – I <u>listened to / heard</u> it on the radio this morning.
3 She turned up the volume but I still couldn't <u>listen to / hear</u> it.
4 I don't know if this is an antique; we'll have to get an expert to come and <u>look at / see</u> it.
5 They wanted to stay and <u>watch / look at</u> the programme, but it was a bit late.
6 I was very angry with Tom – he just wasn't <u>hearing / listening</u> when I spoke to him.
7 Can you bend over and <u>touch / press</u> your toes?
8 You have to <u>touch / press</u> the eject button if you want to get the video out.
9 Could you <u>touch / hold</u> this video for a moment while I move the TV?
10 If you <u>watch / look</u> carefully, you can <u>look / see</u> how the man does the trick with those cards.

95.4 Write down a smell, taste, and sound that you like and hate. Complete these sentences, and then try to compare your answers with someone else.

I love the smell of .... I hate the smell of ....
I love the sound of .... I hate the sound of ....
I love the taste of .... I hate the taste of ....

96 Notices and warnings

A Informative notices

Some notices give you information:

OUT OF ORDER
for a machine that is
not working, e.g. phone
or washing machine

NO VACANCIES
in the window of a B&B
(cheap hotel). It means the
hotel is full

SOLD OUT
outside a cinema or concert
– there are no tickets left. All
sold

B Do this!

Some notices tell you to do certain things:

PLEASE QUEUE OTHER SIDE

(= wait in a line on the other side of
this notice) e.g. in a bank or post office

KEEP RIGHT

(= stay on the right side, and continue on
the right side) e.g. in airports

C Don't do this!

Some notices tell you <u>not</u> to do certain things:

NO EXIT

NO SMOKING

No Parking

**DO NOT LEAN
OUT OF THE WINDOW**

**PLEASE
DO NOT
DISTURB**

**Please Do Not Feed
The Animals**

Keep off the grass

**SILENCE
EXAMINATION IN
PROGRESS**

**DO NOT LEAVE
BAGS
UNATTENDED**

D Watch out!

Some notices are warnings – they tell you to be careful because something bad may happen:

MIND YOUR HEAD
(= be careful you don't hit your
head e.g. in front of a low door)

MIND THE STEP
(= be careful you don't hit the step
and fall e.g. in front of a step)

FRAGILE
(= be careful, this will
break easily)

BEWARE OF PICKPOCKETS
(= be careful, there are people here who will steal
things from your bag or pocket without you knowing)

Exercises

96.1 Can you complete these notices and warnings in possible ways, without looking at the opposite page?

| PLEASE QUEUE .... | BEWARE OF .... |

| MIND THE .... | MIND YOUR .... | SOLD .... |

| PLEASE DO NOT .... | OUT OF .... |

| NO .... | KEEP .... |

96.2 Where would you expect to see these notices or warnings?

1 No vacancies

2 *Beware of pickpockets*

3 Nothing to declare

4 **Please queue other side**

5 OUT OF ORDER

6 Sold out

7 FRAGILE

8 Keep off the grass

96.3 What notice(s) is/are possible in each of these places?

1 a zoo
2 a waiting area in a busy airport
3 the door of a hotel room at 9 o'clock in the morning
4 in front of garage doors
5 above the window of a train
6 inside a theatre
7 on the underground
8 a door going into a low room

96.4 Now write some different notices of your own. Think of six possible notices you could put in one of these places:

1 a school
2 a university
3 a language school
4 a place where people work, e.g. bank, factory, hospital

Where would you put these notices? If possible, do this activity with another person or show it to another person.

96.5 Look for other notices (in English or your first language). Can you understand the English notices? Can you translate the ones in your own language? Try to find six more notices in the next week.

97 Vague language

Vague means 'not clear or precise or exact'. For example, we can say:
I have a **vague idea** where it is. (= I know the general area but I don't know exactly where)
I have a **vague memory** of the game. (= I can remember bits of it but not very clearly)
In spoken English we often use words which are very vague.

A Thing(s)

- To refer to actions, ideas and facts:

    The main **thing** (= fact) about John is that he likes everything to be organised.
    Hitting that young child was a terrible **thing** (= action) to do.

- To refer to <u>countable</u> objects (often the speaker and listener know what the object is, or the speaker has forgotten the name of it at the moment of speaking):

    What's that **thing** (bicycle) doing in the house?
    Put those **things** (cups and saucers) in the cupboard.

- To refer to a general situation:

    How are **things** at school? (= school in general)
    Recently, **things** (= life in general) have been going really well.

B Stuff

We generally use **stuff** (*infml*) to refer to <u>uncountable</u> nouns (or a group of countable nouns) when it is not necessary to be precise and give the exact name. Often the listener knows what the speaker is talking about.

Just leave that **stuff** (= different items of clothes) on the floor. I'll clear it up.
I never use that biological **stuff** (= washing powder) in my machine.

C (A) sort of ...

This is used to describe something when you are not being very exact or precise. Sometimes it is not possible to be exact, and sometimes you cannot find the exact word you want.

The walls are **a sort of** yellowy colour. (= not exactly yellow, but similar to yellow)
It's **a sort of** horror film. (= not exactly a horror film, but similar to one)
He gets ... uh **sort of** ... nervous when you mention the word 'exams'.

D A bit

It often means 'a little', but it is very common in spoken English, and sometimes it may be used more generally to mean a little or even quite a lot.

Could you speak up **a bit** (= a little). I can't hear you very well.
I thought the hotel was **a bit** (= quite) expensive, actually.

E Approximately

These words have the same meaning but **approximately** is more formal than the others:
The train should arrive in **approximately** twenty minutes.
It's **about** three miles to the house.
There were **roughly** twenty people at the party.
We are expecting 100 guests, **more or less**.

Exercises

97.1 What could *thing(s)* and *stuff* refer to in these sentences?

1 I never wear that stuff; it's got such a strong smell.
2 This thing has got stuck in the lock.
3 I bought a couple of bottles when I was in Scotland. It's great stuff.
4 We don't need these things. We can eat the chicken with our fingers.
5 What's that white stuff called that you mix with water to make bread?
6 There was a great thing on television last night about elephants.
7 I couldn't get any more stuff in my suitcase.
8 It's a wonderful thing and keeps my young children occupied for ages.
9 I don't know why I bought that thing – it's too heavy for me to carry even when it's empty.
10 It's good stuff. My hair feels really soft, and it didn't cost a lot.

97.2 Add a few words and phrases from the opposite page to make this conversation less precise and more natural.

A: How many people were at the conference?
B: 400
A: Did you enjoy it?
B: Yes
A: You don't seem very sure.
B: Well, there were some good events, but it was too long.
A: And did you go to John's talk?
B: Naturally
A: How did it go?
B: Well he was nervous at the beginning, but he soon got more confident and I think it went really well.
A: Did he have a big audience?
B: 75
A: That's good, isn't it?
B: I think John was disappointed – he wanted at least a hundred.

97.3 Reply to each of these questions with a suitable 'vague' response.

1 A: Did you get everything you wanted?
  B: Yeah ....
2 A: Was it expensive?
  B: Yeah ....
3 A: Did you say the walls were blue?
  B: Yeah ....
4 A: Will there be twenty chairs in the room?
  B: Yeah ....
5 A: Is it a very serious film?
  B: Yeah ....
6 A: Are you tired?
  B: Yeah ....

97.4 Think about similar words and phrases that you use when speaking your own language. How many direct translations can you find for the words and phrases on the opposite page?

98

American English

A British English and American English

People in Britain and America understand each other perfectly most of the time, but there are differences in grammar, vocabulary, spelling and pronunciation. With vocabulary, the same word may have a different meaning, e.g. British **chips** are American **french fries**; and American **chips** are British **crisps**. Sometimes there are completely different words for the same thing: a **lorry** in British English is called a **truck** in American English.

B Vocabulary

Here are some important differences. The British English word comes first in each case. Most of the words are explained in other units. Use the index to help you.

Roads and transport
taxi / cab/taxi
return (ticket) / round trip
petrol / gas (gasoline)
main road / highway
motorway/interstate
underground/subway
subway/underpass
pavement/sidewalk
lorry/truck
car park / parking lot

Education
secondary school / high school
university/college

Time
autumn/fall
holiday/vacation
fortnight / two weeks

Homes
tap/faucet
rubbish / garbage/trash
dustbin/trashcan
wardrobe/closet

Buildings
flat/apartment
ground floor / first floor
lift/elevator
toilet (gents/ladies) / restroom (men's/ladies' room)

Food

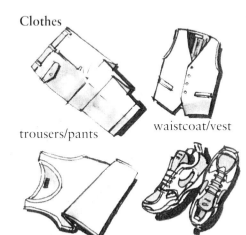

biscuits/cookies

sweets/candy

chips/french fries

crisps/chips

Clothes

trousers/pants

waistcoat/vest

vest/undershirt

trainers/sneakers

Note: Some American English words are now becoming more common in British English, e.g. movie (Br. = film); apartment (Br. = flat); semester (Br. = term). [An academic year may be divided into two semesters or three terms.] One special problem is that **guys** in American English can refer to men and/or women, but in British English it is only used to refer to men.

Exercises

98.1 Decide if the speaker is using British English or American English, and cross out the incorrect answer.

1 We've decided to take our vacation in the <u>autumn/fall</u> this year.
2 At my son's high school the new <u>term/semester</u> starts next week.
3 I never eat biscuits or <u>sweets/candy</u>.
4 Put that garbage in the <u>dustbin/trashcan</u>.
5 The trousers look nice with that <u>waistcoat/vest</u>.
6 The <u>lorry/truck</u> came past us on the highway.
7 My apartment is on the fourth floor but I'm afraid there's no <u>lift/elevator</u>.
8 The people next door are on <u>holiday/vacation</u>. They'll be away for a fortnight.
9 We left the car in the <u>car park / parking lot</u> and took the subway to the centre.
10 My trainers are in the <u>wardrobe/closet</u>.

98.2 Now complete this table.

British English	American English
holiday	vacation
trousers	*pants*
flat	apartment
trainers	....
secondary school	high school
biscuits	....
....	garbage
....	highway
fortnight	*2 weeks*
underground	subway

98.3 This text includes some words used in American English. Underline them and write the British English words on the right-hand side.

It was getting near lunchtime and I needed some gas, so I left the interstate and drove towards the nearest town. There was a gas station just outside the town and I decided to stop and have a look round. I put the car in a parking lot and took a cab to the centre. It was midday and very hot, so I stopped at a little cafe with tables on the sidewalk. I started talking to a truck driver, who gave me a history of the town, and afterwards he took me on a guided tour. It made a very nice break.

1 ....
2 ....
3 ....
4 ....
5 ....
6 ....
7 ....

98.4 Here are some more American English words that are explained in different parts of this book. What is the British English equivalent?

	American English	British English
1	stand/wait in line	
2	drapes	
3	collect call	
4	attorney	
5	check (in a restaurant)	

99 Formal and informal English

Most English that you learn can be used in a wide range of situations. But you will also hear or see language that is formal or informal, and sometimes very formal or very informal. You need to be more careful with this language because it may not be suitable in certain situations. (They are marked *fml* and *infml* throughout the book.)

A Formal English

Formal English is more common in writing than speaking. It is found in notices, business letters, and legal English; but you will also hear examples in spoken English.

Cafe notice: Only food **purchased** (= bought) here may be eaten on the **premises** (= here).
Police statement in court: I **apprehended** (= stopped) the accused outside the supermarket.
Theatre announcement: The play will **commence** (= start) in two minutes.
Formal business situation: The meeting will **resume** (= start again) this afternoon at 2 p.m.
Lawyer: My client had a broken ankle. **Thus** (= so) he could not have driven the car.
Formal letter: I **regret to inform you** (= I am sorry to say) that we **are unable to** (= can't)
    grant (= give) you ...
Announcement: If you **require** (= need) **further assistance** (= more help), please contact ...
Outside a pub: Parking for **patrons** (= customers) only.

B Informal English

In general, informal language is more common in spoken English than written English. Certain types of language are often informal:

– most uses of **get** are informal (See Unit 21 for more details)
– many **phrasal verbs** are informal (See Units 16 and 17 for more details)
– many **idioms** are informal (See Unit 18 for more details)

Here are some examples using words from above and other common informal words:

I had to go and **pick up** (= collect) the **kids** (= children) from school.
My flat is very **handy** for the shops. (= near the shops and very convenient)
I managed to **fix up** (= arrange/make) an appointment for 7.30.
I thought the book was **terrific** (= marvellous).
Most of the students are **bright** (= intelligent) but one or two are really **thick** (= stupid).
I offered him ten **quid** (= pounds) but the **guy** (= man) wasn't interested.
I **reckon** (= think) we'll **get** (= obtain) the money **pretty** (= quite) soon.
What's up? (= What's the matter?)
We must **get in touch with** them (= contact them) very soon.
Do you fancy going out? (= Would you like to go out?) Note the -ing form after **fancy**.
When you **get** (= reach/arrive) there, **have a word with** (= speak to) someone at reception.
I'm just going to the **loo** (= toilet).

C Slang

This is a form of <u>very</u> informal language. It includes words used by particular groups of people (e.g. some young people may refer to 'drugs' as **dope**), and also words which many people think are impolite and unacceptable in most situations. You should probably not use these words, but some of them are quite common . The word **piss** (= urinate / go to the toilet) for example, is often used metaphorically in these slang expressions:

piss off (= go away); he was **pissed** (= drunk); it's **pissing with rain** (= it is raining heavily)

Exercises

99.1 Put the words on the left into the correct columns in the table.

purchase   handy
loo   resume
thus   terrific
quid   commence
apprehend   reckon
guy

Formal	Informal

Now find a synonym for each of the words from this list.

therefore   toilet   convenient   catch/stop   start   man   start again
pound   think   fantastic   buy

99.2 Rewrite these sentences in more informal English.

1 When are you going to collect your bicycle?
2 Most of these children are very clever.
3 I think it'll commence quite soon.
4 Would you like to go out for a meal?
5 My flat is five minutes from where I work, thus it is very convenient.
6 What's the matter?
7 The man in the market wanted twenty pounds for this ring.
8 Where did you purchase that book?
9 They'll never apprehend him.
10 I'm just going to the toilet.

99.3 Now rewrite this letter in more suitable formal English.

```
Dear Mr Collins

We're really sorry to say that we can't lend you the sum of five
hundred quid that you need, but it may be possible to give you a
loan for some of the money.

If you are still interested, do you fancy getting in touch with
our main office to fix up an appointment with the assistant
manager. He will be happy to talk to you about it.

Yours sincerely
```

99.4 Dictionaries will tell you if a word is formal or informal. Use your dictionary to find out if these underlined words are either formal or informal.

1 I couldn't <u>attend</u> the meeting.
2 I thought the film was <u>a drag</u>.
3 Someone has <u>pinched</u> my pen.
4 He's a nice <u>bloke</u>.
5 Smoking isn't <u>permitted</u>.

100 Abbreviations and abbreviated words

A Letters or words?

Some abbreviations are read as individual letters:

BBC	British Broadcasting Corporation	MP	Member of Parliament
UN	United Nations	PM	Prime Minister
UK	United Kingdom	EU	European Union
USA	United States of America	PC	personal computer

Some abbreviations are read as words:

OPEC /əʊpek/   Organisation of Petroleum Exporting Countries
AIDS /eɪdz/   Acquired Immune Deficiency Syndrome

Occasionally an abbreviation can be read as individual letters or a word.

VAT /væt/ *or* V-A-T   Value Added Tax (= a tax on goods/products in EU countries)

B Written forms only

Some abbreviations are written forms only; they are still pronounced as full words.

Mr /mɪstə/
Mrs /mɪsɪz/ (= a married woman)
Ms /məz/ (= a woman who may be single or married)

St. Mark (Saint Mark)
Dean St. (Dean Street)
Dr (Doctor)

C Abbreviations as part of the language

Some abbreviations (from Latin) are used as part of the language.

Abbreviation	*Pronunciation*	*Meaning**	*Latin*
etc.	/et'setrə/	and so on	et cetera
e.g.	E-G	for example	exempli gratia
i.e.	I-E	that's to say, in other words	id est

**Note:* This is also how we say them in spoken English; we write 'e.g.' and we say 'for example'.

D Shortened words

Some English words can be shortened, and it is very common to meet them in this form, particularly in spoken English. Here are some of the most common:

phone (telephone)	fridge (refrigerator)	bike (bicycle)
maths (mathematics)	exam (examination)	TV/telly (television)
board (blackboard)	plane (aeroplane)	a paper (newspaper)
case (suitcase)	photo (photograph)	mum (mother)
dad (father)	ad/advert (advertisement)	sales rep (sales representative)
vet (veterinary surgeon)		

flu (influenza) (= an illness like a cold but more serious)
lab (laboratory) (= a special room where scientists work)
language lab (= room where students can listen and repeat using recording equipment)

Note: Most of these words are explained in other parts of the book. Use the index on pages 248–265.

Exercises

100.1 What do these letters stand for? Complete each one.

1 BBC = British ....
2 MP = Member of ....
3 EU = European ....
4 VAT = Value ....
5 PM = Prime ....
6 UN = United ....
7 UK = ...
8 OPEC = Organisation of Petroleum
....

100.2 Rewrite this note, making it more informal by using short forms where possible.

Michael

Peter had a mathematics examination this afternoon and then he had to take his bicycle to the repair shop, so he'll probably be a bit late home. You can watch television while you're waiting for him, and please help yourself to anything in the refrigerator. If there's a problem (for example, Doctor Brown rings about the influenza vaccination), my telephone number is next to the photographs on the dining room table. I should be home myself by about five o'clock.

Margaret (Peter's mother)

100.3 What abbreviations in written English are often used for these words or phrases?

1 for example
2 and so on
3 Street
4 in other words
5 Mister
6 Doctor

100.4 Complete these sentences with suitable abbreviations or shortened words opposite.

1 If you go to any of the Mediterranean islands .... Sardinia or Corsica, it's a good idea to hire a car.
2 He didn't want to walk so he went on his ....
3 A: Do you always listen to tapes in the classroom?
   B: No, we sometimes listen in the ....
4 I asked the teacher to write the word on the ....
5 If you go there, you can buy books, pens, writing paper, ...
6 She was away from college last week because she had .... I think she's better now, though.
7 When I decided to sell my records, I put an .... in the paper and I had three replies the same day.
8 It was a warm day so I put the milk and butter in the ....
9 If the tickets are very expensive .... more than $75, don't buy any.
10 I put my .... in a left luggage locker.

100.5 Here are some more abbreviations. What does each one stand for, and where will you see them?

PTO   RSVP   c/o   asap

Answer key

Unit 1

There is no key for this unit.

Unit 2

2.1 *Possible answers*

Clothes/accessories	*Railways*	*Words with -ful/-less suffix*
tie	fare	homeless
put on	train	painful
blouse	get on	careful
scarf	journey	helpful
jumper	station	thoughtless
jacket	platform	useless
jeans	ticket	

2.2 1 b   2 c   3 b   4 c   5 b   6 a   7 a and c   8 b

2.3 The answers here will depend on your first language: a translation may or may not be suitable for all of the words. Example sentences are a good idea for most words, and there is usually something else that is also useful to know. Here are some suggestions:

dream: noun and verb; as a verb the past tense and past participle can be 'dreamed' but more common is 'dreamt' /dremt/. As a noun it is used with the verb 'have'; also useful to learn 'nightmare' (= bad dream).

empty: ≠ full. Also useful to learn 'half-empty' (= 'half-full') but seems more negative.

concentrate: the main stress is on the first syllable, and it is followed by the preposition 'on'. The noun is 'concentration'.

forget: irregular verb (forget/forgot/forgotten); ≠ remember.

beard: a picture is the best way to show meaning; it is pronounced /bɪəd/; also useful to know is 'moustache'.

rescue: synonym = save; noun and verb.

nearly: synonym = almost; usually goes before the main verb except the verb 'to be', e.g. We nearly lost the game; It is nearly 4 o'clock.

knife: a picture is the best way to show meaning; the letter 'k' is silent; also important to know are 'fork' and 'spoon'.

2.4 *Possible answers*

take: a picture/photo, time, a bath, a decision
do: your homework, research, someone a favour, an exam, sport, one's best, the shopping (food)
make: a mistake, a decision, a mess, a noise, friends, money, coffee
have: a rest, a bath, a drink, a party, a good time

Unit 3

3.1 1 terrible   2 the same as 'choose'   3 a verb   4 an adjective   5 uncountable
6 complete/total/utter   7 You must choose between A and B; You can choose from ten different colours.   8 *See answers to 7*

3.2 1 choice   2 advise   3 piece   4 chaotic   5 clean   6 'homework' is school or college work that you do at home; 'housework' is work that is necessary in a home e.g. washing, ironing, cleaning   7 win a game   8 gain / put on weight   9 order   10 Is this seat free/taken?

3.3 kni<u>f</u>e; bom<u>b</u>; <u>p</u>sychology; recei<u>p</u>t; cas<u>t</u>le; dou<u>b</u>t; <u>w</u>rist; ca<u>l</u>m

3.4 1 = def. 2   2 = def. 4   3 = def. 1

Unit 4

4.1 1 **in** Seville (preposition)
2 **I** spent (pronoun)
3 **a** beautiful city (indefinite article)
4 **expensive** hotel (adjective)
5 **of** money (preposition)
6 wonderful **hotel/place** (noun)
7 **to** Spain (preposition)
8 **never** stays (adverb)

4.2 uncountable noun: time; traffic
plural noun: shorts; jeans
phrasal verb: put on
idiom: get a move on; get changed

4.3 1 transitive   3 intransitive   5 transitive
2 intransitive   4 transitive   6 intransitive

4.4 *Syllables and main stress (underlined)*

One syllable: noun
Two syllables: <u>Eng</u>lish; de<u>cide</u>; be<u>fore</u>
Three syllables: in<u>for</u>mal; under<u>stand</u>; <u>ad</u>jective; <u>op</u>posite; <u>com</u>fortable (Four syllables are possible here, but the 'or' is silent for most native speakers most of the time. /kʌmftəbl/)
Four syllables: edu<u>ca</u>tion; prepo<u>si</u>tion
Five syllables: pronunci<u>a</u>tion

4.5 1 adjectives
2 happily; correctly; luckily; surely; possibly
3 happy/content; correct/right; lucky/fortunate; sure/certain; no clear synonym for 'possible', although 'maybe' and 'perhaps' are very similar.
4 unhappy; incorrect; unlucky; unsure; impossible
5 correct

Unit 5

5.1 1 row /rəʊ/ and cow /kaʊ/
2 back /bæk/ and bacon /beɪkən/
3 soup /suːp/ and soap /səʊp/
4 vase /vɑːz/ and razor /reɪzə/

5.2 1 dream because it is pronounced /driːm/
2 flood because it is pronounced /flʊd/
3 fast because it is pronounced /fɑːst/
4 wound because it is pronounced /wuːnd/
5 since because it is pronounced /sɪns/
6 symptom because it is pronounced /sɪmptəm/

5.3

first	*second*	*third*
policy	cathedral	understand
palace	police	competition
opposite	advertisement	education
desert	assistance	
organise		

/ə/ appears in: cathedral /kəˈθiːdrəl/ understand /ʌndəˈstænd/
police /pəˈliːs/ competition /kɒmpəˈtɪʃən/
opposite /ˈɒpəsɪt/ advertisement /ədˈvɜːtɪsmənt/
education /edʒʊˈkeɪʃən/ desert /ˈdezət/
assistance /əˈsɪstəns/ organise /ˈɔːgənaɪz/

5.4

Same	*Different*
know/knife	island/islam (**s** in island is silent)
muscle/scissors	aisle/Christmas (**s** in aisle is silent)
climb/bomb	listen/western (**t** in listen is silent)
wrong/wrist	hand/handsome (**d** in handsome is silent)
calf/calm	honest/hope (**h** in honest is silent)

Unit 6

6.2 1 writing   2 a cassette   3 an OHT   4 notes/papers   5 notes/books   6 a plug
7 look up the meaning of a word   8 rub things out / erase them   9 photocopy things
10 because people can't hear it very well

6.3 1 clean the board   2 turn up the tape recorder   3 borrow a dictionary   4 swap places
5 video a programme   6 do an exercise   7 correct mistakes   8 look up a word
9 plug in the OHP / tape recorder

6.5 A: What does 'swap' mean?
A: How do you pronounce it?
A: How do you spell it?
A: How do you use it in a sentence?

Unit 7

7.1 unhappy; impatient; impolite; illegal
incorrect; irregular; invisible; impossible
illegible; unfriendly; unemployed; dishonest
unpack; unlock; disagree; dislike

7.2 1 it's illegal   3 he got undressed   5 she's very impatient
2 it's very untidy   4 it's illegible   6 impolite

7.3

1 misunderstood	4 disagree	7 unlock	10 reopen
2 unpacked	5 redo	8 disliked	11 overworking
3 disappeared	6 overslept	9 redo/retake	12 unwrap

Unit 8

8.1 edu<u>ca</u>tion; im<u>prove</u>ment; <u>jog</u>ging; <u>govern</u>ment; <u>spel</u>ling; hesi<u>ta</u>tion; a<u>rrange</u>ment; stu<u>pi</u>dity; <u>dark</u>ness; <u>weak</u>ness; simi<u>la</u>rity; punctu<u>a</u>lity; <u>sad</u>ness; popu<u>la</u>rity.

8.2	1 television	3 education	5 weakness	7 management
	2 election	4 government	6 stupidity	8 improvement

8.3	1 actor	4 singer	7 economist
	2 employer	5 murderer	8 translator
	3 footballer	6 psychologist	9 manager

8.4
1 writes reports/articles for newspapers
2 dances in ballets
3 directs films
4 manages a bank
5 employs people (employees)
6 sings pop songs and makes records
7 translates books and articles
8 drives a lorry
9 takes pictures (photographs)
10 draws and paints things, e.g. people and landscapes

Unit 9

9.1
thoughtful/less	dirty	painful/less	comfortable
attractive	careful/less	knowledgeable	famous
creative	dangerous	(un)suitable	(un)reliable
foggy	political	sunny	washable
homeless	enjoyable	musical	(un)breakable
useful/less			

9.2	1 careful	4 knowledgeable or helpful	7 useful	10 undrinkable
	2 foggy	5 dangerous	8 reliable	11 inflexible
	3 famous	6 painful	9 industrial	12 homeless

9.3 painless; useless; careless; thoughtless; tactless*
*If someone is 'tactful' they are diplomatic, i.e. they always say the right things. If you are tactless, you are always saying the wrong thing and might be offending someone.

Opposites for the other words:
wonderful (≠ terrible, awful)   awful (≠ wonderful, fantastic)   beautiful (≠ ugly)

9.4 *Possible answers*

1 cloudy, sunny, foggy
2 dangerous, careless, thoughtless, awful
3 musical, creative, famous
4 industrial, famous, beautiful, dirty, attractive

5 famous, creative, knowledgeable
6 reliable, comfortable, economical
7 political, enjoyable, thoughtful
8 ?

Unit 10

10.1
1 We waited a long time.
2 I dreamt about you last night.
3 We queued for half an hour.

4 The holiday cost about £500.
5 I replied to his letter yesterday.

10.2　1　I'll give him a ring this evening.
　　　2　I go on a diet if I put on weight.
　　　3　It was very hot, so we had a rest for a while after lunch.
　　　4　I put on the brakes but I still couldn't stop in time.
　　　5　He gave me a push.
　　　6　Did you have a look in the paper?

10.3　1　same meaning
　　　2　similar (but not exactly the same because 'to water' means 'to pour water over something that is growing'.)
　　　3　completely different (the verb 'to book' = 'to reserve')
　　　4　completely different ('a break' is a rest; 'to break a leg' = to fracture the leg)
　　　5　similar (but not exactly the same because 'a run' here is not just the action of running; it is an activity that the person chooses to do.)

Unit 11

11.1　*Possible answers*

Money: credit card, cheque book, box office (where you buy tickets), income tax
Roads: traffic lights, traffic jam, pedestrian crossing, parking meter, traffic warden
Things we wear: T-shirt, sunglasses, earring
People: baby-sitter, brother-in-law, film star, pop star

11.2　1　traffic jam　　　4　waiting room　　7　income tax　　　9　first aid box
　　　2　film star　　　　5　baby-sitter　　8　parking meter　10　science fiction
　　　3　alarm clock　　　6　sunglasses

11.3　*Possible answers*

sitting room; waiting room
pop star; rock star
birthday card; postcard
toothbrush (= what you clean your teeth with)
traffic jam; traffic warden
sunshade (= parasol); suntan (= when your body goes brown from the sun)
box office; postbox
hairdresser (= person who cuts your hair)

11.4　*Possible answers*

notebook (= a book of plain paper to write notes)
textbook (= a book used for study, especially in schools)
cookery book (= a book that tells you how to prepare and cook food)
telephone book (= the book with telephone numbers; also called a telephone directory)
bookcase (= a piece of furniture with shelves for books)
book shop
greetings card, e.g. birthday card, Christmas card
travel card (= a ticket for travel on buses and trains for a period)
phone card (to use with certain telephones)
postcard

Unit 12

12.1

good-looking	brand-new	well-known	badly-written
easy-going	part-time	north-east	left-handed
ten-pound	first-class	short-sleeved	second-hand

12.2 *Possible answers*

well-done; well-made; well-built; well-dressed
badly-written; badly-designed
right-handed; left-handed
part-time; full-time
north-east; south-east

12.3

1 sleeved	4 new	7 part	10 minute	13 pound
2 star	5 east/west	8 written	11 hand	14 known
3 handed	6 behaved	9 off	12 looking	15 going

Unit 13

13.1

heavy smoker; heavy traffic; heavy rain
miss a bus; miss a person; miss a lesson
tell a joke; tell a lie; tell the truth; tell a story

13.2

1 dry wine	3 weak coffee	5 get off the bus	7 miss the bus
2 a slight accent	4 a loud voice	6 tell a lie	8 get out of the car

13.3

1 terribly; missed	5 start	9 strong
2 told	6 made	10 missed
3 starting	7 vitally	
4 runs	8 heavy; highly	

13.4 1 large size 2 wide range 3 broad shoulders 4 vast majority

Unit 14

14.1 *Prepositions and possible replies*

1 about; I've no idea.
2 at; French and German.
3 for; Her brother, I think.
4 for; Assistant manager.
5 to; I think it's a comedy programme.
6 about; She said the vegetables were cold.
7 for; The fact that she was late twice last week.
8 to; The man over there.
9 at; One of the students in her class.
10 in; Thrillers, I think.
11 on; How much it costs, I expect.
12 of; The fact that she can't get out. She's claustrophobic, you see.

14.2 1 c   2 j   3 a   4 l   5 h   6 b   7 d   8 k   9 g   10 i   11 e   12 f

Possible answers

1 to the waiter / about it
2 to my brother/sister
3 for a job with a charity / in a developing country
4 at English
5 from hay fever
6 in languages
7 on opera
8 of flying
9 from English people
10 London; by/at the number of parks

14.4 fond of; concentrate on; responsible for; rely on

Unit 15

15.1

1 on	3 on	5 on	7 for	9 on	11 in	13 by	15 on	17 at	19 by
2 by	4 on	6 by	8 in	10 by	12 on	14 by	16 in	18 at	20 at

15.2
1 by myself / on my own   5 on TV   9 at the moment
2 in time   6 by mistake   10 by chance
3 out of work   7 in the end
4 on the phone   8 at the end

15.3
1 No, she hit him by accident.
2 No, they went on foot (*or* by bus, by taxi, by train).
3 No, they're here on business.
4 No, I saw it on TV (*or* 'I heard about it on the radio').
5 No, he did it by himself / on his own.
6 No, I'm in a hurry.

Unit 16

16.1

1 picked	3 gone	5 gets	7 look	9 go
2 found	4 get	6 gone	8 carry	10 run

16.2 *Possible answers*

1 her illness
2 bread/coffee/sugar etc.
3 in a dictionary
4 my boss / my parents / the neighbours / my teacher etc.
5 her coat / her jacket / her gloves etc.
6 the fire
7 the cat / the children etc.
8 the car
9 early/late etc.
10 by ten pounds / next week etc.

16.3   1 = def 6   2 = def 2   3 = def 4   4 = def 3   5 = def 1

16.4 *See Page 36 for examples.*

Unit 17

17.1 *Possible answers*

1 excuses/stories
2 on the bed / on the floor
3 the TV / the light / the fire
4 my flat / my house
5 the problem / the mess / the central heating
6 tonight / on Saturday evening
7 the second question / the final part
8 just outside London
9 on your salary / on seventy pounds
10 in a small town / by the sea

17.2
1 no
2 yes (**put** the fire **out**)
3 yes (**turn** the radio **on**)
4 no
5 no
6 yes (**made** that story **up**)
7 no
8 no
9 yes (**turn** the light **off**)
10 yes (**leave** this question **out**)

17.3
1 The cost of living is going up all the time and I find it quite difficult to get by on my salary. But I think I can probably carry on for a few months.
2 She told us to come in but then we had to take off our shoes and I had to put out my cigarette.
3 The teacher told the class to make up a story to go with the picture in their books, and then carry on with Exercise 3. She said they could all leave out Exercise 4.

17.4 Unit 21: get on (with someone); get on (= make progress); get up
Unit 47: grow up; go out (with); split up; break up
Unit 48: wake up; get up; stay in; go out; come round
Unit 56: take sth. off; hang sth. up; put sth. on; try sth. on
Unit 62: get on; get off; get in(to); get out (of)
Unit 75: turn sth. on/off; turn sth. up/down; switch on/off/over; plug sth. in

Unit 18

18.1
1 feel like = want/desire
2 for good = for ever
3 tied-up = busy
4 pulling sb.'s leg = joking by saying that something is true when in fact it is not true.
5 make do = manage

18.2
1 hang on
2 a short cut
3 go ahead
4 make it; Never mind
5 What's up?
6 Keep an eye on
7 get a move on
8 make up your mind

18.3
1 start; matters
2 turns
3 -hand
4 small
5 do; term

18.4 *Examples*

have something / nothing / a little **in common** = to have similar interests (If you 'have nothing in common', it means you don't have similar interests.)
mad about something = to like something very much
get on someone's **nerves** = to make someone angry or irritable by your behaviour.

Unit 19

19.1 1 do 3 make 5 take 7 do 9 doing
2 have 4 do 6 take and do 8 take and make 10 made

19.2 1 have a drink 5 I'm thirsty 8 take/make a decision
2 make 6 do my shopping 9 had a good time
3 do the housework 7 make money 10 making progress
4 had

19.3 *Possible answers*

1 My mother had to do a lot of housework, so I agreed to do the shopping for her.
2 A couple asked me to do them a favour and take a picture of them. *or* I made friends with a couple of people and took some photos of them.
3 I went to the disco and had a great time, but unfortunately I had to do an exam today, which was very difficult.

Unit 20

20.1 break a record / the law; catch the ball / a bus / a cold; keep in touch / a record; give my regards to / me a hand

20.2 1 see 3 give 5 catch 7 keep 9 break
2 keep 4 see 6 keep 8 caught 10 see

20.3 1 break the ice 3 catch a bus
2 give him/her a hand 4 broke the record

Unit 21

21.1 1 buy 3 arrive 5 obtain* 7 becoming 9 receive
2 fetch 4 became 6 receive 8 buy 10 arrive
*obtain is used more frequently in written English than in spoken English.

21.2 1 It's getting cold in here. 4 It's getting late
2 I'm getting hungry 5 It's getting dark
3 I'm getting hot 6 I'm getting worse at English

21.3 1 getting ready to go out 4 get on very well with my boss
2 get dressed very quickly 5 get rid of most of these chairs
3 get to know people in this country 6 How are you getting on?

Unit 22

22.1 1 going 2 coming 3 go 4 take
5 taking ('bringing' is also possible here if the speaker already imagines himself at the party)
6 bring 7 go 8 come

22.2 1 doing 3 turn 5 lead to
2 try 4 How are you? 6 How are you getting on?

22.3 1 shopping 3 for a drink 5 for a swim
2 for a meal / for something to eat 4 sightseeing; for a drive/walk 6 riding

22.4 1 deaf 2 bankrupt 3 grey 4 bald 5 mad

Unit 23

23.1 1 very/terribly/really/awfully 5 apologise; matter
2 I'm; held; problem 6 long; never
3 keep; mind 7 beg; worry
4 kind 8 sort

23.2 *Possible answers*

1 I'm terribly sorry / I beg your pardon.
2 I'm sorry I'm late but I missed the bus.
3 Oh thank you. That's very kind of you.
4 Don't worry. It doesn't matter.
5 Thank you for inviting me. / Thank you for a lovely dinner/meal.
6 Never mind. Don't worry. I'll sort it out.
7 I would like to apologise for not coming to your office last week. Unfortunately, …
8 Please accept our apologies for the delay in sending the information we promised you. Unfortunately we had a fire at the factory last month, and this has resulted in …

Unit 24

24.1 A: <u>Would</u> you like to go out this evening?
B: I'm afraid I haven't got any money. (omit 'but')
A: That's OK, I'll pay. How about <u>going</u> to see a film?
B: No, actually I think I'd rather stay at home and do my homework. (omit 'to' after 'rather')
A: Why <u>don't you</u> do your homework this afternoon?
B: I'm busy this afternoon.
A: OK. How about tomorrow evening, then?
B: Yeah <u>fine</u>. / Good idea.
A: Great. What film shall we go to?
B: <u>I don't mind</u>.

24.2 1 possibly; sure / of course
2 wondering; love to
3 shall; don't; good/great idea
4 shall; how about; could; rather; like
5 would; mind

24.3 *Possible answers*

1 Yeah sure 5 I'd love to, but I'm afraid I can't
2 Yes of course 6 Yeah great
3 I'm afraid not 7 Yes that's a good idea
4 Yes, I'd love to 8 Yes if you like

Unit 25

25.1 *Any combination of these question beginnings:*

What do you think of …
How do you feel about …
What are your feelings about …

25.2 1 of; personally ('actually' would also be correct here)
2 according
3 extent
4 concerned
5 totally ('completely' would also be correct here)

25.3 *Possible answers*

1 Personally I don't think you can learn a language in three months.
2 In my opinion the club needs to buy new players.
3 Yes, I agree with you.
4 The newspaper says that terrorists started the fire.
5 I partly agree with her.

25.4 *Possible answers*

1 Yeah maybe, but I think there are lots of women who don't want to do that.
2 Yes I agree to some extent, but how do you decide if someone doesn't want to work?
3 Yes, I think you're right.
4 You could be right but don't you think that more people would take drugs if we did that?
5 Yes I agree to a large extent – it *can* lead to a lot of conflict between countries.

Unit 26

26.1
1 Happy Christmas *or* Merry Christmas
2 Happy Birthday (*or* Many Happy Returns)
3 Happy New Year
4 Congratulations
5 Good luck
6 See you soon

26.2
1 How do you do?; How do you do?
2 Bless you
3 Have a nice/good weekend; Yes, same to you.
4 Cheers; Cheers

26.3
1 'Excuse me' is enough here, but you could add a little more, e.g. 'Excuse me for one moment' *or* 'Excuse me. I won't be long'.
2 Sorry? (with rising intonation)
3 Goodbye. Nice to meet you. / Nice to have met you.
4 Excuse me.
5 Goodnight. (See you in the morning / tomorrow.)
6 Excuse me. (You would probably add something like 'I think you've dropped something'.)
7 Congratulations
8 Good luck

26.4
We use 'hard luck' to someone who has just failed in something, e.g. failed an exam
We ask people to 'say cheese' when we are about to take a picture of them.
We say 'watch out' as a warning e.g. to warn someone crossing a road that a cyclist is right behind them and could hit them if they aren't careful.
We say 'I beg your pardon' in many situations when we also say 'sorry' e.g. you step on someone's foot; you interrupt someone. It is more formal.
We say 'I've no idea' to show that we definitely do not know the answer to something; in some cases we say it because we are annoyed at being asked the question.

Unit 27

27.1
1 I need some information.
2 We had lovely weather.
3 The furniture is very old.
4 I'm looking for a new pair of jeans. *or* I'm looking for some new jeans.
5 Your hair is getting very long.
6 Do you have any scissors? *or* Do you have a pair of scissors?

7 We had a lot of homework yesterday.
8 Do you think she's making progress with her English?
9 These trousers are too small.
10 She gave me some good advice.

27.2 *countable*: cup; grape; coin
uncountable: butter; travel; housework; money; spaghetti; insurance
countable and uncountable:
television U e.g. Television is bad for your eyes.
            C e.g. We bought a new television yesterday.
work   U e.g. Most people enjoy their work.
            C e.g. The Mona Lisa is a famous work of art.
coffee   U e.g. I love coffee.
            C e.g. I sat down and ordered a coffee (i.e. cup of coffee).

27.3
1 some scissors / a pair of scissors	5 some scales
2 some sunglasses / a pair of sunglasses	6 some headphones
3 some advice	7 some / a pair of (warm) pyjamas
4 some furniture	8 to do more homework

27.4 *uncountable nouns*: traffic; news
plural nouns: roadworks; authorities

Unit 28

28.1
1 to work	3 going	5 to drive / driving	7 to work / working	9 to finish
2 to help	4 to take	6 eating	8 going	10 helping

28.2 *Possible ways to complete Part C.*
1 to have a successful career; to be happy; to have children
2 doing housework; waiting at bus stops; going to the dentist
3 getting up late; walking in the country; going shopping
4 walking long distances; doing sport; drinking coffee
5 to live until they are 75; to have some disappointments; to meet a person they will love
6 making their bed; cooking their dinner; tidying up
7 come home at a certain time; tidy their own rooms; get up at a certain time
8 get up when they like; do what they like; have parties at their home

28.3 1 He let her go on holiday with her friends.
2 He offered to lend her the money for the hotel.
3 He refused to pay for the flight and her entertainment.
4 She promised to bring him back a present and repay her loan in six months.
5 They decided to go to the south of France for two weeks.

Unit 29

29.1 1 She said the film was terrible.
2 He told me it's not possible.
3 Can you explain what to do?
4 She suggested that we go to … / she suggested going to …
5 Can we discuss my report?
6 I want him to leave.
7 I need to confirm the booking.
8 I apologised for my mistake.
9 She advised me to buy a dictionary.
10 She insisted on paying.

29.2 1 showed   3 apologise   5 persuaded   7 confirm   9 explained
          2 complain   4 warn   6 insisted   8 blamed   10 discussed

29.3 *Possible answers*

  1 that we go for a meal.   6 him to go.
  2 them to be quiet.   7 her to go home.
  3 it was great.   8 the manager for the defeat.
  4 it in class.   9 them not to drink it.
  5 on going with her / that we go together 10 how it works.

29.4 *order*
  1 + object, e.g. He ordered a meal.
  2 + object + infinitive, e.g. He ordered us to leave.

  recommend
  1 + object, e.g. She recommended the school.
  2 + 'that' clause, e.g. She recommended that we stay in a hotel.
  3 + preposition, e.g. What would you recommend for young children?
  4 + (object) + -ing, e.g. I recommend (you) reading the book before you see the film.

  prevent
  1 + object, e.g. I couldn't prevent the accident.
  2 + object + preposition, e.g. They prevented us from leaving.

Unit 30

30.1 big/enormous or huge   hot/boiling
          small/tiny   cold/freezing
          tired/exhausted   bad/awful or terrible or dreadful
          surprised/astonished   hungry/starving
          interesting/fascinating   frightened/terrified

30.2 *Sample answer*

Arrived on Sunday. The hotel is fantastic – we've got a huge room and the food is wonderful. It's been boiling every day so far, so we've spent most of the time on the beach, along with everyone else – it's absolutely packed. But the sea is actually freezing – that's because it's the Atlantic coast, I suppose.
Tomorrow we're going to walk to a tiny seaside village about ten kilometres from here – I imagine I'll be really exhausted by the time we get back, but it does sound a fascinating place and I'm looking forward to it.
I'll write again in a couple of days and tell you about it. Until then,

30.3 1 exhausted   2 fascinating   3 terrifying   4 astonished   5 freezing

30.4 1 exhausted   2 disappointed   3 embarrassed   4 confused   5 astonished

Unit 31

31.1 1 on   2 in   3 at   4 at   5 in   6 on   7 on   8 at   9 on   10 in

31.2 1 No, behind the picture.
          2 No, down the hill.
          3 No, under the fence.
          4 No, I saw her get out of the car.
          5 No, above the clouds.
          6 No, the flat below me.

1 across 3 into 5 near 7 between 9 round
  2 through 4 in 6 along 8 at/in 10 through

Unit 32

32.1 1 My brother often visits us on Sunday.
  2 She hardly ever phones me.
  3 I have never broken my leg.
  4 I hardly saw him during his visit.
  5 I occasionally get up early. ('occasionally' could also begin or end the sentence)
  6 She is always early for work on a Monday.

32.2 1 hardly ever / rarely 2 hardly 3 nearly 4 slightly 5 incredibly

32.3 1 No it was rather interesting (actually)
  2 No they were rather quiet (actually)
  3 No, it's rather clean (actually)
  4 No, it was rather good (actually)

32.4 1 I thought they were extremely good.
  2 He's been getting very good marks in his exams.
  3 John said the flat was fairly / quite / a bit small.
  4 They said it was a bit boring.
  5 The clothes were quite/fairly expensive.

Unit 33

33.1 1 get 2 while 3 leaving 4 eventually/finally 5 just as 6 while/as

33.2 *Possible answers*

  1 we went for a swim.
  2 I have finished here.
  3 leaving.
  4 I was getting out of the car.
  5 John looked up the other half.
  6 the bus arrived.
  7 you are not insured to drive it.
  8 I was coming round the corner.

33.3 *Possible answers*

  1 And for another, I've got lots of work to do.
  2 Then finally we came back through the Loire valley and stayed in Tours for a couple of days.
  3 besides/anyway, we can't really afford it.

33.4 *Possible answer*

Dear Sir/Madam
I have just returned from a week's break at The Royal Malvern Hotel and I am writing to express my dissatisfaction with the food and service provided in your restaurant.

To begin with, there was very little variety in the food and sometimes no choice at all. Secondly, the service was very slow most of the time and we had to wait half an hour between courses. And finally, when we complained to the head waiter about these delays, he was very rude and the service did not improve.

I sincerely hope that immediate action will be taken to improve this situation, and I shall expect a letter of apology and explanation for this very poor standard of service in a hotel with such a fine reputation.

Yours faithfully

Unit 34

34.1
1 although
2 in spite of
3 in spite of / despite

4 even though
5 whereas
6 In addition / Moreover

7 however
8 too / as well
9 on the other hand

10 also

34.2
He went to school today even though he didn't feel very well.
He always did his best at school whereas most of his schoolfriends were very lazy.
He's got the right qualifications. What's more, he's the most experienced.
He didn't pass the exam in spite of the help I gave him.
He decided to take the job. However, the pay isn't very good.

34.3
1 despite / in spite of
2 whereas
3 furthermore / in addition / moreover / what's more
4 although / even though / despite the fact that
5 however / on the other hand
6 as well / too

34.4 *Possible answers*

1 she spoke very quickly.
2 the others couldn't.
3 the bad weather.

4 it's much cheaper.
5 I think they'll probably pass.
6 I wasn't bored at all.

Unit 35

35.1
1 similar
2 unlike / different from
3 a lot in common
4 in common
5 live at home / have jobs / like sport / want to become managers
6 went to university

35.2
1 Martin is very different from his brother.
2 The flats are very good value compared with/to the houses.
3 Everyone in the class passed the exam except Carla.
4 The two boys have nothing in common.
5 You don't have to wear a tie apart from (on) Saturday(s).

35.3   1 otherwise   2 in case   3 unless   4 as long as

35.4 *Possible answers*

1 have to finish it at the weekend.
2 a member.
3 pay me back before next week.
4 my cousin comes to stay for a few days.
5 I have to.
6 I want to buy anything.

Unit 36

36.1
1 I didn't phone you as/since/because it was very late. *or*
   It was very late so I didn't phone you.
2 I turned up the radio in the lounge so (that) I could hear it in the kitchen.
3 The restaurant was full so we went to the bar next door. *or*
   We went to the bar next door as/since/because the restaurant was full.
4 I stayed at home as/since/because I was expecting a phone call. *or*
   I was expecting a phone call so I stayed at home.
5 It's a very large city so you have to use public transport a lot. *or*
   You have to use public transport a lot as/since/because it's a very large city.
6 I learnt to drive so that my mother didn't have to take me to … (*purpose*)
   I learnt to drive, so my mother didn't have to take me to … (*result*)

36.2 It is possible to use 'because of / due to / owing to' in all of the answers.
1 She got the job because of her excellent qualifications.
2 We couldn't eat outside because of the terrible weather.
3 She had to stay at home because of her broken ankle.
4 The referee had to stop the game because of the bad light.
5 The flowers died because of the dry weather.
6 Because of the heavy traffic, I was half an hour late. *or*
   I was half an hour late due to the heavy traffic

36.3 1 as/since   2 cause / lead to / result in   3 so that   4 lead to   5 therefore

36.4 *Possible answers*

1 I want to improve my English because I will need it in my job very soon.
2 I bought myself a walkman so that I could listen to English cassettes on the bus.
3 I study English at the weekend as I am very busy during the week.
4 I always write words down in my notebook so that I don't forget them.
5 I don't get many opportunities to practise my English. Consequently, I find it difficult to remember everything I study.
6 My brother has got a number of American friends. As a result, he gets a lot of opportunities to practise his English.
7 If he could speak almost perfect English, it could lead to a job in Britain or America.
8 Some people find English difficult because of the pronunciation.

Unit 37

37.1
1 an ocean	4 a desert	7 a group of islands	10 mountain
2 a mountain range	5 a jungle (a rainforest)	8 a continent	11 Lakes
3 a country	6 a sea	9 islands	12 stars

37.2 My journey took me across the Atlantic Ocean from Europe to South America. I travelled through the Amazon rainforest and down through the interior of Brazil as far as the Iguacu Falls. From there I headed north again, through Bolivia, round Lake Titikaka and up to Cuzco. Then I crossed the Andes and finally arrived in Lima. For the last part of the journey I flew to Jamaica in the West Indies.

37.3 1 hurricane   2 flood   3 drought   4 earthquake   5 volcanic eruption

37.4 1 Sahara Desert   2 River Nile   3 Nigeria   4 Lake Tanganyika
5 Mount Kilimanjaro   6 Victoria Falls   7 Kalahari Desert   8 South Africa
9 Madagascar   10 the equator

Unit 38

38.1 1 foggy   2 snowing   3 cloudy   4 pouring with rain   5 ic(e)y   6 sunny

38.2 1 false   3 true   5 false   7 false   9 true
2 true   4 true   6 true   8 true   10 false

38.3 *The missing words are*
breeze; gale
boiling; freezing

38.4 1 blows   2 hot   3 winds   4 snows   5 spell   6 heavy   7 humid

Unit 39

39.1 1 plant trees (you can 'plant plants' but it sounds unnatural. In this case you would probably say: 'We're going to put some plants in'.
2 water trees/plants
3 pick apples
4 extract coal
5 grow wheat/apples/trees/plants
6 slaughter cows

39.2 1 true   4 true
2 true   5 false (a period when we take crops from the ground)
3 false (a long period without rain)   6 false (iron is used to make steel)

39.3 1 a tin can   3 a knife with a steel blade   5 a gold wedding ring
2 a silver spoon   4 a frying pan with a copper base   6 these iron bars are very strong

39.4 1 vegetable   2 metal   3 dairy   4 cereal   5 crop(s)

Unit 40

40.1 1 same /aɪ/   5 same /aɪ/   8 different /ə/; /ɑː/
2 different /e/; /əʊ/   6 different /ʌ/; /ɒ/   9 same /ɒ/
3 different /eə/; /iː/   7 different /æ/; /eɪ/   10 same /aʊ/
4 different /g/; /ʤ/

40.2 *Suggested answers*

Farm animals: pig, cow, horse, chicken, sheep, goat
Wild animals: lion, tiger, elephant, monkey, camel, leopard, bear
Insects: fly, mosquito, wasp, ant, butterfly

40.3 *Possible answers*

1 eagles   6 blue whales
2 whales or sharks   7 monkeys or giraffes
3 monkeys or dogs are the most probable answer   8 snakes
4 leopards, lions, tigers and other big cats   9 elephants
5 camels   10 sheep

40.4 *Possible answers*

1 mouse/rabbit
2 pigs/horses/chickens
3 leopards (panthers and cheetahs would also be possible)
4 ants/flies/bees/spiders (cockroaches would also be possible)
5 camels

40.5 golden eagle = 270 kph when they dive (= fly in a downward direction)
lion = 80 kph   shark = 64 kph   rabbit = 56 kph   elephant = 40 kph   pig = 18 kph
spider = 1.88 kph   snail = 0.05 kph

Unit 41

41.1
1 Great Britain, the United States of America, Canada, Australia, New Zealand
2 Portuguese
3 Dutch
4 Swiss-German, French, Italian. A small number of people also speak a language called Romansch.
5 Arabic
6 Swedish
7 Spanish
8 Egyptian
9 Hebrew
10 China

41.2 J<u>a</u>pan   Japa<u>ne</u>se   Brazilian   E<u>gy</u>ptian   <u>A</u>rabic   It<u>a</u>lian   <u>Au</u>stria   Au<u>str</u>alia
Chi<u>ne</u>se   Portu<u>gue</u>se   Sa<u>u</u>di Ar<u>a</u>bia
Words ending -ia usually have the stress on the third syllable from the end.
Words ending -ian usually have the main stress on the second syllable from the end.
Words ending -ese usually have the stress on the final syllable, i.e. on the -ese.

41.3 *Possible answers*

1 The Japanese	3 Brazilians	5 The Swiss
2 Israelis	4 The British	6 Greeks

41.4

1 Thailand	3 Turkey	5 Egypt	7 Greece	9 Sweden
2 Argentina	4 South Korea	6 Saudi Arabia	8 Israel	10 Portugal

41.5

1 Russian	4 Japanese	7 Dutch	10 French
2 Korean	5 Greek	8 Spanish	11 Swedish
3 Italian	6 Chinese	9 Swiss German	

Unit 42

42.1

1 forehead	8 foot	15 wrist
2 cheek	9 toe	16 hand
3 chin	10 finger	17 bottom
4 chest	11 neck	18 thigh
5 arm	12 shoulder	19 heel
6 hip	13 waist	
7 knee	14 elbow	

42.2
1 blow your nose
2 shake hands
3 comb your hair
4 fold your arms
5 bend your knees
6 nod your head
7 bite your nails

42.3
1 they're happy or being polite
2 running
3 they're happy or when someone says something funny
4 when they're nervous
5 when they have a cold
6 when they want to say 'no'
7 when they mean 'yes'
8 when they're sad, unhappy, or possibly when they're very happy
9 they're tired or bored

42.4

C	E	L	B	O	W	A
H	T	I	A	E	N	R
I	O	P	C	Y	A	M
N	E	C	K	E	I	H
I	H	A	N	K	L	E
K	C	H	E	S	T	E
C	H	E	E	K	A	L

Unit 43

43.1
1 hair
2 skin
3 hair
4 height/build
5 shoulders
6 chests
7 beard/moustache
8 arms/legs
9 looking
10 hair/skin/eyes

43.2
1 beautiful/pretty
2 plain
3 overweight
4 thin
5 good-looking/handsome

43.3
What does he/she look like?
How tall is he/she?
How much does he/she weigh?

Unit 44

44.1

Positive	Negative
clever	stupid
nice	unpleasant
relaxed	tense
hard-working	lazy
cheerful	miserable
generous	mean

44.2
unkind; unfriendly; unreliable; unambitious; unpleasant
inflexible; insensitive
dishonest

44.3
1 mean
2 has no initiative / doesn't use her initiative
3 unreliable
4 punctual
5 lazy
6 shy
7 flexible
8 sensitive
9 insensitive
10 ambitious

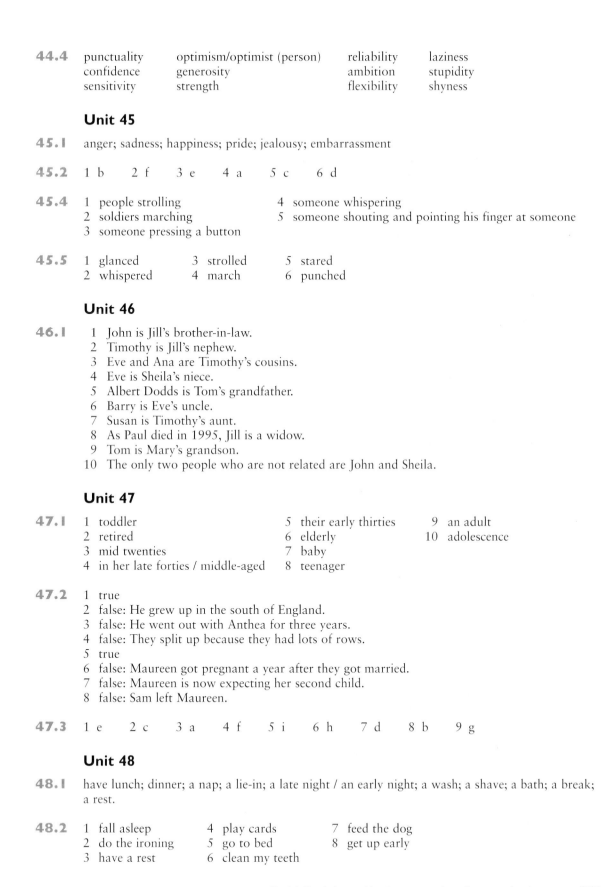

44.4 punctuality optimism/optimist (person) reliability laziness
confidence generosity ambition stupidity
sensitivity strength flexibility shyness

Unit 45

45.1 anger; sadness; happiness; pride; jealousy; embarrassment

45.2 1 b   2 f   3 e   4 a   5 c   6 d

45.4 1 people strolling   4 someone whispering
2 soldiers marching   5 someone shouting and pointing his finger at someone
3 someone pressing a button

45.5 1 glanced   3 strolled   5 stared
2 whispered   4 march   6 punched

Unit 46

46.1 1 John is Jill's brother-in-law.
2 Timothy is Jill's nephew.
3 Eve and Ana are Timothy's cousins.
4 Eve is Sheila's niece.
5 Albert Dodds is Tom's grandfather.
6 Barry is Eve's uncle.
7 Susan is Timothy's aunt.
8 As Paul died in 1995, Jill is a widow.
9 Tom is Mary's grandson.
10 The only two people who are not related are John and Sheila.

Unit 47

47.1 1 toddler   5 their early thirties   9 an adult
2 retired   6 elderly   10 adolescence
3 mid twenties   7 baby
4 in her late forties / middle-aged   8 teenager

47.2 1 true
2 false: He grew up in the south of England.
3 false: He went out with Anthea for three years.
4 false: They split up because they had lots of rows.
5 true
6 false: Maureen got pregnant a year after they got married.
7 false: Maureen is now expecting her second child.
8 false: Sam left Maureen.

47.3 1 e   2 c   3 a   4 f   5 i   6 h   7 d   8 b   9 g

Unit 48

48.1 have lunch; dinner; a nap; a lie-in; a late night / an early night; a wash; a shave; a bath; a break; a rest.

48.2 1 fall asleep   4 play cards   7 feed the dog
2 do the ironing   5 go to bed   8 get up early
3 have a rest   6 clean my teeth

1 bother   3 stay in   5 lie-in   7 on my own / by myself
        2 go out   4 early   6 come round

Unit 49

49.1   1 yes   2 yes   3 no   4 shut   5 three   6 no   7 no   8 no

49.2   1 gate; path; doorbell   3 view   5 belongs; condition
        2 climb; lift   4 rent   6 heat; heating

49.3   *Possible answers*

Positive	*Negative*
the rooms are very light	the rooms are very dark
a good view	no view
quiet	noisy
large rooms	small rooms
in good condition	in bad condition
	draughty

Unit 50

50.1   *Possible answers*

1 sleep
2 cooking and washing-up
3 wash and shower (and bath)
4 sit and relax (and watch TV)
5 eat meals
6 guests sleep / where you keep things you don't use all the time.
7 work/study
8 you have a washing machine / tumble dryer (= machine to dry clothes)

50.2   1 in the fridge   4 in the dishwasher
        2 in the oven   5 in the cupboard
        3 in the washing machine 6 in the cupboard

50.3*   sink (K); curtains (L); carpet (L); dishwasher (K); kettle (K); sofa (L); oven (K); fridge (K);
        armchair (L); cupboard (K); saucepan (K)
        * K = kitchen, L = lounge

50.4   1 in   2 out; back   3 on; in   4 on   5 in   6 out; on

50.6   *Possible answers*

1 oven, TV, radio, hi-fi, washing machine, dishwasher
2 plates, cups, saucers, saucepans, glasses, knives and forks
3 chair, stool, armchair, sofa
4 kettle, saucepan

Unit 51

51.1   1 I cleaned my teeth   5 I had a wash
        2 I went to sleep   6 I put on my pyjamas
        3 I set the alarm clock   7 I got into bed
        4 I switched off the light

        Possible order: 5, 1 (or 1, 5), 6, 3, (could be 3, 6), 7, 4, 2. There are, of course, other variations
            e.g. you might get into bed and then set the alarm clock; etc.

51.2 1 She did the shopping. 4 She hoovered the carpet / did the hoovering.
2 She ironed something. 5 She did the washing.
3 She did the washing-up. 6 She made the bed.

51.3 1 no 3 yes 5 no 7 yes
2 two 4 three 6 yes 8 no

Unit 52

52.1

Infinitive	Past tense	Past participle
burn	burnt (*also* burned)	burnt (*also* burned)
break	broke	broken
drop	dropped	dropped
spill	spilt (also spilled)	spilt (also spilled)
trip	tripped	tripped
lose	lost	lost
leave	left	left

52.2 1 f 2 g 3 e 4 c 5 b 6 a 7 d

52.3 1 someone broke some glasses
2 he has a stain on his trousers
3 he burnt his shirt

52.4 *Possible answers*

1 I dropped it. 5 I'm afraid I lost it.
2 I'm afraid there's something wrong with it. 6 I left it at home.
3 I tripped over. 7 It's not working.
4 It's not working properly. 8 It's out of order.

Unit 53

53.1 1 sold; bought 3 paid 5 won
2 lost; cost; found 4 gave; spent 6 wasted

53.2 1 How much is your gold ring worth?
2 I'm afraid I can't afford it. *or* I'm afraid I can't afford to go.
3 Could you lend me some money?
4 How much did your dictionary cost? *or*
How much did you pay for your dictionary?

53.3 1 yes 2 no 3 yes 4 no 5 yes 6 no 7 no 8 no

Unit 54

54.1 1 a cough, sore throat, sneezing
2 a cough, sore throat, sneezing, temperature, aching muscles
3 runny nose, sneezing, sore eyes
4 headache
5 keep going to the toilet
6 difficulty in breathing

54.2 1 different /dɪ/, /daɪ/ 4 different /aɪ/, /ɪ/
2 same /k/ 5 different /uː/, /ʌ/
3 same /ɜː/ 6 different /ɒ/, /ʌ/

54.3 *Possible answer*

I had terrible toothache, so I made an appoitment to see the dentist. He had a look at the tooth and decided that I needed a filling. It was quite a big one, so I had an injection first. Afterwards it felt so much better.

54.4

1 hurts		3 ache		5 lung		7 asthma		9 myself
2 attack		4 pain		6 prescription		8 disease		10 aches

Unit 55

55.1

Noun	Verb	Noun	Verb
cut	cut	blood	bleed
wound	wound	bandage	bandage
injury	injure	bruise	bruise
shot	shoot	treatment	treat

55.2 *Model answer*

Paul somehow fell from the tree where he was picking apples and he knocked himself unconscious. His wife immediately rang for an ambulance and it soon arrived and rushed him to hospital. He was suffering from concussion and had to have some stitches for a large cut on the side of his head, but fortunately it was nothing more serious than that.

55.3 *Possible answers*

1 I was preparing the dinner and I cut my finger on the vegetable knife.
2 he was in a fight and someone gave him a black eye.
3 I was running for a bus and I hit my foot on something on the pavement and fell over.
4 We were running for the same ball; I'm afraid I didn't see him and he didn't see me, and we collided.

Unit 56

56.1 *Possible answers*

shoes, socks, jeans, trousers, shorts, gloves, tights

56.2 4, 7, 1, 3, 5, 9, 2, 8, 6

56.3 an earring, a ring, a button, a pocket, a necklace, gloves.

56.4 *Most likely answers*

1 blouse *or* *top; skirt   3 tie; shirt   5 too; enough
2 suit; trousers   4 enough; size
(**top* is a general word)

56.5 *Possible answers*

worn by women: dress, blouse, skirt, tights, necklace
worn by both: hat, gloves, jeans, trousers, jacket, scarf, coat, shirt

Unit 57

57.1

1 clothes		3 electrical appliances		5 toys	
2 furniture		4 household goods		6 stationery	

57.2 newsagent: envelopes, a newspaper
chemist: toothbrush, aspirin
department store: envelopes, an armchair, gloves (and possibly the apples, carrots, coca cola, chicken and a loaf of bread)
butcher: a chicken
greengrocer: apples and carrots
supermarket: a chicken, a toothbrush, a loaf of bread, coca cola, apples, carrots, a newspaper

Other things you could buy in each shop:
newsagent: cigarettes, sweets, greeting cards
chemist: soap, shampoo, perfume, toothpaste
department store: clothes, washing machines, saucepans
butcher: steak, sausages, bacon, lamb
greengrocer: onions, oranges, peas, lemons
supermarket: coffee, wine, cakes, biscuits, cheese

57.3
1 boutique	3 shop/sales assistant	5 till / cash desk	7 butcher('s)
2 shopping centre	4 changing/fitting room	6 window shopping	8 chemist('s)

57.4
1 looking for	3 being served	5 take it
2 size	4 changing room	6 till / cash desk

Unit 58

58.1
1 peas/potato; peach/pear
2 beans; banana
3 mushroom; melon
4 carrot/cauliflower/cabbage; cherry
5 aubergine; apple

58.2
lettuce/chicken /ɪ/
onion/mushroom /ʌ/
orange/cauliflower /ɒ/
banana/melon /ə/
aubergine/tomato /əʊ/
salmon/lamb /æ/

58.3
1 salmon; the others are types of meat but salmon is a fish
2 salmon; the others are types of shellfish but salmon is a fish
3 aubergine; the others are found in salad but aubergine isn't
4 peach; the others are vegetables but a peach is a fruit
5 mussels; the others are types of meat but mussels is a shellfish

58.4 *Most likely answers:*

always	*usually*	*never*
cherries	apples	bananas
grapes	peaches	pineapples
strawberries	pears	melons
		lemons
		oranges
		mangoes

Unit 59

59.2
1 chicken liver pate
2 tagliatelle with courgettes, cream and bacon
3 fillet steak
4 baked salmon
5 steak with a <u>pepper</u> sauce
6 breast of chicken in a <u>white wine</u> sauce
7 fillet steak
8 ice cream and chocolate mousse
9 fruit salad
10 probably the soup, salmon, and fruit salad

59.3 *Possible answers*

lemon – bitter   chicken – bland or tender   honey – sweet   bacon – salty or fatty or tasty
ice cream – sweet   fillet steak – tender or fatty or lean   chillies – hot and spicy
avocado – bland

Unit 60

60.1
Towns	*Villages*
noisy	quiet and peaceful
dirty and polluted	clean air
exciting	boring
stressful	relaxing
crowded	lots of open space
lots to do	nothing to do in the evening
dangerous	safe

60.2 *Possible answers*

Town	*Country*	*Town and country*
factories	fields	gates
shopping centres	woods	car parks
pollution	tractors	footpaths
night-life	villages	libraries
Town Hall, suburbs	valleys	traffic

60.3
1 gate	3 path	5 valley	7 valley
2 tractor	4 field	6 wood	8 village

Unit 61

61.1 Go <u>along this road</u> and take <u>the first turning</u> at the junction. Then you <u>keep going</u> and <u>turn</u> right when you <u>get to</u> the <u>school</u>. Then <u>turn right</u> again <u>into Maldon</u> Road, and the bank is <u>on the left-hand side</u> just <u>after the</u> cinema.

61.2
1 fasten your seat belt; get in / start	4 braked; crashed	7 traffic jam
2 injured; damaged	5 pavement	8 lane; overtook
3 rush hour	6 broke down	

61.3
1 park	4 one lane	7 lights
2 speed limit	5 motorway	8 bridge
3 turn right	6 park	9 roadworks

Unit 62

62.1 1 ride 3 fares 5 fly 7 take
2 get in 4 run 6 timetable 8 missed

62.2 *Possible answers*

1 bus fare; train fare; air fare; taxi fare
2 get on the bus; get on the coach; get on the train; get on the plane
3 bus station; railway station; coach station
4 bus driver; train driver; taxi driver; van driver
5 get in the car; get in the taxi; get in the van. (People also sometimes say 'get on the bus' or 'get in the train'.)
6 train journey; bus journey; taxi journey; coach journey

62.3 1 coach 2 van 3 lorry 4 motorbike 5 bike

62.4 1 platform 3 full up 5 punctual 7 journey
2 bus stop 4 arrival 6 queue 8 due

Unit 63

63.1 1 earn £500 3 pay income tax 5 deal with clients
2 work overtime 4 go to meetings 6 run a shop

63.2 1 What's your job?
2 My salary is $50,000.
3 My total income is £30,000.
4 I work for a pharmaceutical company.
5 My job involves looking after and maintaining all the hardware.
6 I'm in charge of one of the smaller departments.

63.3 A: What are your working hours?
A: Do you do/work any overtime?
A: How much holiday / how many weeks' holiday do you get?
A: Teachers don't earn very much, do they?

Unit 64

64.1 *Possible answers*

1 a lawyer or doctor 5 a policeman 9 a doctor, nurse, surgeon, or vet
2 a pilot 6 a vet 10 a soldier, sailor, or someone in the air force
3 a sailor 7 a fireman
4 a mechanic 8 an accountant

64.2 *Possible answers*

1 an architect designs buildings 6 plans the construction of roads and bridges
2 lectures in a university 7 builds walls
3 controls the financial affairs of a company 8 buys and sells shares
4 treats animals 9 repairs cars
5 advises people on legal problems 10 operates on people

64.3 1 Really. When did he join the army? 3 Really. When did he join the air force?
2 Really. When did he join the navy? 4 Really. When did he join the fire brigade?

64.4 *Possible answers*

an architect to design your house
a lawyer to give you legal advice
a carpenter to make cupboards and fit doors
a plumber to fit the kitchen and bathroom
an electrician to do all the electrical work
an accountant to calculate how much everything will cost

Unit 65

65.1 1 sacked/dismissed   3 resigned   5 prospects   7 employees
2 unemployed   4 promoted   6 retired

65.2 1 b   2 e   3 d   4 a   5 f   6 c

65.3 1 part-time   3 challenge   5 rise   7 over
2 course   4 market   6 her   8 apply

65.4

Verb	General noun	Personal noun
promote	promotion	–
employ	employment	employer (boss)/employee (worker)
resign	resignation	–
retire	retirement	–
train	training	trainer (gives the training) / trainee (receives it)

Unit 66

66.1 *Possible answers*

1 write: a letter, a report, a memo, a cheque
2 send: a letter, a report, a fax, an invoice
3 make: phone calls, products, the tea, mistakes
4 arrange: meetings, conferences, visits, training courses

66.2 1 noticeboard   3 filing cabinet; briefcase   5 wastepaper basket/bin
2 assembly line   4 paperwork

66.3 1 warehouse   3 goods   5 diary   7 retailer
2 automation   4 calendar   6 invoice   8 drawer

66.4 1 manufactured   4 stored
2 fit   5 deliver ('send' would also be possible)
3 examines/checks

Unit 67

67.1 1 loan   3 inflation   5 it breaks even
2 interest   4 aims/goals/objectives   6 recession

67.2 1 gradual   3 thriving   5 aims
2 sharp   4 expanding   6 gone up

67.3 1 rose   3 sharp fall   5 rose sharply
2 fell slightly   4 steady rise   6 rose

67.4 1 public expenditure   3 tax cuts   5 raw material(s)
2 political/economic stability   4 interest/inflation rate*   6 profit and loss
*(**Rate of inflation** is also commonly used.)

Unit 68

68.1 product, price, promotion, place

68.2 sales manager; sales figures; sales forecast; market share; market leader; market research; marketing manager; marketing department.

1 forecast   3 figures   5 research
2 manager; department   4 leader; share

68.3 1 representative   3 products   5 consumers
2 products   4 competitors   6 customers/clients

68.4

Noun	Adjective	Noun	Adjective
excitement	exciting	prestige	prestigious
glamour	glamorous	luxury	luxurious
competition	competitive	reliability	reliable
fashion	fashionable	danger	dangerous

Unit 69

69.1 *Possible answers*

1 cards, musical instruments, board games
2 stamps, coins, antiques
3 hiking, rock climbing, jogging, hunting, camping

69.2 1 photography   4 jogging   7 DIY
2 collecting antiques   5 makes her own clothes
3 playing a musical instrument   6 chess

69.3 1 go   3 made   5 do   7 joined
2 took up; gave it up   4 collects   6 play   8 do

Unit 70

70.1 head it; pass it; catch it; throw it; hit it; kick it

70.2 *Possible answers*

1 tennis, table tennis, squash, badminton (shuttlecock), cricket, baseball, hockey
2 football, rugby, American football, hockey, basketball
3 rugby, American football, cricket, baseball, basketball
4 football, rugby
5 football

70.3

Sport	Place	Equipment
swimming	pool	trunks (men); costume (women)
football	pitch	boots, shorts; goals; net (for the goal); whistle (referee)
motor racing	track	crash helmet
golf	course	clubs
boxing	ring	shorts, boots, gloves, vest
tennis	court	racket, shorts, net, training shoes

70.4
1 false (they are the crowd/spectators) 5 true
2 true   6 false (it is played on a court)
3 true   7 true
4 true   8 false (they wear a swimming costume)

Unit 71

71.1
Infinitive	Past tense	Past participle
win	won	won
lose	lost	lost
beat	beat	beaten
lead	led	led
catch	caught	caught
draw	drew	drawn

71.2
1 nil–nil two–one four all   2 fifteen love forty thirty deuce

71.3
1 beat   5 lost   9 set   13 match
2 penalty   6 won   10 lost   14 score
3 score   7 lost   11 set
4 extra time 8 won   12 tie-break

71.4
1 true
2 false (it has a referee)
3 false (it is only decided on a tie-break if the score reaches 6–6)
4 true
5 true
6 false (it is still in progress)
7 true
8 false (if you lose you are out of the competition)

71.5
1 rugby   3 tennis   5 motor racing   7 swimming
2 football   4 basketball 6 football   8 athletics

Unit 72

72.1
1 stalls   2 C   3 yes   4 no

72.2
1 musical   3 the audience 5 director   7 reviews   9 to book
2 the cast   4 clap   6 critics   8 subtitles 10 stars

72.3
1 *Dirty Harry* could be described as an action film or a thriller.
2 *Blade Runner* is a science fiction film.
3 *Four Weddings and a Funeral* is a comedy.
4 *Schindler's List* could be described as a war film or a thriller.
5 *Dances with Wolves* is a western.

Unit 73

73.1
1 Tolstoy – novelist   7 Verdi – composer
2 Wordsworth – poet   8 Mick Jagger – singer and songwriter
3 Ibsen – dramatist   9 Nascimento – singer-songwriter
4 Mishima – novelist   10 Paul Tortelier – cellist
5 Chekhov – dramatist   11 Paul Simon – singer and songwriter
6 Mozart – composer   12 Mark Knopfler – singer, songwriter, guitarist

13 Henry Moore – sculptor
14 Borges – novelist and short story writer
15 Picasso – painter
16 Saki – short story writer
17 Bernstein – composer and conductor
18 Giacometti – sculptor

73.2 pianist; guitarist; drummer; violinist; cellist; flautist

73.3 1 a landscape   2 a portrait   3 an abstract

73.4
1 orchestra
2 group/band; solo artist
3 classical; composer
4 exhibition; gallery
5 write; performs/plays
6 opera
7 novel
8 play

Unit 74

74.2 Minister to leave his/her job / resign
Government reduces spending ...
New attempt/try to reduce ...
Bad weather has a terrible effect on farmers
Germany supports ...
Minister in argument about tax
Police discover important witness
Japan and US enter fresh discussions

Unit 75

75.1
1 Could you turn it up, please?
2 Could you turn/switch over?
3 Could you turn it down?
4 Could you turn/switch it off?

75.2 *Documentary*: Cutting Edge and World in Action
Game show: Bruce's Price is Right (The Krypton Factor is also a game show)
Quiz show: Telly Addicts
Drama series: Cracker
Current affairs: World in Action
The soap operas are: Coronation Street and EastEnders.
The comedy series is Two Point Four Children.

Unit 76

76.1 *Possible answers*

phone number; phone card; phone box; telephone directory; answerphone; on the phone

76.2 A 1 My name is   2 message   3 out / not here
      4 ring you / call you back   5 number
B 6 Is that   7 afraid   8 be back   9 leave (a) message
      10 phone me / ring me / ring me back
C 11 Is that   12 it's   13 rang   14 get through   15 engaged   16 on

Unit 77

77.1 *Possible answers*

1 software	5 computer-literate	9 laser printer
2 a word processor	6 keyboard	10 laptop
3 floppy disk	7 a computer program/programmer/game	11 spreadsheet
4 user-friendly	8 CD-ROM	12 e-mail

77.2
1 cut
2 print
3 save the data in this document
4 open a new document
5 open an existing document
6 copy
7 paste

77.3

1 computer	3 down	5 back-up	7 cut	9 save
2 printed	4 save	6 graphics	8 graphics	10 back-up

Unit 78

78.1

1 Maths	3 Science	5 Technology	7 Art	9 French
2 History	4 English	6 Geography	8 Music	10 Economics

78.2
1 3
2 5
3 comprehensive
4 16
5 French and German
6 12
7 They leave
8 Go to university or get a job

78.4

1 to school	3 to bed	5 to church
2 into hospital	4 to university	

Unit 79

79.1

1 medicine	3 agriculture	5 business studies	7 politics
2 architecture	4 psychology	6 history of art	8 law

79.2

1 a grant	3 undergraduates	5 graduates	7 research
2 degree	4 lecturers	6 postgraduates	8 lecture

79.3

1 doing	3 get	5 doing	7 make
2 get	4 go to	6 doing/conducting	8 lasts

Unit 80

80.1 3, 9, 7, 8, 2, 6, 4, 1, 5

80.2

1 the police	3 prisoners	5 barristers (lawyers)
2 the judge	4 the jury	6 criminals

80.3

1 broken; committed	3 fine	5 guilty	7 convicted; sentence
2 against	4 prove	6 evidence	8 offence

80.4
1 Yes
2 Visit the people who were broken into and take fingerprints if possible.
3 Probably not
4 burglary
5 No, not at 15.
6 Probably a suspended sentence (= the boys are free but if they commit another crime in the next year or two years, they will receive a much tougher punishment) unless the boys already have a record for burglary. In this case, they could be sent to a centre for young offenders.

Unit 81

81.1

Crimes	People	Places
murder	thief	prison
robbery	barrister	cell
rape	burglar	court
manslaughter	judge	police station
shoplifting	criminal	
	prisoner	
	jury	

81.2
1 burglary   3 charged with shoplifting   5 charged with theft
2 with murder   4 with manslaughter

81.4
1 carry   3 punishment   5 defence
2 allowed/able   4 spray   6 reduce/cut

Unit 82

82.1

Abstract noun	Person	Adjective
politics	politician	political
democracy	democrat	democratic
dictatorship	dictator	dictatorial
socialism	socialist	socialist
conservatism	conservative	conservative
liberalism	liberal	liberal

82.2
1 elections   4 parliament   7 majority
2 Prime   5 system   8 form
3 votes   6 party   9 power

Possible reasons to justify this system are:

One single party has power, so there is little compromise which produces a strong government; there is a single set of policies; the government has a majority and so is relatively stable and does not need to call elections often.

Unit 83

83.1
1 identity/landing card   3 driving/TV licence
2 birth/marriage/exam certificate   4 application/enrolment/registration form

83.2
1 get/obtain   4 sign   7 enrolment
2 checked   5 runs out / expires; renew
3 fill in   6 queues

83.4
1 when were you born?   4 When did you arrive?
2 Where do you come from?   5 When are you leaving?
3 Are you single or married?

83.5 *Problems mentioned were:*

1 long queues
2 waiting in one queue, then you discover you should be in another queue
3 delays e.g. in getting a new passport
4 officials putting the wrong information on documents, which then need to be changed, e.g. driving licence
5 officials losing information you have given them

6 being asked to explain the same information over and over again to different officials, especially over the telephone
7 spending a long time getting a document in one country, then you discover that nobody is interested in it when you arrive in another country
8 officials who act like policemen

Unit 84

84.1
1 ally = friendly country
2 release = permit to go free
3 conflict = strong disagreement
4 troops = large group of soldiers
5 invade = enter another country by force and in large numbers
6 wound = injure from fighting
7 territory = land controlled by a country
8 ceasefire = stop fighting

84.2
1 carry on fighting / continue to fight
2 they will retreat
3 run out of food
4 mostly civilians
5 release them

84.3

First mention	repeated as ...
ordinary people	civilians
soldiers	troops
shelling	firing
hit	wounded
allow them to enter	let anyone in
captured	take control of
soldiers	army

84.4 *Possible answers*

1 Terrorists use hostages for bargaining, e.g. they release hostages if governments give them money or release political prisoners. Hostages also give the terrorists protection.
2 Some governments refuse on moral grounds, i.e. they believe it is wrong to bargain with hostages. Some governments believe that if you agree to terrorists demands on one occasion, terrorists will attack again.

Unit 85

85.1
1 the ozone layer
2 acid rain
3 industrial waste
4 a bottle bank
5 global warming
6 exhaust fumes
7 tropical rainforests
8 natural or human resources

85.2

Noun	Verb	Noun	Adjective
waste	waste	damage	damaging
protection	protect	environment	environmental
destruction	destroy	harm	harmful (≠ harmless)
pollution	pollute	danger	dangerous
damage	damage	safety	safe

85.3
1 plants and animals
2 smoke from factories
3 the earth
4 carbon dioxide
5 destroys the ozone layer

85.4 We should: recycle paper etc.; save/keep/protect tropical rainforests; plant more trees; save water and energy

We shouldn't: throw away paper etc.; destroy the ozone layer; waste water and energy; cut down tropical rainforests

85.5 1 false   2 true   3 true   4 true   5 true

Unit 86

86.1
1 boarding card
2 baggage reclaim
3 excess baggage
4 passport control
5 hand luggage
6 duty tree
7 overhead locker
8 take-off
9 departure lounge
10 check-in

86.2
1 check-in
2 boarding card
3 excess baggage
4 departure lounge
5 hand luggage
6 overhead locker
7 runway
8 stewards (or cabin crew)
9 terminal building
10 baggage reclaim

86.3
1 took off
2 captain/pilot
3 fasten
4 flew
5 landed
6 get off
7 flight

Unit 87

87.1 7, 9, 2, 4, 12, 8, 5, 6, 10, 11, 1, 3

87.2 *Possible answers*

1 I'd like to book a double room for two nights for next Thursday and Friday, please? *or* Do you have a double room free for next Friday and Saturday?
2 Could I have my bill, please? *or* Could you order a taxi for me, please?
3 Could I have a call tomorrow morning at 7 a.m., please?
4 Could you put it on my bill, please?
5 I'm afraid there's something wrong with the shower in my room. *or* I'm afraid the shower in my room isn't working very well.
6 How do I get to the nearest bank from here? *or* Could you tell me the way to the nearest bank, please?

Unit 88

88.1
1 great/lovely time
2 sightseeing
3 packed
4 a look
5 souvenirs
6 galleries
7 lost
8 market
9 go out
10 spent
11 taken

88.3 *Possible answers*

1 Yes, it's a great place.
2 Yes, it's very cosmopolitan.
3 Yes, it was absolutely packed.
4 Yes, the night-life is fantastic.
5 Yes, we had a great time.

Unit 89

89.1 *Possible answers*

sunshine; suntan; suntan lotion; sun cream; sunburn; sunglasses; sunbed; sunbathe; sunlight; sunblock; sunset; sunrise; sunshade; sunstroke

89.2
1	sandy beach	3	beach umbrella	5	sunbathe	7	big waves
2	suntan lotion	4	rough sea	6	seaside	8	steep cliff

1 to spend time on the beach
2 because they want a suntan
3 to protect themselves from the sun
4 to protect themselves and also help to get a suntan
5 very painful
6 surfing

89.3
1	get away	3	quiet	5	walk/stroll
2	country/countryside	4	lie/sunbathe	6	picnic

89.4
1	resort	3	lying/sunbathing	5	picnic
2	different/various	4	rent	6	quiet

Unit 90

90.1
1	at	3	at	5	on	7	on	9	on	11	in
2	in	4	in	6	at	8	at	10	at	12	on

90.2
1	by	3	since	5	during	7	in	9	throughout
2	until	4	for	6	for	8	during	10	for

90.3
1	two	3	1963	5	ten
2	17th	4	12 hours 30 minutes	6	1960s

90.4
1	a few days ago	4	for ages
2	for the time being	5	a long time ago
3	recently/lately		

Unit 91

91.1
1 four hundred and sixty-two
2 two and a half
3 two thousand three hundred and forty-five
4 six point seven five
5 nought point two five
6 three and a third
7 one million two hundred and fifty thousand
8 ten point oh four
9 forty-seven per cent
10 the tenth of September *or* September the tenth
11 the third of July *or* July the third
12 six oh two eight four seven seven *or* double seven
13 five degrees below zero *or* minus five degrees centigrade
14 nineteen oh three *or* nineteen hundred and three
15 eighteen seventy six

1 thousand   4 twenty-five out of forty
2 the tenth of September   5 the thirty-first of August
3 two hundred and twenty   6 seven two three six oh nine

91.3   1 59   2 192   3 60   4 5   5 8   6 15

Unit 92

92.2   *Possible questions*

How tall is she?
What size shoes does she take?
How high is the mountain? / What's the height of the mountain?
How far is it from one side of the lake to the other?
How big is the lake? / What's the size of the lake?
How deep is it? / What's the depth of the lake?
How long is the pitch? / What's the length of the pitch?
How wide is the pitch? / What's the width of the pitch?

92.3   1 No, he's quite thin.   5 No, it's a great place.
2 No, it's very shallow.   6 No, he's fairly short.
3 No, it's a tall building, actually.   7 No, it's a great big place.
4 No, it's quite narrow.

Unit 93

93.1   1 a rectangular table   6 an oval-shaped plate
2 a star-shaped ring   7 diamond-shaped earrings
3 a round window   8 a striped sofa
4 a check shirt   9 a pointed nose
5 a tartan tie   10 light grey jeans

93.2   1 pencil/pen   6 the sea
2 salmon   7 an egg
3 football/rugby/hockey pitch or tennis court   8 a 'warning' triangle
4 carrot   9 a coat hanger
5 moon   10 a square

Unit 94

94.1   1 bottle   3 bowl   5 packet   7 tin
2 jug   4 box   6 bag   8 jar

94.2   *Probable answers*

The most surprising and unlikely are: a vase of coffee; a tube of cigarettes; a carton of toothpaste
It may also be quite unusual to have a 'glass of soup'.

94.3   1 bunch (also 'bouquet')   7 group
2 gang   8 team
3 slices (also pieces and bits)   9 piece (also bit)
4 piece (also bit)   10 drop (also bit)
5 bit   11 pair
6 sheet (also piece and bit)   12 bit

Wrong answers

1 none
2 sheet
3 gang   (gang would be appropriate if you have a negative view of journalists)
4 group
5 none
6 piece
7 none
8 piece

Unit 95

95.1

1 ripe	4 water	7 photo	10 washing powder
2 new	5 sore	8 donkey	11 doorbell
3 horrible	6 fresh	9 cod	12 silk

95.2 *Possible answers*

1 looks sad.
2 looks/feels soft.
3 tastes horrible.

95.3 *Correct answers*

1 listening to; heard	6 listening
2 heard	7 touch
3 hear	8 press
4 look at	9 hold
5 watch	10 watch ('look' is also possible here but less likely); see

Unit 96

96.1 *Possible answers*

Please queue other side
Beware of pickpockets
Mind the step
Mind your head
Sold-out
Please do not disturb; Please do not feed the animals
Out of order
No exit; No smoking; No parking
Keep right; Keep off the grass

96.2 *Possible answers*

1 In a Bed & Breakfast (cheap hotel)	5 Public telephone
2 On the underground	6 Theatre or cinema
3 Customs at an airport or port	7 On the outside of a parcel/package
4 Bank or post office	8 In a park

96.3

1 Please do not feed the animals	5 Do not lean out of the window
2 Do not leave bags unattended	6 No smoking
3 Please do not disturb	7 Keep right; No smoking; No exit
4 No parking	8 Mind your head

Unit 97

97.1 *Possible answers*

1 a type of perfume or after shave	6 programme
2 the key	7 clothes or belongings
3 whisky	8 a type of toy
4 knife and fork	9 a suitcase
5 flour	10 shampoo or conditioner

97.2 *Possible additions*

A: How many people were at the conference?
B: <u>Roughly</u> 400.
A: Did you enjoy it?
B: Yes, <u>sort of</u>.
A: You don't seem very sure.
B: Well, there were some good <u>things</u>, but it was <u>a bit</u> too long.
A: And did you go to John's talk?
B: Naturally.
A: How did it go?
B: Well he was <u>sort of</u> nervous at the beginning, but he soon got more confident and I think it went really well.
A: Did he have a big audience?
B: <u>About</u> 75.
A: That's good, isn't it?
B: I think John was <u>a bit</u> disappointed – he wanted at least a hundred.

97.3 *Possible answers*

1 more or less	3 sort of	5 sort of
2 a bit	4 more or less/roughly	6 a bit / sort of

Unit 98

98.1
1 American (because of vacation): fall
2 American (because of high school): semester
3 British (because of biscuits): sweets
4 American (because of garbage): trashcan
5 British (because of trousers): waistcoat
6 American (because of truck): highway
7 Probably American (because of apartment): elevator
8 British (because of fortnight): holiday
9 American (because of subway with this meaning): parking lot
10 British (because of trainers): wardrobe

98.2

British	American
holiday	vacation
trousers	pants
flat	apartment
trainers	sneakers
secondary school	high school
biscuits	cookies
rubbish	garbage
main road	highway
fortnight	two weeks / fourteen days
underground (tube)	subway

1 gas/petrol
2 freeway/motorway
3 gas station / petrol station or garage
4 parking lot / car park

5 cab/taxi
6 sidewalk/pavement
7 truck driver / lorry driver

98.4 1 queue   2 curtains   3 reverse charge call   4 barrister   5 bill

Unit 99

99.1
Formal	Informal
purchase	handy
resume	loo
thus	terrific
commence	quid
apprehend	reckon
	guy

purchase/buy; handy/convenient; loo/toilet; resume / start again; thus/therefore; terrific/fantastic; quid/pounds; commence/start; apprehend/catch; reckon/think; guy/man

99.2
1 When are you going to pick up your bike?
2 Most of the kids are very bright.
3 I reckon it'll start pretty soon.
4 Do you fancy going out for a meal?
5 My flat is five minutes from where I work, so it's very handy.
6 What's up?
7 The guy in the market wanted 20 quid for this ring.
8 Where did you buy/get that book?
9 They'll never catch him.
10 I'm just going to the loo.

99.3 We regret to inform you that we are unable to lend you the sum of £500 that you require, but it may be possible to grant you a loan for part of the sum.

If you are still interested, would you like to contact our main office to arrange an appointment with the assistant manager. He will be happy to discuss the matter further.

99.4
1 attend (*fml*) = go to
2 a drag (*infml*) = boring
3 pinched (*infml*) = stolen

4 bloke (*infml*) = man
5 permitted (*fml*) = allowed

Unit 100

100.1
1 British Broadcasting Corporation
2 Member of Parliament
3 European Union
4 Value Added Tax

5 Prime Minister
6 United Nations
7 United Kingdom
8 Organisation of Petroleum Exporting Countries

100.2 Michael
Pete had a maths exam this afternoon and then he had to take his bike to the repair shop, so he'll probably be a bit late home. You can watch TV while you're waiting for him and please help yourself to anything from the fridge. If there's a problem (e.g. Dr Brown rings about the flu vaccination) my phone number is next to the photos on the dining room table. I should be home myself by about 5 p.m.
Margaret (Peter's mum)

100.3   1 e.g.   2 etc.   3 St.   4 i.e.   5 Mr   6 Dr

100.4   1 e.g.   3 language lab   5 etc.   7 ad(vert)   9 i.e.
            2 bike   4 board   6 flu   8 fridge   10 case

100.5   PTO stands for 'please turn over' at the bottom of a page.
            RSVP means 'please reply' (from the French 'repondez, s'il vous plaît') and is found at the bottom
            of formal invitations e.g. to a reception or wedding. The French do not use this expression or
            abbreviation however.
            c/o stands for 'care of'. You put this on an envelope when the person you write to does not live at
            the address on the letter but can be reached there.
            asap stands for 'as soon as possible' and is commonly used in faxes; the letters are read
            individually a-s-a-p.

Phonetic symbols

Vowel sounds

Symbol	Examples		
/iː/	sleep	me	
/i/	happy	recipe	
/ɪ/	pin	dinner	
/ʊ/	foot	could	pull
/uː/	do	shoe	through
/e/	red	head	said
/ə/	arrive	father	colour
/ɜː/	turn	bird	work
/ɔː/	sort	thought	walk
/æ/	cat	black	
/ʌ/	sun	enough	wonder
/ɒ/	got	watch	sock
/ɑː/	part	heart	laugh
/eɪ/	name	late	aim
/aɪ/	my	idea	time
/ɔɪ/	boy	noise	
/eə/	pair	where	bear
/ɪə/	hear	beer	
/əʊ/	go	home	show
/aʊ/	out	cow	
/ʊə/	pure	fewer	

Consonant sounds

Symbol	Examples		
/p/	put		
/b/	book		
/t/	take		
/d/	dog		
/k/	car	kick	
/g/	go	guarantee	
/tʃ/	catch	church	
/dʒ/	age	lounge	
/f/	for	cough	
/v/	love	vehicle	
/θ/	thick	path	
/ð/	this	mother	
/s/	since	rice	
/z/	zoo	houses	
/ʃ/	shop	sugar	machine
/ʒ/	pleasure	usual	vision
/h/	hear	hotel	
/m/	make		
/n/	name	now	
/ŋ/	bring		
/l/	look	while	
/r/	road		
/j/	young		
/w/	wear		

Pronunciation problems

when 'a' is /eɪ/	when 'u' is /ʌ/	when 'i' is /aɪ/	when 'o' or 'oo' is /ʌ/
p<u>a</u>tient	p<u>u</u>nctual	p<u>i</u>lot	gl<u>o</u>ves
<u>A</u>sia	l<u>u</u>ggage	v<u>i</u>rus	<u>o</u>ven
d<u>a</u>ngerous	h<u>u</u>ngry	d<u>i</u>al	m<u>o</u>nth
p<u>a</u>vement	disc<u>u</u>ss	hepat<u>i</u>tis	fr<u>o</u>nt
b<u>a</u>con	f<u>u</u>nction	m<u>i</u>nus	m<u>o</u>nkey
phr<u>a</u>se	p<u>u</u>blish	l<u>i</u>cence	g<u>o</u>vernment
eng<u>a</u>ged	c<u>u</u>stoms	d<u>i</u>et	w<u>o</u>rry
sunb<u>a</u>the	l<u>u</u>ck	str<u>i</u>ped	fl<u>oo</u>d
l<u>a</u>tely	bankr<u>u</u>pt	t<u>i</u>ny	bl<u>oo</u>d

When ow is /əʊ/ e.g. r<u>ow</u> (= line), thr<u>ow</u>, bl<u>ow</u>, sh<u>ow</u>, kn<u>ow</u>, elb<u>ow</u>
When ou or ow is /aʊ/ e.g. l<u>ou</u>nge, dr<u>ou</u>ght, r<u>ow</u> (= argument), t<u>ow</u>el, all<u>ow</u>ed, bl<u>ou</u>se, sh<u>ow</u>er
When ou is /uː/ e.g. s<u>ou</u>p, gr<u>ou</u>p, thr<u>ou</u>gh, w<u>ou</u>nd, s<u>ou</u>venir, r<u>ou</u>tine
When ou is /ʌ/ e.g. c<u>ou</u>sin, c<u>ou</u>ple, tr<u>ou</u>ble, t<u>ou</u>gh, r<u>ou</u>gh, en<u>ou</u>gh
When a, au or aw is /ɔː/ e.g. dr<u>a</u>w, r<u>a</u>w, l<u>a</u>w, st<u>a</u>ll, f<u>a</u>ll, c<u>au</u>se, <u>au</u>dience, l<u>au</u>nch, exh<u>au</u>sted
When a or au is /ɑː/ e.g. v<u>a</u>se, c<u>a</u>lm, l<u>au</u>gh, dr<u>au</u>ghty, h<u>a</u>lf
When a or u is /ɪ/ e.g. b<u>u</u>sy, b<u>u</u>siness, min<u>u</u>te, lett<u>u</u>ce, purch<u>a</u>se, surf<u>a</u>ce, or<u>a</u>nge, dam<u>a</u>ge
When o is /uː/ e.g. m<u>o</u>ve, pr<u>o</u>ve, impr<u>o</u>ve, l<u>o</u>se
When or or ur is /ɜː/ e.g. p<u>ur</u>ple, b<u>ur</u>n, b<u>ur</u>glary, w<u>or</u>th, w<u>or</u>k, c<u>ur</u>tain
When ea is /e/ e.g. dr<u>ea</u>dful, j<u>ea</u>lous, h<u>ea</u>lth, d<u>ea</u>d, br<u>ea</u>d, inst<u>ea</u>d, pl<u>ea</u>sant, w<u>ea</u>ther, w<u>ea</u>pon

Silent letters (the underlined letters are silent):
<u>i</u>sland, <u>k</u>nee, <u>k</u>nife, <u>k</u>now, <u>k</u>nock, <u>k</u>nowledge, <u>w</u>rong, <u>w</u>rist, mus<u>c</u>le, cas<u>t</u>le, whis<u>t</u>le, fas<u>t</u>en, lis<u>t</u>en, bom<u>b</u>, lam<u>b</u>, thum<u>b</u>, com<u>b</u>, s<u>c</u>issors, p<u>s</u>ychology, <u>h</u>onest, <u>h</u>our, cup<u>b</u>oard, ans<u>w</u>er, <u>g</u>uess, hand<u>s</u>ome, ai<u>s</u>le, hal<u>f</u>, ca<u>l</u>m, Chris<u>t</u>mas, mor<u>t</u>gage

Short syllables (the underlined letters often disappear or are only a /ə/):
fatt<u>e</u>ning; mis<u>e</u>rable; comf<u>or</u>table; fash<u>io</u>nable; rest<u>au</u>rant; strawb<u>e</u>rry, eventu<u>a</u>lly, parli<u>a</u>ment, actu<u>a</u>lly occasi<u>o</u>nally, pris<u>o</u>ner, medi<u>c</u>ine, fav<u>ou</u>rite, temp<u>e</u>rature, lit<u>e</u>rature

Problem pairs:
quite /kwaɪt/ and quiet /'kwaɪət/   desert /'dezət/ and dessert /də'zɜːt/
soup /suːp/ and soap /səʊp/

Note: The pronunciation of these letters at the end of words is often like this:
-ous /əs/ e.g. famous, dangerous, unconscious, ambitious, cautious, jealous
-age /ɪdʒ/ e.g. luggage, baggage, village, damage, cabbage, bandage, message, manage, garage
-able /əbl/ e.g. comfortable, reliable, suitable, unbreakable, vegetable, fashionable, miserable
-are /eə/ e.g. care, spare, square, beware, stare, fare, aware, rare(ly), barely
-ile /aɪl/ e.g. fragile, mobile, file, while
-tory/tary /təri/ e.g. directory, history, secretary, documentary
-ture /tʃə/ e.g. picture, signature, departure, capture, temperature, literature, feature
-ate /eɪt/ at the end of verbs e.g. educate, operate, communicate
-ate /ət/ at the end of nouns and adjectives e.g. graduate, approximate, certificate

Index

badminton 70 /'bædmɪntən/
bag 94 /bæg/
baggage reclaim 86 /'bægɪdʒ/
bake 59 /beɪk/
balcony 49 /'bælkəni/
banana 58 /bə'nɑːnə/
band 73 /bænd/
bandage 55 /'bændɪdʒ/
barely 32 /'beəli/
barrister 80 /'bærɪstə/
baseball 70 /'beɪsbɔːl/
basket 94 /'bɑːskɪt/
basketball 70 /'bɑːskɪtbɔːl/
bat 70 /bæt/
bathroom 50, 98 /'bɑːθrʊm/
batteries 52 /bætəriːz/
BBC 100 /biː biː siː/
be back 76
be down 67
be in power 82
be unable to 99
be up 67
be/get delayed / held up 23
beach /biːtʃ/ ~ umbrella 89
bear 40 /beə/
beard 43 /bɪəd/
beat 71 /biːt/
beautiful 43 /'bjuːtɪfəl/
because (of) 36 /bɪ'kɒz/
bed & breakfast 87
bedroom 50 /'bedrʊm/
bedside table 51 /'bedsaɪd/
bee 40 /biː/
beef 58 /biːf/
before (+ -ing) 33 /bɪ'fɔː/
behind 31 /bɪ'haɪnd/
beige 93 /beɪʒ/
belongs to 14, 49 /bɪ'lɒŋz
    tuː/
below 31 /bɪ'ləʊ/
belt 56 /belt/
bend (n, v) 42, 61 /bend/
besides 33 /bɪ'saɪdz/
best friend 46
between 31 /bɪ'twiːn/
beware of 96 /bɪ'weə əv/
bicycle 62 /'baɪsɪkəl/
bid 74 /bɪd/
bike 100 /baɪk/
bill 59, 87 /bɪl/
billion 91 /'bɪlɪən/

birth certificate 83
    /bɜːθ sə'tɪfɪkət/
bit 94 /bɪt/
bite your nails 42 /baɪt/
bitter 59 /'bɪtə/
blame (sb. for) 29 /bleɪm/
bland 59 /blænd/
bleed 55 /bliːd/
bless you 26 /bles juː/
block of flats 49 /blɒk/
bloke 99 /bləʊk/
blond(e) 43 /blɒnd/
blood test 55 /blʌd test/
blouse 56 /blaʊz/
blow your nose 42
board (black/white) 6, 100
    /bɔːd/
board (v) 86 /bɔːd/
board games 69
board pen 6
boarding card 86 /'bɔːdɪŋ
    kɑːd/
boil 59 /bɔɪl/
boiling 30, 38 /'bɔɪlɪŋ/
bon appetit 26 /bɒn æpəti/
book (v) 59, 72, 87 /bʊk/
bookcase 50 /'bʊkkeɪs/
boots 56 /buːts/
born (be born) 47 /bɔːn/
borrow 6, 53 /'bɒrəʊ/
both 35 /bəʊθ/
bother 48 /'bɒðə/
bottle 94 /'bɒtəl/
bottom 42 /'bɒtəm/
boutique 57 /buː'tiːk/
bowl 94 /bəʊl/
box 94 /bɒks/
box office 11
boxing 70 /'bɒksɪŋ/
boyfriend 47 /'bɔɪfrend/
brackets 1, 4 /'brækɪts/
brake (n, v) 10, 61 /breɪk/
branch (e.g. of a tree) 39
    /brɑːntʃ/
brand-new 12 /bræ'njuː/
Brazil 41 /brə'zɪl/
Brazilian 41 /brə'zɪlɪən/
break (n) 78 /breɪk/
break a record 20
break down 17, 61
break even 67

break in(to) 17, 81
break one's arm 55
break the ice 20
break the law 20, 80
break up 47
breathe 42 /briːð/
breathing 54 /'briːðɪŋ/
breeze 38 /briːz/
bricklayer 64 /'brɪkleɪə/
bridge 61 /brɪdʒ/
briefcase 6, 66 /'briːfkeɪs/
bright (clever) 44, 99 /braɪt/
bring 22 /brɪŋ/
Britain 41 /'brɪtən/
British 41 /'brɪtɪʃ/
broad shoulders 43 /brɔːd/
broadsheet 74 /'brɔːdʃiːt/
broker 64 /'brəʊkə/
brother-in-law 11, 46
bruise (n, v) 55 /bruːz/
brush one's teeth 48, 51
BSc 79 /biː əs siː/
build 43 /bɪld/
bullet/knife wound 55
bunch (of flowers) 94 /bʌntʃ/
bureaucracy 83
    /bjʊə'rɒkrəsi/
bureaucrat 83
    /'bjʊərəʊkræt/
burglar 81 /'bɜːglə/ ~ alarm
    81
burglary 81 /'bɜːgləri/
burgle 81 /'bɜːgəl/
burn 52 /bɜːn/
bus station/stop 62
business studies 79
butcher 57 /'bʊtʃə/
butterfly 40 /'bʌtəflaɪ/
button 56 /'bʌtən/
by (e.g. Dickens, Spielberg,
    etc.) 15
by accident 15
by car/train/bus/plane 15
by chance 15
by hand 15
by mistake 15
by myself 15, 48 /baɪ/
by 90

cab (US) 98 /kæb/
cabbage 58 /'kæbɪdʒ/

division 91 /dɪ'vɪʒən/
Do you think you could ...? 24
do/don't 96
do (a bit of / lots of) hiking, etc. 69
do (the) housework 19
do a course 19, 65
do a subject 19, 78
do homework 3, 19
do overtime 63
do research (in/into) 19, 79
do something/nothing 19
do the ironing 48
do the shopping 19, 48, 57
do the washing 48
do the washing-up 48
do well 67
do-it-yourself (DIY) 69
document 77, 83 /'dɒkjəmənt/
documentary 75 /dɒkjə'mentəri/
don't worry 23
doorbell 49 /'dɔːbel/
double room 87 /'dʌbəl ruːm/
down (the computer's down) 77 /daʊn/
down 31 /daʊn/
down in the dumps 18
downmarket 68 /daʊn'mɑːkɪt/
Dr 100 /'dɒktə/
drag 99 /dræg/
drama series 75 /'drɑːmə/
dramatic 67 /drə'mætɪk/
dramatist 73 /'dræmətɪst/
drapes (US) 50 /dreɪps/
draughty 49 /'drɑːfti/
draw (n, v) 71 /drɔː/
drawers 66 /drɔːz/
drawing 73 /'drɔːɪŋ/
dreadful 30 /'dredfəl/
dream (n, v) 10 /driːm/
drinkable 9 /'drɪŋkəbəl/
driving licence 83 /'draɪvɪŋ laɪsəns/
drop (n) 94 /drɒp/
drop (v) 52
drought 37, 39 /draʊt/

drummer 73 /'drʌmə/
drums 73 /drʌmz/
dry weather 13
dubbed 72 /dʌbd/
due to 36, 62 /djuː tuː/
dumping 85 /'dʌmpɪŋ/
during 90 /'djʊərɪŋ/
Dutch 41 /dʌtʃ/
duty-free 86 /djuːti friː/
duvet 51 /'djuːveɪ/

e-mail 77 /'iː meɪl/
e.g. 100 /iː dʒiː/
eagle 40 /'iːgəl/
earache 54 /'ɪəreɪk/
early morning call 87
early twenties/thirties etc. 47
earn 63 /ɜːn/
earrings 11, 56 /'ɪərɪŋz/
earth 37 /ɜːθ/
earthquake 37 /'ɜːθkweɪk/
easy-going 12 /'iːzi gəʊɪŋ/
economic policy 82 /iːkə'nɒmɪk/
economic stability 67
economical 9 /iːkə'nɒmɪkəl/
economics 78 /iːkə'nɒmɪks/
economist 8 /iː'kɒnəmɪst/
editor 74 /'edɪtə/
education 5, 78, 79 /edʒʊ'keɪʃən/
effective 1 /ɪ'fektɪv/
Egypt 41 /'iːdʒɪpt/
Egyptian 41 /ɪ'dʒɪpʃən/
elbow 42 /'elbəʊ/
elderly 47 /'eldəli/
elect 8, 82 /ɪ'lekt/
election 8, 82 /ɪ'lekʃən/
electrical appliances 57 /ɪ'lektrɪkəl ə'plaɪənsɪz/
electrician 64 /elɪk'trɪʃən/
elephant 40 /'elɪfənt/
elevator (US) 98 /'elɪveɪtə/
embarrassed/embarrassing 30, 45 /ɪm'bærəst/ /ɪm'bærəsɪŋ/
embarrassment 45 /ɪm'bærəsmənt/
emergency services 64 /ɪ'mɜːdʒəntsi/

emotional 44 /ɪ'məʊʃənəl/
employer 65 /ɪm'plɔɪə/
employment 65 /ɪm'plɔɪmənt/
engaged 76 /ɪŋ'geɪdʒd/
engineer 64 /endʒɪ'nɪə/
engineering 79 /endʒɪ'nɪərɪŋ/
enjoy 28 /ɪn'dʒɔɪ/
enjoyable 9 /ɪn'dʒɔɪəbəl/
enormous 30, 49 /ɪ'nɔːməs/
enough 5, 56 /ɪ'nʌf/
enrol 83 /ɪn'rəʊl/
enrolment form 83
environment 85 /ɪn'vaɪərənmənt/
equator 37 /ɪ'kweɪtə/
equipment 27, 70 /ɪ'kwɪpmənt/
etc. 100 /ɪt'setərə/
EU 100 /iː juː/
even 91 /'iːvən/
even though 34
eventually 33 /ɪ'ventʃuəli/
evidence 80 /'evɪdəns/
ex- 46 /eks/
exam 100 /ɪg'zæm/
examine 66 /ɪg'zæmɪn/
except (for) 35 /ɪk'sept/
excess baggage 86 /ekses 'bægɪdʒ/
excited/exciting 30, 68 /ɪk'saɪtəd/ /ɪk'saɪtɪŋ/
excuse 23 /ɪk'skjuːs/
excuse me 26 /ɪk'skjuːz mi/
exhaust fumes 85 /ɪg'zɔːst fjuːmz/
exhausted/exhausting 30 /ɪg'zɔːstəd/ /ɪg'zɔːstɪŋ/
exhibition 73 /eksɪ'bɪʃən/
expand 67 /ɪk'spænd/
expecting (a baby) 47 /ɪkspekɪŋ/
expect (think) 28 /ɪk'spekt/
expenditure 67 /ɪk'spendɪtʃə/
expensive 53 /ɪk'spensɪv/
expire 83 /ɪk'spaɪə/
explain 29 /ɪk'spleɪn/
extent 25 /ɪk'stent/
extra time 71 /'ekstrə taɪm/
extract 39 /'ekstrækt/
extreme 82 /ɪk'striːm/

extremely 32 /ɪk'striːmli/
eyebrows 42 /'aɪbraʊz/

factory 60, 85 /'fæktəri/
fair 43 /feə/
fairly 32 /'feəli/
fall (n, v) 67 /fɔːl/
fall asleep 48 /fɔːl/
fall in love 47 /fɔːl/
fall over 16 /fɔːl/
fall slowly/sharply 2 /fɔːl/
fall (n) (US) 98 /fɔːl/
falls 37 /fɔːlz/
family name 46
famous 9 /'feɪməs/
fancy 99 /'fænsi/
far 92 /fɑː/
fare 62 /feə/
farewell 26 /feə'wel/
farmer 8 /'fɑːmə/
farming 39 /'fɑːmɪŋ/
fascinated/fascinating 30
    /'fæsɪneɪtəd/ /'fæsɪneɪtɪŋ/
fascism 82 /'fæʃɪzəm/
fascist 82 /'fæʃɪst/
fashion 68 /'fæʃən/
fashionable 68 /'fæʃənəbəl/
fasten 5 /'fɑːsən/
fasten your seat belt 61, 86
fat 43, 92 /fæt/
father-in-law 11, 46
fattening 5, 59 /'fætənɪŋ/
fatty 59 /'fæti/
faucet (US) 98 /'fɔːsɪt/
favourite 75 /'feɪvərɪt/
fear 45 /fɪə/
features 74 /'fiːtʃəz/
feel (n, v) 95 /fiːl/
feel like … 18, 28
feel sick 54
feels + adj; feels like + noun
    95
fence 49 /fens/
field 60 /'fiːld/
fifteen-minute (drive) 12
fifty-pence piece 53
fight crime 81 /faɪt/
file (for papers) (n, v) 6
    /faɪl/
files 66 /faɪəlz/

filing cabinet 66 /'faɪlɪŋ
    'kæbɪnət/
fill in (a form) 83
film star 11 /fɪlm stɑː/
final score 71 /'faɪnəl skɔː/
finally 33 /'faɪnəli/
finance (v) 67 /'faɪnæns/
find out 16
fine (n) 80 /faɪn/
finger 2, 42 /'fɪŋɡə/
finish 28 /'fɪnɪʃ/
fire (v) 84 /faɪə/
fire brigade 64 /faɪə brɪɡeɪd/
firefighter 64 /'faɪəfaɪtə/
first aid 11
first class 12
first name 46
first of all 33
first(ly) 33 /fɜːstli/
fishermen 39 /fɪʃəmən/
fishing 39 /'fɪʃɪŋ/
fishing boat 39
fit 56, 64, 66 /fɪt/
fitting room 57 /'fɪtɪŋ rʊm/
five-pound (note) 12
fix up 99 /fɪks/
flats 49 /flæts/
flexi-time 63 /'fleksitaɪm/
flexible 44 /'fleksɪbəl/
flight 62, 86 /flaɪt/
flood 37 /flʌd/
floor 49 /flɔː/
floppy disk 77 /'flɒpi dɪsk/
floral 93 /'flɔːrəl/
flu (influenza) 54, 100 /fluː/
fly 40, 62 /flaɪ/
fog 38 /fɒɡ/
foggy 38 /'fɒɡi/
fold your arms 42
food mixer 50
foot 42 /fʊt/
football 70 /'fʊtbɔːl/
footpath 60 /'fʊtpɑːθ/
for 90 /fɔː/
for a start 18
for a walk/swim/drive/run
    15
for ages 90
for another thing 33
for example 100
for good 18

for one thing 33
for the time being 90
force (sb. to do sth.) 28
    /fɔːs/
forehead 42 /'fɒrɪd/
foreign news 74 /'fɒrɪn/
foreign policy 82
forest 37 /'fɒrɪst/
forget 28 /fə'ɡet/
form (a government) 82
    /fɔːm/
fortnight 90 /'fɔːtnaɪt/
fortunately 48 /'fɔːtʃənətli/
fountain 88 /'faʊntɪn/
fraction 91 /'frækʃən/
fragile 96 /'frædʒaɪl/
France 41 /frɑːns/
freelance 74 /'friːlɑːns/
freeway (US) 98 /'friːweɪ/
freezing 30, 38 /'friːzɪŋ/
French 41, 78 /frentʃ/
french fries (US) 98
frequently 32 /'friːkwəntli/
fresh 59 /freʃ/
fridge (refrigerator) 50, 100
    /frɪdʒ/
friendly 44 /'frendli/
frightened/frightening 30
    /fraɪtənd/ /fraɪtənɪŋ/
front door 49
front garden 49
fruit 58 /fruːt/
fry 59 /fraɪ/
frying pan 50
full (of) 14 /fʊl/
full board 87
full name 46
full stop 4
full up 62
full-time 12
fully aware 13
fully-booked 87
furniture 27 /'fɜːnɪtʃə/
further 99 /'fɜːðə/
furthermore 34 /fɜːðə'mɔː/

gain (weight) 3 /ɡeɪn/
gale 38 /ɡeɪl/
game 71 /ɡeɪm/
gang 94 /ɡæŋ/
garage 49 /'ɡærɪdʒ/

hardworking 44
/ˈhɑːdˈwɜːkɪŋ/
harmful 85 /ˈhɑːmfəl/
harvest 39 /ˈhɑːvɪst/
hate 28 /heɪt/
have a baby 19
have a break 48
have a dream 10
have a drink 19
have a go 22
have a good/great time 19,
88
have a lie-in 48
have a look 10, 50
have a nice weekend 26
have a party 19
have a rest 10, 19, 48
have a shower/bath/wash/
shave 19, 48
have a word (with) 99
have a(n) early/late night 48
have breakfast 48
have friends for dinner 48
have something to eat 19
have something/nothing in
common 35
hay fever 54 /heɪ fiːvə/
head (v) 70 /hed/
headache 54 /ˈhedeɪk/
headline 74 /ˈhedlaɪn/
headphones 27 /ˈhedfəʊnz/
health 54 /helθ/
healthy (economy) 67
/ˈhelθi/
hear 95 /hɪə/
hearing 95 /ˈhɪərɪŋ/
heart 54 /hɑːt/
heart attack 54
heat (v) 49 /hiːt/
heat (n) 38 /hiːt/
heavy rain 13, 38
heavy smoker 13
heavy traffic 13
Hebrew 41 /ˈhiːbruː/
hedge 60 /hedʒ/
heel 42 /hiːl/
height 43, 92 /haɪt/
held up 23 /held/
help yourself 24
helpful 9 /ˈhelpfəl/
hepatitis 54 /hepəˈtaɪtɪs/

high 92 /haɪ/
high school (US) 98
highlighter pen 6 /ˈhaɪlaɪtə/
highlights 75 /ˈhaɪlaɪts/
highly (unlikely) 13 /ˈhaɪli/
highway (US) 98 /ˈhaɪweɪ/
hijacking 84 /haɪdʒækɪŋ/
hiking 69, 89 /ˈhaɪkɪŋ/
hips 42 /hɪps/
hire 86 /haɪə/
historical monuments 88
history 78 /ˈhɪstəri/
history of art 79
hit 70 /hɪt/
hit (affect badly) 74 /hɪt/
hobby 69 /ˈhɒbi/
hockey 70 /ˈhɒki/
hold (an election) 82 /həʊld/
hold 95 /həʊld/
hole punch (n, v) 6 /həʊl/
holiday pay 63 /ˈhɒlədeɪ/
Holland 41 /ˈhɒlənd/
home news 74
homeless 9 /ˈhəʊmləs/
homesick 3 /ˈhəʊmsɪk/
homework 27 /ˈhəʊmwɜːk/
honest 44 /ˈɒnɪst/
hoover 51 /ˈhuːvə/
hope 28 /həʊp/
horror film 72 /ˈhɒrə/
hospitality 23 /hɒspɪˈtæləti/
hostage 84 /ˈhɒstɪdʒ/
household (goods) 57
/ˈhaʊshəʊld/
housework 3, 27, 51
/ˈhaʊswɜːk/
How about …? 24
How are you getting on? 21
How are you? 26
How do I get to …? 87
How do you do? 26
How do you feel about …?
25
How do you pronounce …?
6
How do you spell …? 6
How do you use …? 6
How long/tall/wide is …?
92
How much does he/she
weigh? 43

How tall is he/she? 43
How's it going? 22
however 34 /haʊˈevə/
huge 30, 49 /hjuːdʒ/
human resources 85
/ˈhjuːmən rɪzɔːsɪz/
humid 38 /ˈhjuːmɪd/
humidity 38 /hjuːˈmɪdəti/
hundred 91 /ˈhʌndrəd/
hunting 69 /ˈhʌntɪŋ/
hurricane 37, 38 /ˈhʌrɪkən/
hurry up 16 /ˈhʌri/
hurt (oneself) 54 /hɜːt/
hyphen 4 /ˈhaɪfən/

I agree with you 25
I beg your pardon 23, 26
I don't mind 24
I don't think … 25
I regret to inform you 99
I think you're right 25
I was wondering if …? 24
I won't be long 23
I'd love to 24
I'd prefer to / I'd rather …
24
I'll clear it up 23
I'll leave it 57
I'll sort it out 23
I'll take it/them 57
I'm (terribly/very/so) sorry
23
I'm afraid I can't 24
I'm afraid not 24
I'm being served 57
I'm just looking 57
I'm looking for a … 57
I'm sorry I'm late 23
i.e. 100 /aɪ iː/
ic(e)y 38 /aɪsi/
ice 38 /aɪs/
ice hockey 70 /aɪs/
icons 77 /ˈaɪkɒnz/
identity card 83 /aɪˈdentəti
kɑːd/
idiom 4 /ˈɪdiəm/
if you like 24 /ɪf/
illegal 7, 80, 81 /ɪˈliːgəl/
illegible 7 /ɪˈledʒəbəl/
illness 54 /ˈɪlnəs/
image 68 /ˈɪmɪdʒ/

lane 61 /leɪn/

language lab 100 /'læŋgwɪʤ læb/

laptop 77 /'læptɒp/

laser printer 77 /'leɪzə/

last (v) 79 /lɑːst/

last 90 /lɑːst/

late arrival 62

late at night 81 /leɪt/

late twenties/thirties etc. 47

lately 90 /'leɪtli/

latest 71 /'leɪtɪst/

laugh (n, v) 10, 42 /lɑːf/

launch 68 /lɔːnʧ/

law 79 /lɔː/

law and order 3, 80

lawyer 64 /'lɔɪə/

lazy 44 /'leɪzi/

lead 71 /liːd/

lead (electrical) 6 /liːd/

lead to 36

league 71 /liːg/

lean 59 /liːn/

leave a job (resign) 65 /liːv/

leave a message 76

leave home/work (depart) 48

leave lights on 81

leave out (omit) 17

leave sb. (permanent separation) 47

leave sth. behind (forget sth.) 52

leaves (on a tree) 39 /liːvz/

lecture 79 /'lekʧə/

lecturer 64, 79 /'lekʧərə/

left-wing 82 /leftwɪŋ/

lemon 58 /'lemən/

lend 53 /lend/

length 92 /leŋkθ/

leopard 40 /'lepəd/

lesson 78 /'lesən/

let (sb. do sth.) 28 /let/

lettuce 58 /'letɪs/

liberal 82 /'lɪbərəl/

liberalism 82 /'lɪbərəlɪzəm/

library 60 /'laɪbrəri/

licence 75 /'laɪsəns/

lie (on the beach) 89 /laɪ/

lie down 16, 17

lie in bed 48

lift 49, 87, 98 /lɪft/

light (colour) 93 /laɪt/

lightning 38 /'laɪtnɪŋ/

like 28, 95 /laɪk/

line (phone) 76 /laɪn/

line (US) 62 /laɪn/

line judge 70

lion 40 /laɪən/

lips 42 /lɪps/

listen (to) 14, 95 /'lɪsən/

literature 73 /'lɪtrəʧə/

live (adj) 75 /laɪv/

lively 88 /'laɪvli/

liver 54 /'lɪvə/

living room 50 /'lɪvɪŋ/

loan 67 /ləʊn/

lobster 58 /'lɒbstə/

local call 76 /'ləʊkəl/

lock 7 /lɒk/

long 92 /lɒŋ/

long distance call 76

loo 99 /luː/

look (at) 95 /lʊk/

look after sth./sb. 16, 64

look round (e.g. the shops) 88

look up (a word) 6, 16

looks + adj; looks like + noun 95

lorry 61, 62 /'lɒri/

lose (a game) 3, 71 /luːz/

lose sth. (e.g. money) 52

lose weight 3

loss 67 /lɒs/

lounge 50 /laʊnʤ/

love (tennis) 71, 91 /lʌv/

love 28 /lʌv/

luggage 27, 86 /'lʌgɪʤ/

lung 54 /lʌŋ/

lung cancer 54

luxury 68 /'lʌkʃəri/

luxurious 68 /lʌg'ʒʊərɪəs/

MA 79 /em eɪ/

machine 5 /mə'ʃiːn/

mad about sb./sth. 69

main course 59

main road 61

maintain 1 /meɪn'teɪn/

majority 82, 91 /mə'ʤɒrəti/

make a decision 2, 19 /meɪk/

make a loss 67

make a meal of 19

make a mess 2

make a mistake 2, 13, 19

make a profit 67

make coffee 50

make do (with) 18

make friends 19

make it 18

make money 19

make my own breakfast/dinner 48

make my own clothes 69

make notes 79

make (sb. do sth.) 28

make up (a story) 17

make up your mind 18

manage (be able to) 28 /'mænɪʤ/

manage (a shop) 8 /'mænɪʤ/

management 8 /'mænɪʤmənt/

manager (sport) 70 /'mænɪʤə/

Mandarin (also Cantonese) 41 /'mændərɪn/

manslaughter 81 /'mænslɔːtə/

manual 64 /'mænjʊəl/

manufacture 66 /mænjə'fækʧə/

Many Happy Returns 26

map 88 /mæp/

march (walk) (n, v) 45 /mɑːʧ/

marital status 83 /'mærɪtəl steɪtəs/

market 88 /'mɑːkɪt/

marketing /'mɑːkɪtɪŋ/ ~mix 68

market leader/research/share 68 /'mɑːkɪt/

marriage 47 /'mærɪʤ/

marvellous 30 /'mɑːvələs/

mass-produced 68 /mæsprə'ʤuːst/

match 71 /mæʧ/

maths (mathematics) 78, 100 /mæθs/

optimistic 44 /ˌɒptɪˈmɪstɪk/
orange 58 /ˈɒrɪndʒ/
orchestra 73 /ˈɔːkɪstrə/
order 29, 66, 87 /ˈɔːdə/
ordinary-looking 43
otherwise 35 /ˈʌðəwaɪz/
out loud 1
out of 31
out of order 52, 96
out of work 15, 65
outbreak 84 /ˈaʊtbreɪk/
oval 93 /ˈəʊvəl/
oven 50 /ˈʌvən/
over 31 /ˈəʊvə/
overcharge 7 /əʊvəˈtʃɑːdʒ/
overcoat 56 /ˈəʊvəkəʊt/
overdo 7 /əʊvəˈduː/
overhead locker 86
oversleep 7, 48 /əʊvəˈsliːp/
overtake 61 /əʊvəˈteɪk/
overtime 63 /ˈəʊvətaɪm/
overweight 43 /əʊvəˈweɪt/
owing to 36 /ˈəʊɪŋ tu/
own 49 /əʊn/
ozone layer 85 /ˈəʊzəʊn leɪə/

pack (a suitcase) 7 /pæk/
package (v) 66 /ˈpækɪdʒ/
packed 30, 88 /pækt/
packet 94 /ˈpækɪt/
pain 54 /peɪn/
painful 9, 54, 55 /ˈpeɪnfəl/
painless 9 /ˈpeɪnləs/
painter 73 /ˈpeɪntə/
painting 73 /ˈpeɪntɪŋ/
pair (of) 94 /peə/
palace 88 /ˈpælɪs/
pale 43, 93 /peɪl/
pants (US) 98 /pænts/
paperwork 63, 66
    /ˈpeɪpəwɜːk/
park (v) 61 /pɑːk/
parking lot (US) 98
parking meter 11
part-time 12, 65
partly 25 /ˈpɑːtli/
partner 46 /ˈpɑːtnə/
pass a ball 70 /pɑːs/
pass an exam 79
pass through customs 86
passenger 62 /ˈpæsəndʒə/

passport 83 /ˈpɑːspɔːt/
passport control 86
past 31 /pɑːst/
paste 77 /peɪst/
path 49 /pɑːθ/
pattern 93 /ˈpætən/
pavement 61 /ˈpeɪvmənt/
pay (for) 53 /peɪ/
pay back 67
pay by cheque/credit card
    57
pay interest 67
pay rise 65
PC 100 /piː siː/
peace 84 /piːs/
peace and quiet 89
peace settlement 84
peace talks 84
peaceful 60 /ˈpiːsfəl/
peach 58 /piːtʃ/
pear 58 /peə/
peas 58 /piːz/
pedestrian 61 /pɪˈdestriən/
pedestrian crossing 11, 61
penalty 71 /ˈpenəlti/
pepper 59 /ˈpepə/
peppers 58 /ˈpepəz/
percentage 91 /pəˈsentɪdʒ/
perform 72 /pəˈfɔːm/
performance 72 /pəˈfɔːməns/
perhaps 25 /pəˈhæps/
permit 99 /ˈpɜːmɪt/
personally 25 /ˈpɜːsənəli/
persuade 29 /pəˈsweɪd/
pessimistic 44 /pesɪˈmɪstɪk/
pet 40 /pet/
petrol station 61 /ˈpetrəl/
PhD 79 /piː eɪtʃ diː/
philosophy 79 /fɪˈlɒsəfi/
phone 100 /fəʊn/
phone book/box/card/
    number 76
phone sb. back 76
photo 100 /ˈfəʊtəʊ/
photocopier 6 /ˈfəʊtəʊkɒpiə/
photocopy 6 /ˈfəʊtəʊkɒpi/
photography 69 /fəˈtɒgrəfi/
phrasal verb 4
physical education 78
    /ˈfɪzɪkəl/
pianist 73 /ˈpiːənɪst/

piano 73 /piˈænəʊ/
pick 39 /pɪk/
pick sth./sb. up (collect) 16,
    99
pick sth. up (gather) 16
picnic 89 /ˈpɪknɪk/
piece 94 /piːs/
pig 40 /pɪg/
pillow 51 /ˈpɪləʊ/
pilot 62, 64 /ˈpaɪlət/
pinch (steal) 99 /pɪntʃ/
pineapple 58 /ˈpaɪnæpəl/
pink 93 /pɪŋk/
piss 99 /pɪs/
pitch 70 /pɪtʃ/
place 88 /pleɪs/
plain 43 /pleɪn/
plane 100 /pleɪn/
plant (n, v) 39 /plɑːnt/
plaster 55 /ˈplɑːstə/
platform 62 /ˈplætfɔːm/
play (n) 72, 73
play a game 71 /pleɪ/
play a musical instrument
    69
play cards 48, 69
player 70 /ˈpleɪə/
playroom 50 /ˈpleɪrʊm/
playwright 73 /ˈpleɪraɪt/
pleasant 44 /ˈplezənt/
please do not disturb 96
please do not feed the
    animals 96
please queue other side 96
plenty 60 /ˈplenti/
plug 6 /plʌg/
plug sth. in 6, 75
plumber 5, 64 /ˈplʌmə/
plural noun 4 /ˈplʊərəl/
plus 91 /plʌs/
PM 100 /piː em/
pocket 56 /ˈpɒkɪt/
poem 73 /ˈpəʊɪm/
poet 73 /ˈpəʊɪt/
point (at sth.) 45 /pɔɪnt/
point (decimal) 91 /pɔɪnt/
police force 64 /pəˈliːs/
police officer 64
policy 82 /ˈpɒləsi/
polish 51 /ˈpɒlɪʃ/
polite 3 /pəˈlaɪt/

political 9 /pə'lɪtɪkəl/
political leader/party 82
political stability 67
politics 78, 79, 82
    /'pɒlətɪks/
pollution 60, 85 /pə'luːʃən/
pond 2 /pɒnd/
pool 70 /puːl/
pop music 73
pop star 11
popular press 74
pork 58 /pɔːk/
porter 87 /'pɔːtə/
portrait 73 /'pɔːtrɪt/
Portugal 41 /'pɔːtʃəgəl/
Portuguese 41 /pɔːtʃə'giːz/
post office 11
postgraduate 79
    /pəʊst'grædʒuət/
potato 5, 58 /pə'teɪtəʊ/
pour (with rain) 38 /pɔː/
powerful 72 /'paʊəfəl/
precious 39 /'preʃəs/
prefer 5, 24, 28 /prɪ'fɜː/
prefix 4 /'priːfɪks/
pregnant 47 /'pregnənt/
preposition 4 /prepə'zɪʃən/
prescription 54
    /prɪ'skrɪpʃən/
press (a button) 45, 95
prestige 68 /pres'tiːʒ/
prestigious 68 /pres'tɪdʒəs/
pretty 32, 99 /'prɪti/
prevent 29, 61 /prɪ'vent/
prevent sth. (from) 81
pride 45 /praɪd/
price 68 /praɪs/
primary (school) 78
    /'praɪməri/
Prime Minister 82
print 77 /prɪnt/
printer 77 /'prɪntə/
prison 80 /'prɪzən/
product 68 /'prɒdʌkt/
profession 64 /prə'feʃən/
profit 67 /'prɒfɪt/
promise 28 /'prɒmɪs/
promote 65 /prə'məʊt/
promotion 65, 68
    /prə'məʊʃən/
pronoun 4 /'prəʊnaʊn/

properly 52 /'prɒpəli/
property 81 /'prɒpəti/
propose 29 /prə'pəʊz/
prospects 65 /'prɒspekts/
protect (oneself) 81, 89
    /prə'tekt/
protection 85 /prə'tekʃən/
proud 45 /praʊd/
prove 80 /pruːv/
psychology 79 /saɪ'kɒlədʒi/
public expenditure 67
public school 78
publish 74 /'pʌblɪʃ/
pull (n, v) 10 /pʊl/
pull sb.'s leg 18
pullover 56 /'pʊləʊvə/
punch sb. 45 /pʌntʃ/
punctual 8, 44, 62
    /'pʌŋktʃuəl/
punctuality 8 /pʌŋktʃu'æləti/
punishment 80, 81
    /'pʌnɪʃmənt/
pupil 78 /'pjuːpəl/
purchase 99 /'pɜːtʃəs/
purple 93 /'pɜːpəl/
purpose 36 /'pɜːpəs/
push (n, v) 10 /pʊʃ/
put on the brakes 10
put on weight 59
put on (clothes) 2, 17, 51,
    56
put one's feet up 89
put sb. through (connect)
    76
put sth. back (return) 50
put sth. out (extinguish) 16
pyjamas 27, 51 /pə'dʒɑːməz/
pyramid 93 /'pɪrəmɪd/

quality 68 /'kwɒləti/
quality press 74
quarter 91 /'kwɔːtə/
question (v) 80 /'kwestʃən/
question mark 4
queue (n, v) 10, 62, 83
    /kjuː/
quid 99 /kwɪd/
quit 65, 74 /kwɪt/
quite 32, 92 /kwaɪt/
quiz show 75 /kwɪz ʃəʊ/

rabbit 40 /'ræbɪt/
racket 70 /'rækɪt/
railway station 62 /'reɪlweɪ/
rain (n, v) 10 /reɪn/
rainforest 37 /'reɪnfɒrɪst/
rape 81 /reɪp/
rapist 81 /reɪpɪst/
rare (meat) 59 /reə/
rarely 32 /'reəli/
rather 24, 32 /'rɑːðə/
raw 59 /rɔː/
raw material 67
reasonable 53 /'riːzənəbəl/
recently 90 /'riːsəntli/
reception 87 /rɪ'sepʃən/
recession 67 /rɪ'seʃən/
reckon 99 /'rekən/
recommend 29 /rekə'mend/
recorded highlights 75
rectangle 93 /'rektæŋgəl/
recycle 85 /riː'saɪkəl/
redo (homework) 7 /riː'duː/
reduce 67, 81 /rɪ'djuːs/
referee 70 /refər'iː/
refuse 28 /refjuːs/
registration (form) 83
    /redʒɪ'streɪʃən/
regularly 32 /'regjələli/
relaxed 44 /rɪ'lækst/
release 84 /rɪ'liːs/
reliable 44, 68 /rɪ'laɪəbəl/
religious (education) 78
    /rɪ'lɪdʒəs/
remember 28 /rɪ'membə/
remind 86 /rɪ'maɪnd/
renew 83 /rɪ'njuː/
rent (v, n) 49, 86 /rent/
reopen 7 /riː'əʊpən/
repair 64 /rɪ'peə/
repeat 6 /rɪ'piːt/
reply (n, v) 10 /rɪ'plaɪ/
reporter 74 /rɪ'pɔːtə/
republic 82 /rɪ'pʌblɪk/
republican 82 /rɪ'pʌblɪkən/
require 99 /rɪ'kwaɪə/
research 79 /rɪ'sɜːtʃ/
reserved 44 /rɪ'zɜːvd/
resign 65 /rɪ'zaɪn/
resignation 65 /rezɪg'neɪʃən/
resort 89 /rɪ'zɔːt/
resources 85 /rɪ'zɔːsɪz/

responsibilities 63
/rɪspɒnsɪˈbɪlɪtiːz/
responsible (for) 63, 65
/rɪˈspɒntsəbəl/
result (in) 36 /rɪˈzʌlt/
resume 99 /rɪˈzjuːm/
retailer 66 /ˈriːteɪlə/
retake (an exam) 7 /ˈriːteɪk/
retired 47 /rɪˈtaɪəd/
retirement 47, 65
/rɪˈtaɪəmənt/
reverse charge call 76
review 72, 74 /rɪˈvjuː/
revise 1 /rɪˈvaɪz/
revision 1 /rɪˈvɪʒən/
ride (a bike) 62 /raɪd/
right angle 93 /raɪt æŋgəl/
right-wing 82 /raɪtwɪŋ/
ring (boxing) 70 /rɪŋ/
ring (v, n) 10
rise (n, v) 67 /raɪz/
rise slowly/sharply 2
river 37 /ˈrɪvə/
roadworks 61 /ˈrəʊdwɜːks/
roast 59 /rəʊst/
rob 81 /rɒb/
robber 81 /ˈrɒbə/
robbery 81 /ˈrɒbəri/
rock climbing 69 /rɒk/
rock star 11 /rɒk/
rocks 89 /rɒks/
romance 47 /rəʊˈmæns/
root 39 /ruːt/
rough (sea) 89 /rʌf/
roughly 97 /ˈrʌfli/
round (adj) 93 /raʊnd/
round (preposition) 31
round trip (US) 98
routine 1, 63 /ruːˈtiːn/
row (argument) 47, 74 /raʊ/
row (line) 72 /rəʊ/
rub sth. off (the board) 6
/rʌb/
rub sth. out 1, 6
rubber 6 /ˈrʌbə/
rugby 70 /ˈrʌgbi/
ruin 52 /ˈrʊɪn/
run (a shop/company) 13,
63
run (frequency) 62

run out (of sth.) 16, 52, 83,
84
runny nose 54 /ˈrʌni/
runway 86 /ˈrʌnweɪ/
rushed (to hospital) 55
/rʌʃt/
rush-hour 61 /rʌʃaʊə/
Russia 41 /ˈrʌʃə/
Russian 41 /ˈrʌʃən/

sack 65 /sæk/
sadness 45 /ˈsædnəs/
safe (n) 81 /seɪf/
sailor 64 /ˈseɪlə/
salad 58 /ˈsæləd/
salary 63 /ˈsæləri/
sales 68 /seɪlz/
sales figures/forecast/
manager/target 68
sales rep 68, 100
salmon 58 /ˈsæmən/
salt 59 /sɔːlt/
salty 59 /ˈsɔːlti/
same to you 26
sand 89 /sænd/
satellite 75 /ˈsætəlaɪt/
satellite dish 75
saucepan 50 /ˈsɔːspən/
Saudi Arabia 41 /saʊdi
əˈreɪbɪə/
Saudi Arabian 41 /saʊdi
əˈreɪbɪən/
save (data) 77 /seɪv/
save (up) 16, 53 /seɪv/
saxophone 69, 73
/ˈsæksəfəʊn/
saxophonist 73
/sækˈsɒfənɪst/
say (the paper / TV says
that …) 25 /seɪ/
say cheese 26
scales 27 /skeɪlz/
scar 43 /skɑː/
scarce 39 /skeəs/
scarf 56 /skɑːf/
science 78 /saɪəns/
science fiction 11, 72
scissors 27 /ˈsɪzəz/
score 71 /skɔː/
screen (computer) 77
/skriːn/

screen (cinema) 72 /skriːn/
sculptor 73 /ˈskʌlptə/
sculpture 73 /ˈskʌlptʃə/
sea 37 /siː/
seafood 58 /ˈsiːfuːd/
seaside 89 /ˈsiːsaɪd/
season 87 /ˈsiːzən/
seat 3 /siːt/
seats (in parliament) 82
second (n) 90 /ˈsekənd/
second(ly) 33 /ˈsekəndli/
second-hand 12
secondary (school) 78
/ˈsekəndəri/
see 95 /siː/
see (understand / find out)
20
see you later/soon 26 /siː/
seem 28 /siːm/
seldom 32 /ˈseldəm/
self-confident 44
self-defence 81
self-portrait 73
self-study 1
semester (US) 98 /sɪˈmestə/
semi-circle 93
send off (a letter) 16 /send/
senses 95 /ˈsensɪz/
sensible 44 /ˈsentsɪbəl/
sensitive 44 /ˈsentsɪtɪv/
sentence (prison) 80
/ˈsentəns/
series 75 /ˈsɪəriːz/
serious (illness) 13 /ˈsɪərɪəs/
set 71 /set/
set the alarm 51
shade 93 /ʃeɪd/
shake 42 /ʃeɪk/
shake hands 42
shallow 92 /ˈʃæləʊ/
shape 93 /ʃeɪp/
shark 40 /ʃɑːk/
sharp(ly) 67 /ˈʃɑːpli/
sheet (of paper) 94 /ʃiːt/
shelling 84 /ˈʃelɪŋ/
shiftwork 63 /ˈʃɪftwɜːk/
shirt 56 /ʃɜːt/
shoot 55 /ʃuːt/
shop assistant 57
shop window 57
shoplift 81 /ˈʃɒplɪft/

still 34 /stɪl/
stocks and shares 64
stomach 54 /ˈstʌmək/
stomache-ache 54
    /ˈstʌməkeɪk/
stool 50 /stuːl/
store 66 /stɔː/
straight 43 /streɪt/
strawberry 58 /ˈstrɔːbəri/
stress 4 /stres/
stressful 60 /ˈstresfʊl/
striped 93 /straɪpt/
stroll (n, v) 45, 89 /strəʊl/
strong 44 /strɒŋ/
strong accent/coffee 13
strong economy 67
study (n) 50 /ˈstʌdi/
stuff 97 /stʌf/
stupid 8 /ˈstjuːpɪd/
stupidity 8 /stjuːˈpɪdəti/
subject 78 /ˈsʌbdʒɪkt/
subtitles 72 /ˈsʌbtaɪtəlz/
subtraction 91 /səbˈtrækʃən/
suburbs 60 /ˈsʌbɜːbz/
subway (US) 98 /ˈsʌbweɪ/
suffer (from) 14 /ˈsʌfə/
suffix 4 /ˈsʌfɪks/
suggest 29 /səˈdʒest/
suggestion 24 /səˈdʒestʃən/
suit (v) 3 /suːt/ (n) 56
suitable 9 /ˈsuːtəbəl/
sunbathe 89 /ˈsʌnbeɪð/
sunblock 89 /ˈsʌnblɒk/
sunburn 89 /ˈsʌnbɜːn/
sunglasses 11, 27
    /ˈsʌnglɑːsɪz/
sunny 38 /ˈsʌni/
suntan lotion 89 /ˈsʌntæn
    ləʊʃən/
supermarket 57
    /ˈsuːpəmɑːkɪt/
supervisor 66 /ˈsuːpəvaɪzə/
supplies 84 /səˈplaɪz/
surgeon 64 /ˈsɜːdʒən/
surname 46 /ˈsɜːneɪm/
surprised (at/by) 14, 30
    /səˈpraɪzd/
surprising 30 /səˈpraɪzɪŋ/
swap (places) 6 /swɒp/
Sweden 41 /ˈswiːdən/
Swedish 41 /ˈswiːdɪʃ/

sweet 59 /swiːt/
swimming 70 /ˈswɪmɪŋ/
    ~ costume 70
Swiss 41 /swɪs/
switch sth. on/off/over 75
    /swɪtʃ/
Switzerland 41 /ˈswɪtsələnd/
swollen 55 /ˈswəʊlən/
syllable 4 /ˈsɪləbəl/
symptom 54 /ˈsɪmptəm/
synonym 4 /ˈsɪnənɪm/

T-shirt 11
table tennis 11, 70 /ˈteɪbl/
tabloid 74 /ˈtæblɔɪd/
take 22, 90 /teɪk/
take a bus/train/taxi 19
take a decision 2, 19
take a photograph 2, 19
take a shower 2, 19
take an exam 19
take control (of) 84
take it in turns 18
take notes 79
take off (leave the ground)
    16, 17, 86
take off (remove) 16, 56
take over 65
take photographs 88
take place 82
take the first/second turning
    on the left/right 61
take time 2
take up (a hobby) 69
take-off (n) 86 /ˈteɪkɒf/
talks 74 /tɔːks/
tall 43, 92 /tɔːl/
tan 89 /tæn/
tartan 93 /ˈtɑːtən/
taste (n, v) 10, 95 /teɪst/
tastes + adj; tastes like +
    noun 95
tasty 59 /ˈteɪsti/
tax cut 67
taxi (v) 86 /ˈtæksi/
taxi rank 62
team 70 /tiːm/
teenager 47 /ˈtiːneɪdʒə/
telephone directory 76
    /ˈtelɪfəʊn dɪˈrektri/
tell 29 /tel/

tell a joke/story 13
tell the truth 13
telly 100 /ˈteli/
temperature 38 /ˈtemprətʃə/
temple 88 /ˈtempəl/
ten-pound note 53
ten-year-old (boy) 12
tender 59 /ˈtendə/
tennis 70 /ˈtenɪs/
tense 44 /tens/
tent 89 /tent/
term 78 /tɜːm/
terminal building 86
    /ˈtɜːmɪnəl bɪldɪŋ/
terrible (pain) 54 /ˈterəbəl/
terribly (sorry) 13 /ˈterɪbli/
terrific 30, 99 /təˈrɪfɪk/
terrified/terrifying 30
    /ˈterɪfaɪd/ /ˈterɪfaɪɪŋ/
territory 84 /ˈterɪtəri/
terrorism 84 /ˈterərɪzəm/
terrorist 84 /ˈterərɪst/
text book 6
Thai 41 /taɪ/
Thailand 41 /ˈtaɪlænd/
thank you (very much) 23
thanks 23 /θæŋks/
that's a good idea 24
that's to say (i.e.) 100
that's true 25
that's very kind of you 23
theft 81 /θeft/
therefore 36 /ˈðeəfɔː/
thick (stupid) 44, 99 /θɪk/
thick 92 /θɪk/
thief 81 /θiːf/
thin 43, 92 /θɪn/
thing(s) 97
third 91 /θɜːd/
though 34 /ðəʊ/
thoughtful 9 /ˈθɔːtfəl/
thoughtless 9 /ˈθɔːtləs/
thousand 91 /ˈθaʊzənd/
three-quarters 91
    /θriːˈkwɔːtəz/
thriller 72 /ˈθrɪlə/
through 5, 31 /θruː/
throughout 90 /θruːˈaʊt/
throw 70 /θrəʊ/
throw away 85

throw sth. (at sb. / to sb.) 14

thumb 2, 42 /θʌm/

thunder and lightning 38 /ˈθʌndə ənd ˈlaɪtnɪŋ/

thunderstorm 38 /ˈθʌndəstɔːm/

thus 99 /ðʌs/

ticket office 11

tidy 51 /ˈtaɪdi/

tie 56 /taɪ/

tie-break 71 /ˈtaɪbreɪk/

tied-up 18 /ˈtaɪdʌp/

tiger 40 /ˈtaɪgə/

tights 56 /taɪts/

times 91 /taɪmz/

timetable 78 /ˈtaɪmteɪbəl/

tin 39, 94 /tɪn/

tin opener 11 /tɪn/

tiny 30, 49 /ˈtaɪni/

tip (n, v) 59, 87 /tɪp/

tired (of) 14, 30 /taɪəd/

tiring 30 /ˈtaɪərɪŋ/

to a certain/large extent 25

to begin with 33

to make matters worse 18

to start with 33

toddler 47 /ˈtɒdlə/

toe 42 /təʊ/

toilet 51 /ˈtɔɪlət/

tomato 58 /təˈmɑːtəʊ/

too (+ adj) 56

too (as well) 34

too (far) to (walk) 92

toothache 54 /ˈtuːθeɪk/

touch (v) 95 /tʌʧ/

tough 59, 81 /tʌf/

touristy 88 /ˈtʊəristi/

towards 31 /təwɔːdz/

towel 51 /taʊəl/

toys 57 /tɔɪz/

track 70 /træk/

tractor 60 /ˈtræktə/

traffic 60 /ˈtræfɪk/

traffic jam 11, 61

traffic lights 11, 61

traffic warden 11

trainee 65 /treɪˈniː/

training /ˈtreɪnɪŋ/ ~ course 65

training shoes 70

transitive/intransitive verb 4

translator 8 /trænsˈleɪtə/

trash (US) 98 /træʃ/

treat 64 /triːt/

trial 80 /traɪl/

triangle 93 /ˈtraɪæŋgəl/

trip (over) 52 /trɪp/

troops 84 /truːps/

tropical (rainforest) 85 /ˈtrɒpɪkəl/

truck (US) 98 /trʌk/

trunks 70 /trʌŋks/

try (sth.) on 56

tube /tjuːb/

tuition 79 /tjuˈɪʃən/

Turkey 41 /ˈtɜːki/

Turkish 41 /ˈtɜːkɪʃ/

turn left/right 61 /tɜːn/

turn sth. down 75

turn sth. off 75

turn sth. on 17, 50, 75

turn sth. up 6, 75

turnover 67 /ˈtɜːnəʊvə/

turquoise 93 /ˈtɜːkwɑːz/

twin room 87

twist one's ankle 55

two-hour (delay) 12

ugly 2, 43 /ˈʌgli/

UK 100 /juː keɪ/

ulcer 54 /ˈʌlsə/

umpire 70 /ˈʌmpaɪə/

UN 100 /juː en/

unbreakable 9 /ʌnˈbreɪkəbəl/

uncle 46 /ˈʌŋkɛl/

unconscious 55 /ʌnˈkɒnʧəs/

uncountable (noun) 4 /ʌnˈkaʊntəbəl/

under 31 /ˈʌndə/

under sb. (under their authority) 65

undergraduate 79 /ʌndəˈgrædʒuət/

underpass (US) 98 /ˈʌndəpɑːs/

undershirt (US) 98 /ˈʌndəʃɜːt/

undrinkable 9 /ʌnˈdrɪŋkəbəl/

unemployed 7, 65 /ʌnɪmˈplɔɪd/

unfriendly 44 /ʌnˈfrendli/

unhappy 7 /ʌnˈhæpi/

unkind 44 /ʌnˈkaɪnd/

unless 35 /ənˈles/

unlike 35 /ʌnˈlaɪk/

unlock 7 /ʌnˈlɒk/

unpack (a suitcase) 7 /ʌnˈpæk/

unpleasant 44 /ʌnˈplezənt/

unreliable 9, 44 /ʌnrɪˈlaɪəbəl/

unsuitable 9 /ʌnˈsuːtəbəl/

untidy 7, 51 /ʌnˈtaɪdi/

until 90 /ənˈtɪl/

up 31 /ʌp/

upright 86 /ˈʌpraɪt/

USA 100 /juː es eɪ/

useful 9 /ˈjuːsfəl/

useless 9 /ˈjuːsləs/

user-friendly 77

utility room 50

vacation (US) 98 /vəˈkeɪʃən/

vague 97 /veɪg/

vague idea/memory 97

valley 60 /ˈvæli/

valuables 81 /ˈvæljuəbəlz/

value 53 /ˈvæljuː/

van 62 /væn/

various 89 /ˈveəriəs/

vase 50, 94 /vɑːz/

VAT 100 /viː eɪ tiː/

veal 58 /viːl/

vegetable 5, 58 /ˈveʤtəbəl/

vehicle 62 /ˈvɪəkəl/

verb 4 /vɜːb/

vest (US) 98 /vest/

vet 64, 100 /vet/

video (n, v) /ˈvɪdɪəʊ/

view 49 /vjuː/

villa 89 /ˈvɪlə/

village 60 /ˈvɪlɪʤ/

vinegar 58 /ˈvɪnɪgə/

violent 72 /ˈvaɪələnt/

violin 73 /vaɪəˈlɪn/

violinist 73 /vaɪəˈlɪnɪst/

virus 54 /ˈvaɪərəs/

visa 83 /ˈviːzə/

vitally (important) 13 /ˈvaɪtəli/

vocational 78 /vəʊˈkeɪʃənəl/

volcanic 37 /vɒlˈkænɪk/

volcano 37 /vɒl'keɪnəʊ/
volleyball 70 /'vɒlibɔːl/
vomit 54 /'vɒmɪt/
vote (for) 82 /vəʊt/

waist 42 /weɪst/
wait (for) 14 /weɪt/
waiting room 11
wake up 16, 17, 48
want 28, 29 /wɒnt/
war /wɔː/ ~ zone 84
war film 72
wardrobe 51 /'wɔːdrəʊb/
warehouse 66 /'weəhaʊs/
warn 29 /wɔːn/
warning 96 /'wɔːnɪŋ/
wash 48 /wɒʃ/
washable 9 /wɒʃəbəl/
washbasin 51 /'wɒʃbeɪsən/
washing machine 11, 50
washing-up 48
waste 53, 85 /weɪst/
wastepaper basket 66
watch 95 /wɒtʃ/
watch out 26
water (v) 39 /'wɔːtə/
wave 45 /weɪv/
waves 89 /weɪvz/
wavy 43 /'weɪvi/
weak 8, 44 /wiːk/
weakness 8 /'wiːknəs/
weapon 55, 81 /'wepən/
weather 27 /'weðə/
weather forecast 74
weekly 74 /'wiːkli/
weigh 86 /weɪ/
well done 26 /wiːl/
well-directed/known/made/
    off/written 12
well-done (meat) 59
western 72 /'westən/
whale 40 /weɪl/
what about ...? 24
what do you do? 63
what do you think of ...?
    25
what does he/she look like?
    43
what does X mean? 6
what shall we do? 24
what size are you?

what size do you take? 92
what do you do for a
    living? 63
what's on? 75
what's the difference
    between X and Y? 6
what's the height/width of
    ...? 92
what's up? 18, 99
what's more 34
when 33 /wen/
whereas 34 /weə'ræz/
while 33 /'waɪl/
whisper (n, v) 45 /'hwɪspə/
who's calling? 76
why don't we ...? 24
wide 92 /waɪd/
wide range 60
widow 46 /'wɪdəʊ/
widower 46 /'wɪdəʊə/
width 92 /wɪtθ/
win 71 /wɪn/
wind 38 /wɪnd/
window shopping 57
windy 38 /'wɪndi/
wonderful 30 /'wʌndəfəl/
wood 60 /wʊd/
word processing 77
word processor 77
work (function) 87 /wɜːk/
work 63
work out (calculate) 91
work overtime 63
working hours 63
worry (about) 14 /'wʌri/
worth (+ -ing) 53, 88 /wɜːθ/
would you like to ...? 24
wound 55, 84 /wuːnd/
wrist 2, 42 /rɪst/
write (sth. down) 6 /raɪt/
writer 73 /'raɪtə/
writing paper 11
wrong 5, 14, 76 /rɒŋ/
wrong number 76

yacht 89 /jɒt/
yawn 42 /jɔːn/

zebra 40 /'zebrə/
zero 91 /'zɪərəʊ/
zoo 40 /zəʊ/

Acknowledgements

I owe a great debt to Gillian Lazar for the extremely meticulous and valuable comments she has made on every single unit in the book, and also for her continued support and encouragement. Others have reported on parts of the manuscript, and for their valuable and supportive feedback I would also like to thank: Phillip N. Hewitt, Mike McCarthy, Geraldine Mark, Karl E. Schuhmacher, Roy Sprenger, Liz Walter.

Much of the material has been piloted in different parts of the world. I would like to thank Mark Appleby (Barcelona, Spain), Helen Barnes (British Council, Barcelona, Spain), Frank Carney (British Council, Pozan, Poland), Cliff Parry (British Council, Athens, Greece), Chris Powell (International House, Pisa, Italy), Sean Power (ELCRA Bell S.A., Geneva, Switzerland), Pat Rich (British Council, Barcelona, Spain), Karen Williams (British Council, Barcelona, Spain). Sean Power and Mark Appleby have not only given me very useful feedback but also valuable suggestions for improving the material. For help with American English equivalents I would like to thank Emilie Thomson.

Geraldine Mark has not only commented on the material, she has also edited it, and with remarkable incisiveness, efficiency, and constant good humour. My thanks to her.

At Cambridge University Press, I would like to thank Jeanne McCarten for the inspiration behind this project; Nóirín Burke for all her work in organising reports and piloting; and Isabella Wigan for her work in collating the final stages of the project.

On the production side, I would like to thank Randell Harris and Nick Newton for their design, Peter Byatt for his illustrations, and the rest of the team at Cambridge University Press.

Finally my thanks, as always, to Ruth Gairns for her support, advice and encouragement.

Vocabulary notes

Vocabulary notes